Early Literacy Matters

Early Literacy Matters is an innovative action guide for elementary school leaders and instructional coaches dedicated to accelerating literacy performance in the early grades, when prevention of reading difficulties matters most. As a unique father-daughter team with combined expertise in literacy education and instructional leadership, the authors share best practices for literacy success. Readers will learn how to...

♦ establish and lead a literacy team,
♦ implement embedded professional development,
♦ utilize key assessments to frame daily instruction, and
♦ illustrate specific organizational and scheduling models needed to support systemic change based on the science of reading.

Each chapter features reflection questions and explicit strategies and tools leaders can implement immediately in today's classrooms.

Carol E. Canady, Ph.D. is a Pre-K–5 literacy coordinator and a literacy consultant for various school districts. She has served as a K–8 teacher and counselor and has taught literacy courses as an Assistant Professor at Miami University and as an instructor at Wright State and Cincinnati Christian Universities. She received her Ph.D. in Reading Education from the University of Virginia, and has received distinguished recognition for teaching and community service, including recent demonstration of high leverage teaching practices in a national video series. Among other publications, *Early Literacy Matters* is the second book she has co-authored.

Robert Lynn Canady, Ed.D. is Professor Emeritus and former chair of the Department of Leadership, Foundations and Policy Studies at the University of Virginia, and a national consultant on innovative scheduling and grading practices. He has served as principal of elementary, middle, and junior high schools, and held leadership positions in two school district central offices. He has received numerous awards for outstanding teaching and service and is co-author of four bestselling books, including *Elementary School Scheduling: Enhancing instruction for School achievement* with Michael D. Rettig, School Scheduling Associates, Inc.

Also Available from Routledge
(www.routledge.com/k-12)

Evaluating the K–12 Literacy Curriculum: A Step-by-Step Guide for Auditing Programs, Materials, and Instructional Approaches
Colleen Pennell

Matching Reading Data to Interventions: A Simple Tool for Elementary Educators
Jill Dunlap Brown, Jana Schmidt

Close Reading in Elementary School: Bringing Readers and Texts Together
Diana Sisson and Betsy Sisson

Building Effective Professional Development in Elementary School: Designing a Path for Excellent Teaching
Judy Johnson

The Elementary School Grammar Toolkit: Using Mentor Texts to Teach Standards-Based Language and Grammar in Grades 3-5
Sean Ruday

Passionate Readers: The Art of Reaching and Engaging Every Child
Pernille Ripp

Culturally Relevant Teaching in the English Language Arts Classroom: A Guide for Teachers
Sean Ruday

Early Literacy Matters

A Leader's Guide to Systematic Change

Carol E. Canady and Robert Lynn Canady

Routledge
Taylor & Francis Group

NEW YORK AND LONDON

First published 2021
by Routledge
52 Vanderbilt Avenue, New York, NY 10017

and by Routledge
2 Park Square, Milton Park, Abingdon, Oxon, OX14 4RN

Routledge is an imprint of the Taylor & Francis Group, an informa business

© 2021 Taylor & Francis

Library of Congress Cataloging-in-Publication Data
Names: Canady, Carol E, author. | Canady, Robert Lynn, author.
Title: Early literacy matters : a leader's guide to systematic change /
    Carol E Canady and Robert Lynn Canady.
Description: New York, NY : Routledge, 2021. | Includes bibliographical
    references. |
Identifiers: LCCN 2020041170 | ISBN 9780367367206 (hardback) | ISBN
    9780367367190 (paperback) | ISBN 9780429350955 (ebook)
Subjects: LCSH: Language arts (Early childhood)
Classification: LCC LB1139.5.L35 C36 2021 | DDC 372.6/044--dc23
LC record available at https://lccn.loc.gov/2020041170

ISBN: 978-0-367-36720-6 (hbk)
ISBN: 978-0-367-36719-0 (pbk)
ISBN: 978-0-429-35095-5 (ebk)

Typeset in Palatino
by KnowledgeWorks Global Ltd.

Visit the eResources: www.routledge.com/9780367367190

■ Support Material

The Forms and Reflection Questions in this book are also available as free downloads, so you can easily print and use them for book studies and schoolwide staff development.

The downloadable versions can be found on the book's product page on our website, www.routledge.com/9780367367190.

The website also contains bonus resources not in the book, including instructional and scheduling resources.

Contents

Author Inspirations

The ideas for this text were developed by this father-daughter instructional leadership and literacy educator team over a period of several decades. The mid-sixties marks the first time the second author, **Robert Lynn Canady**, Ed.D., understood the "big picture" on the variability across schools and within individual teacher classrooms. As a central office administrator for a large school system in the South, he was charged with integrating teachers and then students. From this vantage point, he viewed data from multiple schools and became convinced that the education of children is highly related to where they live, the school they attend, the school's principal, and, most critically, their teachers.

When the first author, **Carol E. Canady**, Ph.D., was hired as a literacy coach at a high poverty school, she developed and enjoyed remarkable gains in the primary grades by using literacy teams to provide assessment-based literacy intervention. Similar successes at other schools and at a preschool led her to intensify her efforts in the primary grades. Increasingly convinced by the research that after Grade 3 intervention with less than proficient readers was both difficult and costly, the first and second authors became engaged in consulting and other collaborative efforts to structure and to provide early literacy intervention in PK–3 grades.

A cumulation of such experiences motivated and guided these two authors to develop the systematic approach described in this text to address both a school's organizational and instructional needs. If implemented with fidelity, the model has demonstrated the potential of significantly increasing the reading proficiency of many students before leaving Grade 3.

■ Acknowledgements

We begin by acknowledging **James N. Canady** who worked with Grandpa in preparing most of the schedules and some of the other figures and forms included in this book. James demonstrated expertise as well as tremendous patience and persistence throughout the publication process.

In 2011, we first met **Joan Gordon** and described our structural and instructional developments. With the support of her then superintendent, **Pam Vogel**, Joan's East Union Elementary School in Afton, Iowa now is ranked among the state's high-achieving schools. Dr. Vogel later supported major tenets of our accelerated literacy model in Iowa and Connecticut. Joan and Pam are valuable resources for educators who seek to implement our accelerated literacy model in schools.

Laura Jo Darcy, Division Reading Specialist in King George County, was one of the first leaders in Virginia to fully implement Early Literacy Groups (ELGs) on a daily basis. Laura possesses an in-depth understanding of how young children learn to read and of the school structures necessary to fully implement fluid groupings in the early grades. She was a valuable resource in reviewing our manuscript, and she is a rich resource for readers of this book as they support *Early Literacy Matters*.

Harriet J. Hopkins, a long-time friend and colleague, was one of the second author's early students who quickly realized the importance of a well-crafted elementary school master schedule and particularly the benefits of parallel block scheduling (PBS). Beyond embracing PBS to facilitate reduced, assessment-based reading groups, she also reported that PBS reduced fragmentation of the school day by integrating multiple types of support programs. One of her incidental findings was that both "pull out" and "push in" programs not only stereotyped participating students but also disrupted students who were not involved in interventions.

Harriet K. Dawson, also a long-time friend and colleague, has supported our work as a director of staff development, a coordinator of literacy workshops, a superintendent of schools and an educational consultant for the Virginia Department of Education (VDE). She also led us to our work with Lauderdale County, TN schools and the district's superintendent, **Shawn Kimble**. As superintendent of schools in Lauderdale, County, TN, for the past decade Shawn has emphasized literacy throughout the PK–12 grades in his district. He, too, initially provided each of his elementary principals master schedules that served as catalysts for developing the current integrated, accelerated literacy programs that have received state-wide attention.

As an administrator as well as a former student of the second author, **Mary B. Maschal** embraced the benefits of PBS and became a strong advocate for accelerating reading proficiency in the early grades. More recently she has worked as a consultant with the VA DOE and as a University of Virginia Adjunct Professor. She also critiqued sections of this manuscript and encouraged us throughout the writing process. She, too, is a valuable resource for administrators who seek to implement the major tenets of our model.

Kathy C. Tucker has served in the roles of elementary teacher, principal and differentiation coordinator, regional preschool program coordinator, and university professor in reading education. We thank Kathy for being one of our early cheerleaders as she encouraged and critiqued our scripts.

As an elementary school principal in a rural Tennessee county, with a limited budget **Tracy McAbee** used PBS, creative staffing, and building-level professional development to change the school's culture by intensifying a schoolwide focus on literacy. He particularly made a difference for PK–1 students. Currently a superintendent as of July 2020, Tracy remains a valuable resource for principals and superintendents willing to begin the journey of using our literacy acceleration model to increase the percentage of proficient readers leaving Grade 3.

As a superintendent of schools in three school districts, **Daniel V. Brigman** promoted early literacy acceleration by implementing various elements of our model, including a heavy emphasis on scheduling (organizational) structures that allow integrated instruction to thrive.

Rhonda S. Reece, is one of the few elementary principals with whom we have worked who had a primary teaching background plus training in reading recovery. After participating in one of our two-day workshops, she stated: "I have been looking for such a holistic model for years!" With her instructional leadership, accelerated literacy gains were reported after only one year. She later reported to the authors that developing the school's master schedule was the catalyst for the growth she encountered.

We conclude by honoring the late **Rebecca (Becky) DuFour** for her early support of the model by implementing its major tenets in multiple schools and by conferencing with us during the early stages of preparing this text. We shall always remember Becky for her dedication to excellence in education.

Introduction

Alarmed that for over a decade barely one-third of U.S. fourth and eighth grade students have shown proficiency as readers (National Assessment of Educational Progress [NAEP], 2019), state lawmakers are enacting a flurry of new laws focused on literacy instruction in the primary grades (Gewertz, 2020). Many of these laws have a sharper focus than previous ones—stipulating the 2000 National Reading Panel report's "big five" components of reading (i.e., phonemic awareness, phonics, fluency, vocabulary, comprehension), or citing other foundational reading skills, such as building students' content knowledge base. While state laws can provide a powerful impetus for teacher change, reading experts say "giving them a little information or dropping a new reading curriculum into their classrooms isn't going to be enough" (p. 4). A systematic change as proposed in this text is required.

The Unlocked Potential of Early Literacy

In 2018–2019, public schools identified students between ages 3 and 21 for special education services at a rate of 14% (National Center for Education Statistics [NCES], 2020); however, the evidence on specific reading disability suggests that difficulties of non-proficient readers often stem from inadequate instruction or other experiential factors (Vellutino et al., 2004). Researchers also have confirmed that "appropriate instruction can improve the odds of success for all students learning to read" (Lapp, 2020, p. 4), and reading difficulties can be addressed or even prevented with effective instruction and intervention (Lapp, 2020; Allington, 2011; Vellutino, Fletcher, Snowling, & Scanlon, 2004; Vellutino & Scanlon, 2002).

From a cost perspective, funding for high-quality early learning programs has demonstrated a "significant, positive return on investment" (Kay & Pennucci, 2014, p. 1). After Grade 3, the estimated cost of correcting a reading difficulty is about eight times more than preventing it in the first place (Hernandez, 2011; Annie E. Casey Foundation, 2010). This research highlights student literacy potential and serves as an impetus for devoting resources toward the early elementary grades, with an appropriate expectation of a high return on investment.

Providing Systematic Organizational and Instructional Change

Unlike many reading publications focused solely on changing teaching practice, this book offers both organizational and instructional initiatives school leaders can implement to achieve higher levels of reading proficiency. Applied to reading, "only when both classroom level (instructional) and school level (organizational) are attended to can aspirations be met to improve literacy for all students" (Taylor, Pressley, & Pearson, 2000). We begin by committing to literacy acceleration; then we describe a systematic plan involving both instructional and organizational approaches for accelerating literacy in the primary grades.

Providing Comprehensive Literacy Instruction

To progress toward literacy proficiency and beyond, we must develop literacy instruction and interventions based on the extensive research base available to us (Lapp, 2020). Our literacy block offers a comprehensive multi-tiered literacy program (Sisson & Sisson, 2016; Tyner, 2009; Taylor, 2004). Reading difficulties are addressed or even prevented with a focus on reading words correctly, making sense of text ideas, and building world knowledge. This type of instruction is targeted to specific students' needs and students work toward meeting their goals (Lapp, 2020; Vellutino & Scanlon, 2002). In this book, we show how a comprehensive literacy program can be implemented within a schoolwide structure.

Organizing Literacy Teams and Structuring the Master Schedule

Teachers are important, but responsibility for improving the odds for student success in learning to read also requires schoolwide structure and coordination (Lapp, 2020). In this section, we trace developments in our consulting practice, leading to the instructional and organizational change initiatives illustrated in this book.

As an alternative to within-class grouping, the second author pioneered the concept of Parallel Block Scheduling (PBS), which involves parallel scheduling of core with specialist instruction, and consequently coordinating general and specialist teachers to offer need-based grouping of students across two or more classrooms (Canady, Canady, & Meek, 2017; Alkin, 1992; Canady, 1988, 1990). More recently, the second author has successfully paired core subjects with technology instruction as a means for accomplishing small group instruction as well as for building background knowledge.

To ensure strategic organization and staffing in the delivery of small group instruction and intervention, in her practice as a literacy coordinator and consultant, the first author trained a Literacy Team (LT) to "flood" or cover classrooms to provide all students with need-based instruction. Early results of the LT model were promising with K–1 students at a rural high-poverty school.

The LT is the primary means for applying and monitoring structured literacy instruction and intervention prior to, and ideally instead of, a special education referral. In contrast to a more traditional model, in which individual classroom teachers attempt to meet the differentiated needs of all students, the support of the LT is enlisted to ensure that targeted, effective instruction is consistently provided.

As an extension of their work in classrooms, the LT leader and LT members have a natural opportunity to provide embedded Professional Development (PD), which is important in developing collective teacher capacity.

> Based on a synthesis of over 800 meta-analyses related to student achievement, Hattie (2017) found that among 250+ factors, *collective teacher efficacy* has the greatest influence on student achievement. Increasing collective capacity involves individuals becoming a team with daily embedded professional development at the school and classroom levels.

During extended planning time, LTs collaborate to analyze assessment data, to plan instruction, and to process embedded PD efforts.

We, the authors, further developed and piloted the LT concept in selected schools in five states. Similar to the potential of the parallel block schedule, described in Chapter 7 of this book, we recommend the LT approach when sufficiently trained staff is available to implement the LTs successfully. When staff is limited, we recommend using PBS to provide reduced Early Literacy Groups (ELGs) and to increase student access to content knowledge in the areas of science and social studies through the use of technology. Although the primary purpose of our consulting was not to conduct research, educators who have implemented even some elements of the plan have experienced increases in student achievement.

The LT approach fits well within a Professional Learning Community (PLC) concept, "an ongoing process in which educators work collaboratively in recurring cycles of collective inquiry and action research to achieve better results for the students they serve" (DuFour, DuFour, Eaker, Many, & Mattos, 2016, p. 10). The focus is student learning at high levels, with the assumption that student learning improves when educators are engaged in job-embedded PD as a routine part of their work. Collaborative teams "work interdependently to achieve common goals for which members are held mutually accountable" (p. 12). There is a results orientation. Collaborative teams understand that the typical expectation—one year of student literacy achievement for one year of schooling—does not allow less proficient readers to "catch up" to on- or above-grade level peers, and does not maximize student literacy potential; therefore, they are committed to yearly accelerated reading growth (Allington, 2011; Cunningham & Allington, 2011). Effectiveness is assessed based on evidence of student learning, and these results are used to inform teaching practice and to plan student intervention and enrichment.

This Book's Audience and Organization

Because both schoolwide organizational and instructional changes are critical to accelerated reading gains, this book is a guide not only for teachers and reading specialists, but also for district and school administrators, teacher leaders, and LT members.

In **Chapter 1**, we document the need for higher literacy performance and report organizational and instructional initiatives that have not resulted in accelerated literacy growth. We then propose a systematic plan for leading the change. First, the term literacy acceleration is defined by grade level for PK–3, and then actions are suggested for making literacy a schoolwide priority. In **Chapter 2**, we further define LTs and highlight their multiple benefits over more traditional approaches. With this understanding, we describe the role of the LT leader in developing and coordinating the LT to provide responsive literacy instruction in primary grade classrooms. We also describe how the LT provides embedded professional development.

In **Chapter 3**, we introduce characteristics of effective literacy assessment. From there, we propose a systematic framework for selecting appropriate literacy assessments, and we establish a yearly schedule for the administration of both summative and formative assessments. When used appropriately, these data serve as reliable and valid measures of academic progress, and also contribute to flexible assessment-based grouping and responsive instructional delivery. Recommendations for training members of the LT to administer, score, and interpret assessment information also are offered. In **Chapter 4**, we demonstrate how to deliver focused, need-based literacy instruction in grades PK–3 that results in literacy acceleration. We start by showing strategic use of curriculum, instruction, and text within an extended literacy block. Goal-based small groups, interventions, and enrichments are highlighted, where we demonstrate how to flexibly group students into these services based on data. Four types of data-driven small group instruction and intervention lessons are detailed, and sequential goals are charted for each. Sample goal-based lesson formats and ideas for enrichment units also are shared.

In Chapters 5 through 7, we explain how to craft a master schedule that reflects literacy priorities. In **Chapter 5**, we start with guiding principles for crafting a master schedule. From there, we provide sample master schedules illustrating when the LT "floods" individual K–1 core teachers' classrooms to offer Early Literacy Groups (ELGs), pre-scheduled data-driven small groups, and we include explanations for decision-making. We also offer examples of how to schedule extended common planning time for

LTs. In **Chapter 6**, we lead the scheduling team through a series of steps in crafting a master schedule for their individual school, including models for scheduling Intervention/Enrichment (I/E) periods. The I/E period provides additional time for students who are less proficient in reading and math to receive intervention and for those who have reached proficiency to receive enrichment.

In **Chapter 7**, we illustrate how to utilize principles of PBS, where approximately half of one class is scheduled parallel to approximately half of another class, to provide reduced groups for need-based literacy instruction. Today some educators would refer to PBS as a form of blended learning, because students have the opportunity to participate both in small group literacy instruction and utilize technology to build background knowledge in various core subjects. If staff for LTs is limited, PBS should be considered. We also illustrate schedules with a pre-teach, co-teach, and re-teach model built into the master schedule and explain how this model can be implemented to provide support for special education and other students who can benefit from receiving extra support to master academic content.

In **Chapter 8**, we discuss how to develop effective out-of-school-time (OST) programs focused on the supplemental literacy instruction needed to obtain accelerated literacy gains. OST options are envisioned at various levels of intensity for before- and after-school programs, summer school programs, as well as for at-home online and virtual learning connections. In **Chapter 9**, we discuss the program evaluation process. We offer a survey for use when evaluating these systematic initiatives, with a focus on continuous improvement each year. Based on initiatives offered by others as well as our own experiences, we offer this comprehensive guide for educators committed to significantly increasing reading proficiency by the end of Grade 3.

Chapter 1

A Systematic Approach to Literacy Acceleration

For students reading below grade level, waiting to intervene rarely works, rather "late bloomers usually just wilt" (Wattenberg, Hansel, Hendricks, & Chang, 2004). Instead of watching children wilt, in this chapter we offer a systematic approach to accelerating literacy in the early grades, provide evidence that traditional strategies have not produced needed results, and explain both instructional and organizational strategies needed for accelerating literacy outcomes.

Why Early Literacy Is Priority

As our workforce increasingly requires higher levels of education, the demand for high levels of literacy continues to increase; however, current initiatives are not meeting performance expectations, particularly for special populations. When early literacy receives priority, students can achieve at much higher rates than ever thought possible.

Demands for High Levels of Literacy

Demands for schools to produce students who have higher levels of literacy are clear. Here are a few reasons why such demands exist.

- ♦ Literacy is the spine that holds all other subjects together. Until literacy skills are well mastered, it is very difficult for students to be successful in other subjects (Ronan, 2017; Schmoker, 2011).
- ♦ The gap between less and more proficient readers tends to grow larger each year a child is in school (i.e., the Matthew Effect) and "catching up" (reading at grade level) becomes extremely difficult when content demands increase and students who are still learning to read are ill-equipped to process text at higher levels (Wren, 2000; Stanovich, 1986; Walberg & Tsai, 1983).

- ♦ The task of successful correction can be very difficult, for nearly 90% of the students who leave Grade 1 with reading difficulties, these difficulties remain in Grade 4 (Wattenberg et al., 2004; Juel, 1988).
- ♦ After Grade 3, correcting reading difficulties costs about eight times more than prevention in the first place (Annie E. Casey Foundation, 2010).
- ♦ Students who fail to graduate from high school are more likely to be unemployed, and are 63 more times likely to be incarcerated (Breslow, 2012).

Given the importance of literacy to academic achievement, graduation rates, career, and lifelong learning possibilities, the systemic problems associated with weak literacy skills, and the intractability of later reading difficulties, "[r]eading proficiently by the end of Grade 3 can be a 'make-or-break' benchmark in a child's educational development" (Annie E. Casey Foundation, 2010, p. 9).

Lack of Results Collectively

Although reading proficiency by Grade 3 has been established as a national imperative, low levels of national literacy performance are well-documented. The National Assessment of Educational Progress (NAEP), often referred to as "our nation's report card," is the largest nationally representative and continuous assessment of student achievement in various subjects. Although the 2019 Nation's Report Card reports a 7% increase in reading achievement since implementation in 1992, only 35% of our students scored proficient. In the past decade, 4th and 8th Grade students have made no progress; and between 2017 and 2019, reading performance actually showed a 1% decline.

In addition to low proficiency on national reading assessments, international comparisons of reading achievement show the United States has much room to improve. On the 2016 Progress in International Reading Literacy Study (PIRLS) (Snyder, de Brey, & Dillow, 2019) of 4th Grade reading literacy, the average reading literacy score of fourth graders in the United States was higher than the average score in 24 of the 42 other participating countries, lower than seven countries, and not measurably different from the remaining 11 countries. Seven countries outperformed the United States: Finland, Ireland, Latvia, Norway, Poland, the Russian Federation, and Singapore. While our educational system differs in many ways from top performing countries, we can learn from the educational systems of other nations (DuFour, 2015).

Educators and researchers have raised valid concerns about standardized testing – particularly for early elementary school students (Kohn, 2000; McGill-Franzen & Allington, 1993); however, the NAEP (2019) does not report individual student performance. Instead, student results are reported demographically such as by gender, ethnicity, disability, and English language learner status, by type of school, and by locations, such as region, state, and district.

Lack of Results for Specific Student Groups

Furthermore, despite national and state education policies aimed at closing achievement gaps, low levels of reading proficiency continue to be particularly pronounced among certain groups of students. Children eligible for free or reduced lunch, a proxy for low socioeconomic status (SES), continue to perform at significantly lower levels in reading than higher SES children. On the 2019 NAEP report, 21% of children who were eligible for the National School Lunch Program (NSLP) scored proficient or above in reading as compared with 51% of children who were not eligible for the NSLP. These statistics show huge disparities in reading proficiency based on SES factors.

Although some racial and ethnic achievement gaps have narrowed since 1992, large disparities remain based on certain demographic characteristics including race/ethnicity, disability status, and English Language Learners (ELLs). On the 2019 NAEP, 45% of Caucasian students scored at or above proficient as compared with

- 18% of African-American,
- 23% of Hispanic,
- 55% of Asian or Pacific Islander,
- 57% of Asian,
- 25% of Native Hawaiian or other Pacific Islander,
- 19% of Native American or Alaska Native, and
- 40% of students who reported two or more races.

Gaps by ethnicity continue in spite of multiple interventions and associated costs.

Performance gaps for ELLs and students with disabilities continue to be substantial. For ELLs, 10% scored at or above proficient as compared with 39% who were non-ELLs. For students with disabilities, 12% performed at or above proficient as compared with 39% who did not report a disability. These percentages show significant disparities in national reading achievement based on ELL status and for students with disabilities. An important indicator of equity in education will be the reduction or elimination of these gaps.

While there is evidence that special education can be successful when based on principles of effective instruction (Kavale, 2005; Kavale, Forness, & Siperstein, 1999), there also is evidence that when compared to regular education classes, special education programs do not improve children's academic outcomes (Kvande, Bjørklund, Lydersen, Belsky, & Wichstrøm, 2018; Carlberg & Kavale, 1980). Furthermore, once students are identified as requiring special education services, they are less likely to catch up to grade level or ever be dismissed from special education (DuFour, 2015).

The Potential of Early Literacy

As introduced previously, "appropriate instruction can improve the odds of success for all students learning to read" (Lapp, 2020, p. 4), and reading difficulties can be addressed or even prevented with effective instruction and intervention (Lapp, 2020; Allington, 2011; Vellutino, Fletcher, Snowling, & Scanlon, 2004; Vellutino & Scanlon, 2002). Impairments in learning to read often are related to word identification due to basic alphabetic coding deficits. In most cases, deficits in reading-related cognitive areas are related to phonological skills deficiencies associated with phonological coding deficits. In some cases, reading difficulties also are associated with general language deficits. With a focus on the early grades, by providing our recommended instructional and organizational initiatives, these impairments can be prevented.

Typical Instructional and Organizational Improvement Initiatives

Typically, improving instructional or organizational effectiveness has focused on *what* change is needed. Specifics of *how* to make change have not been delineated such that accelerated results are accomplished. In the field of reading, an overarching structure for supporting students who enter school with limited literacy proficiency has involved establishing an effective multi-tiered system of support (MTSS). Reading professionals also strive to resolve continued literacy debates over best ways to teach reading.

Multi-Tiered Systems of Support

In 2004, Response to Intervention (RTI), a federal legislation initiative offering non-proficient readers the opportunity to respond to expert and intense reading intervention before being placed in special education services, was enacted (Allington, 2009, 2011; Fuchs et al, 2008). A review of 16 studies on the impact of RTI on student achievement shows some improvement (Hughes & Dexter, 2020), largely attributed to the multi-tiered instruction offered. A higher level of support was found for early reading skills than for other subjects, and at the elementary grades than at middle or high school grades. Rates of referral to special education remained constant, with some studies showing declines, but studies lacked consistency regarding how students were placed in interventions and how they were found eligible for special education services. Results of these studies were qualified, due to lack of controls; RTI models were not implemented for the purpose of conducting large-scale evaluations. More recently, a broader MTSS (Rosen, 2020) is being implemented in many schools to encompass RTI and Positive Behavioral Interventions and Supports (PBIS). These systems seek to identify students in a timely manner and to provide academic and other forms of support for overall well-being. Preliminary research supports a multi-tiered approach to literacy instruction, but these models in themselves have not produced accelerated literacy gains.

Continued Literacy Debates

Over two decades since the National Reading Panel report (National Institute of Child Health and Human Development [NICHD], 2000) documenting scientifically based research evidence on teaching children to read, debate over how to teach reading continues. Current debates ensue between proponents of balanced literacy and structured literacy approaches. The term balanced literacy implies an effort to balance the use of direct skill and strategy instruction with application to authentic reading and writing tasks (Pressley, 1998). An important component of early reading instruction for balanced literacy advocates is to explicitly instruct students in strategic actions (i.e., look at the picture, make the beginning sound, find the magic rime, ask if it looks right) (Richardson & Lewis, 2018; Fountas & Pinnell, 2016). Students apply these strategic actions to read leveled readers containing a mix of decodable and less decodable words. They also engage in writing as a follow-up to reading. Typically, students are grouped by reading level.

Structured literacy advocates emphasize systematic and cumulative instruction (International Dyslexia Association [IDA], 2020). Systematic means the teacher follows a sequence from easiest to most difficult concepts and elements, and cumulative means current lesson concepts build from previous ones. Direct teaching of concepts with continuous teacher-student interaction is important. Diagnostic teaching occurs within and apart from each lesson, with emphasis on adjusting instruction to help students make progress on a specific goal as well as on overall reading abilities. Once students demonstrate accuracy, assessment of word reading and overall reading abilities include measures of automaticity. Automatic word reading is associated with comprehension.

Balanced literacy has been criticized for de-emphasizing the role of phonics in learning to read (IDA, 2020; Hanford, 2019; Denton, Fletcher, Taylor, Barth, & Vaughn, 2014). As most students learn to read words accurately and with automaticity, they abandon less mature or unnecessary strategies; however, some students who may not easily learn phonics, either because of poor instruction or disability, are thought to hang onto poor or partially learned strategies. Balanced literacy also has been criticized by systematic literacy advocates for its use of guided reading groups based on reading level, with the teacher in more of a facilitator than a direct instruction role, and with its use of leveled rather than more highly decodable readers.

In his response to a teacher's question regarding types of text to use with early readers, Shanahan (2019b) offers the following insight relevant to the current literacy debate:

> "Sadly, advocates of various beginning reading schemes usually appear oblivious to the problems their favorite support systems present to beginning readers. They love the fact that the texts they champion allow kids to read early on. But they ignore the fact that their beginning reading texts – like everyone else's – differ from the actual universe of texts that we read, and the more these texts diverge the greater the danger that they will be misleading to at least some kids" (p. 2).

Shanahan (2019b) acknowledges the importance of using a variety of beginning reader texts to ease the way for beginning readers as well as the need to "make serious efforts to try to avoid the downsides" (p. 2). Structured literacy has similarities to the Reading First federal program created by the 2001 No Child Left Behind Act (NCLB) in its emphasis on teaching phonics and its lesser emphasis on the reading of authentic texts. The Reading First Impact Study's Final Report (Gamse et al., 2008) on average impacts on classroom instruction over the course of three years shows a positive and statistically significant impact (equivalent to an effect size of 0.17 standard deviations) on decoding among Grade 1 students tested in one school year, but no statistically significant difference on students' reading comprehension in Grades 1, 2, or 3. Administrators and LT leaders do well to rely on strong research evidence, and capitalize on merits while avoiding drawbacks of structured and balanced literacy approaches. Analysis of student assessment data also is imperative as teachers adjust instruction to meet student needs.

We also will discuss the history of self-contained classrooms in the primary grades, and the use of small group instruction to address diverse academic needs. Without specialized scheduling, however, students typically receive less than optimal literacy instruction as we discuss.

Self-Contained Classrooms in the Primary Grades

Upper elementary grades often utilize a departmentalized (students have a different teacher for each subject) or semi-departmental approach (students receive one teacher for English and social studies and another teacher for math and science, for example) (Alkin, 1992); however, in the primary grades, assigning students to self-contained classrooms is common practice, where students are instructed in all academic or core subjects with their homeroom teacher, with the exception of transitioning to a related arts teacher during related arts or encore block of time. Basically, students interact with the same peer group all day.

Small Group Instruction Without Specialized Scheduling

Although the need for self-contained classrooms in the primary grades is understood – primary grade teachers can build relationships with and provide guidance to fewer students – these self-contained classrooms usually are composed of a heterogenous group of students who vary in levels of academic proficiency (Alkin, 1992). To address the diverse academic needs of students, typically students have been placed in small groups based on reading and math performances. While the teacher meets with a reading or math group, the other students often have independent reading and writing time. This independent literacy time can be difficult for the teacher to monitor while providing intensive small group instruction, and therefore, an unproductive use of time for many primary grade students, especially for less proficient readers.

Strategies focused on providing additional instructional time include having specialists "push in" to provide supplemental instruction in the regular classroom or "pull out" to provide this instruction outside of the regular classroom. While research suggests potential benefits to these approaches, there are also several unintended negative consequences (Obiakor, Harris, Mutua, Rotatori, & Algozzine, 2012; Allington & Walmsley, 1995). Core teachers have reported that both "push in" and "pull out" programs often interrupt the flow of their classrooms (Downing & Anderson, 2006). They also report that the programs stigmatize and isolate students and that, without specialized scheduling, students assigned to special "pull out" support programs often miss instruction by the core teacher (Obiakor et al., 2012; Downing & Anderson, 2006).

The amount of time for these programs also has been reported as insufficient. At best, schools provide students who have not achieved reading proficiency with 20–30 minutes of reading instruction beyond regular classroom instruction (Allington, 2012). For the remaining six-plus hours of the school day, few less proficient students are receiving appropriate instruction to "catch up" to their on- or above-grade-level peers. Furthermore, few of them have access to appropriate reading materials and resources throughout the school day.

OST Programming Issues

Another strategy focused on providing additional instructional time is to offer extended-day and extended-year programs such as before school, after school, and summer school programs. In this book, we refer to these as out-of-school-time (OST) programs. OST programs in themselves are not likely to accelerate literacy proficiency (Allington, 2011). Thus, they are supplemental to the progress expected during the regular school day.

An ongoing issue is that students who need OST programs most are least likely to attend. Because attendance is important to success, schools often strongly recommend or require OST programs for promotion in grade. As a result, OST programs have been viewed as punitive. In Chapter 8, we offer OST options of various intensities with the understanding that OST programs are a continuation of quality, high-interest instruction offered during the regular school day or year.

Achieving Accelerated Literacy

Strategies needed to increase the likelihood of reading acceleration are introduced below. We encourage school and Literacy Team (LT) leaders to view these items as a checklist to guide you as you determine the initiatives to take toward implementing literacy acceleration at your school.

Defining Accelerated Reading

As shared in the introduction, we expect PK–3 students to learn to read at accelerated rates, which means we must expect *six years of growth in a four-year span*, an average of 1.5 years of literacy growth per school year in Grades K-3 (Allington, 2011). Where intensive literacy support is in place, we actually strive to achieve *double or triple rates of reading growth* (Cunningham & Allington, 2011). In our commitment to literacy acceleration, we also recommend using accelerated expectations to evaluate the effectiveness of literacy program practices in achieving learning outcomes. Students who are not achieving at accelerated rates receive additional intensive early intervention services. In this book, a student's reading growth is defined as *accelerated* when the growth rates shown in Figure 1.1 have occurred.

For less proficient readers, 2–3 years of growth are expected in PK–1 and 1.5 years of growth are expected in Grades 2–3. For example, students entering Grade 1 reading one-year behind are expected to make at least two years of progress, which would place them on-grade level before entering Grade 2. Proficient readers who receive Early Literacy Group (ELG) instruction are

Figure 1.1 Expected Grade-Level Reading Growth by Level of Student Proficiency

	PK	K	1	2	3
Proficient and Beyond	1–3 years of reading growth each year			From proficient to advanced in enrichment areas.	
Less Proficient	2–3 years of reading growth each year			At least 1.5 years of growth each year	

expected to show similar gains to less than proficient readers. If they receive enrichment they are expected to advance from proficient to advanced proficient in the area of focus in enrichment, typically in social studies or in science. Also, note, LT leaders would track the data for an entire school year to be sure that accelerated reading expectation is maintained through the summer. For example, if a Grade 1 student made 2 years of progress from Fall to Spring to read on-grade level, but was assessed in the Fall of the following year and found to be reading below grade level, then the student did not make 2 years of progress in one year. With a strong commitment to early reading acceleration, administrators lay a firm foundation for success in the upper elementary grades.

Developing Schoolwide Priorities

The RTI and the broader MTSS models usually entail three tiers of instruction, with Tier 1 representing instruction that all students receive. Like the base of a pyramid, to prevent reading difficulties, the first tier must be weighted the heaviest (Shapiro, 2008). With a strong Tier 1 instructional program, quality need-based interventions are more feasible to offer for the smaller number of students who require additional support.

To accomplish accelerated reading gains, we recommend that school leaders develop strategies for accelerating literacy in PK–3 with these three schoolwide goals in mind:

- ◆ Focus on increasing prevention efforts (i.e., Tier 1), resulting in reduced numbers of students who require interventions.
- ◆ Provide quality need-based interventions (i.e., Tiers 2 and 3).
- ◆ Permit few, if any, retentions (Intercultural Development Research Association, 2018).

To accomplish this focus on prevention, *what if* we spend 15% of the money currently allocated to special education on prevention strategies in the early grades? Such an expenditure can be justified and is recommended to improve Tier 1 availability and results (Allington, 2011; Ohio Department of Education, 2015).

Developing a Highly Trained Literacy Team Within a Professional Learning Community

To begin the process of school reform, "someone" must decide change is both needed and possible. That "someone" typically is a central office administrator or an elementary school principal. This leader of organizational and instructional change begins with a thorough examination of all available data, comparing the school to other schools in the district, area, state, and nation. Grade level and individual student data also should be studied. The administrator uses convincing data to show the need for change. A well-documented need for change must be established and explained to multiple stakeholders, including school board members. Next, a Literacy Leader must be identified who has qualifications and characteristics further described in Chapter 2.

We advocate assembling well-trained LTs to function according to the principles of Professional Learning Communities (PLCs) (DuFour, DuFour, Eaker, Many, & Mattos, 2016). LTs are led by competent literacy specialists, often called Literacy Coaches or LT Leaders. These leaders possess the literacy expertise, leadership characteristics, and energy to train all team members, including Teacher Assistants (TAs), throughout the school year with a focus on continuous improvement.

ELGs are goal-oriented small groups instructed by LT members – classroom teachers, reading specialists, special education teachers, or teacher assistants, for example – who have been trained to provide specific skills and strategies. Students are rotated to instructors specifically trained in the skills and strategies students need. Specifics of the LT leader and the LT are delineated in Chapter 2.

Providing Quality (Mostly Embedded) Professional Development

Over 90% of teachers participate in traditional one-shot workshop-style training sessions during a school year (Darling-Hammond, Wei, Andree, Richardson, & Orphanos, 2009). This method is expensive, and transfer to actual classroom practice often does not occur (D'Orio, 2017). Basically, these sessions result in little or no influence on student achievement. Perhaps this lack of influence is because they have been conducted sporadically, with professionals isolated from their work environment, subject matter, and colleagues (Smith & Gillespie, 2007).

In contrast to typical one-shot workshop-style training sessions, LTs provide job-embedded professional development (PD) within the daily work environment. Change is nurtured, because learning is ongoing and occurs within the routine work of the school (DuFour et al., 2016). The LT leader trains the LT, and all LT members receive embedded PD as they perform daily classroom responsibilities (Canady & Canady, 2012). PD can be developed and adapted as short and long-term PD needs arise. Extended planning time provided within the master schedule allows LTs time to process embedded PD opportunities.

When this kind of PD is combined with a shared culture and a well-articulated mission, a spirit of synergy often emerges (DuFour et al., 2016). In a synergistic organization, employees feel competent in their roles or, when uncertain, ask for assistance without apology; admitting need and asking for help are common behaviors in organizations committed to continuous improvement. In Chapter 2, more information on PD opportunities offered by the LT leader are shared. In Chapter 5, we also demonstrate how to build a master schedule with extended planning time for assessment and instructional planning, but also for processing PD.

Assessing Students and Monitoring Progress

Literacy acceleration in the early grades requires the use of assessment to form fluid small groups, and then frequent monitoring of student progress. Both formative and summative assessments are needed. Simple daily/weekly assessments are critical during the early stages of literacy development. Informal reading inventories or running records, skill-based quick checks, and trained teacher observations are a must for frequent assessment-based groupings and re-groupings to occur (Templeton & Gehsmann, 2014; Walpole & McKenna, 2017; Walpole & McKenna, 2009). In Chapter 3, further detail can be found on assessment and progress monitoring.

Providing Systematic Literacy Instruction Within a Literacy Block

Highly effective teachers are masters at appropriately providing direct instruction with a gradual release of responsibility leading to the goal of students reaching independence as learners (Sisson & Sisson, 2016; Tyner, 2009; Taylor, 2004). To ensure that this occurs, we recommend systematically building this model of direct instruction with gradual release of responsibility into the literacy block. As an essential literacy block feature, we also show how systematic small group literacy instruction and an Intervention option can be utilized as a modification of Independent reading time (Canady & Canady, 2012). When ELGs are implemented as intended within a multi-leveled support system, fewer students should require more intensive interventions in later grades (Allington, 2011); however, we also show how intervention and enrichment can be scheduled and implemented within an Intervention/Enrichment (I/E) period.

The instruction provided for each literacy element includes the five essentials of effective reading instruction (NICHD, 2000): phonemic awareness, phonics, fluency, vocabulary, and comprehension. These essentials are offered in an integrated lesson designed to teach a particular skill or strategy and apply the skill or strategy to authentic reading or writing tasks. An integrated lesson plan facilitates student transfer of learning. A structured literacy block and its various elements as well as sample integrated small group lesson plans are shared in Chapter 4.

The success of small group interventions and enrichments depends on the quality of supplemental instruction provided as compared to the quality of instruction the student would have received if he or she had not missed the instruction in the regular classroom (DuFour, 2015). Scheduling ELGs and I/E periods into the master school schedule prevents less proficient readers from missing valuable core instruction.

Early Literacy Groups

Small group reading instruction, the heart of a reading program, is the most important time of the school day for students to receive the targeted instruction they need to progress as readers. Because small group time is so valuable, it must be protected. Rather than expecting teachers to lead small groups while simultaneously overseeing the remainder of the classroom, we propose enlisting trained LT members to provide differentiated literacy instruction, which represents a connected rather than fragmented approach to literacy instruction.

Successfully combined with previously developed organizational and scheduling concepts (Canady & Canady, 2012), ELGs are structured goal-oriented small groups instructed by specifically trained LT members. All students in a grade level receive ELGs, and they are built into the master schedule. In the accelerated plan presented in this book, students receive a minimum of 300 minutes of ELG instruction on a weekly basis. ELGs provide literacy instruction for all students at a particular grade level such as at Kindergarten and Grade 1. On a limited basis, they also are offered in Grade PK and Grade 2. Homogeneous groups of students are assigned to ELGs based on assessed needs. Students work toward mastery of sequential literacy goals.

In our model, coordinated ELGs work well within a larger RTI system or the broader MTSS (Rosen, 2020). Typically, each is built around providing three tiers of support. Since all students are served, ELGs are a critical component of Tier 1 instruction.

For the purposes of this book, we are defining Tiers 1–3 as follows:

Tier 1 = Grade-level core instruction within an evidence-based literacy program that includes daily (or short-term intensive) differentiated Early Literacy Group (ELG) lessons delivered to all students during the course of a school year.
Tier 2 = Additional targeted small group intervention for students who require instruction beyond Tier 1 to become proficient readers.
Tier 3 = Intensive small group intervention for students whose significant gaps have not been successfully addressed in Tier 1 or Tier 2 instruction.

For students who require additional support, Tier 2 and Tier 3 Interventions can be offered during Independent reading time following the ELG time or during a pre-scheduled I/E period to be discussed in the next section.

Formative assessments are used frequently (i.e., daily, weekly) to monitor progress and to move students from one group to another based on skill or strategy needs (Walpole & McKenna, 2016). ELGs also can be formed across classrooms based on student needs. When ELGs are fully implemented in Grades PK–1 or K–1 for multiple years within a functioning multi-tiered system, the percentage of students needing additional Title 1 and special education support services is likely to be reduced (Allington, 2011).

Intervention/Enrichment Periods

An I/E period can be built into the master schedule to provide: (1) intervention services for students who are not meeting proficiency goals in reading or mathematics; and (2) enrichment services for students who have met proficiency goals in reading and in mathematics. The instruction in the Intervention period is similar to ELG instruction, except ELGs serve all students, but students must be identified for Intervention. Also, the time often is longer for Intervention groups than for ELGs. Assuming ELGs are in place in K-1, I/E periods usually appear in the master schedule in Grades 2–5. Typical I/E periods of time are between 35 and 50 minutes, depending on the number of minutes in the school day.

Enrichment is designed to provide selected students who have achieved proficiency (i.e., on-grade-level performance) in reading and mathematics with opportunities to deepen their thinking or learning on a particular topic related to a specific discipline. Enrichment units typically are constructed with content from social studies or science. These units are multidisciplinary; therefore, subjects such as reading, writing, math, technology, and research are incorporated into the units as applicable. For example, although the primary discipline for a unit on immigration is social studies, perhaps disciplines of reading, writing, math, science, and technology would be built into the unit. The goal of enrichment is to move students from *proficiency* to *advanced proficiency* in social studies or science by offering targeted multidisciplinary enrichment units taught by highly qualified personnel.

Flexibly Grouping Students Based on Data

For students to receive maximal benefit, ELG and Intervention instruction must be fluid or flexibly grouped throughout the school year as students master specific and overall goals. The LT leader ensures student grouping and regrouping based on frequent assessments of identified foundational reading goals, with consideration to overall reading abilities.

Options for high, moderate, and reduced ELG and Intervention support are available. Depending on various factors (i.e., grade level, reading level, skill needs, funding), a variety of flexible grouping options, including enrichment activities, also are available to students who read on or above grade level.

Crafting a Master Schedule to Reflect Instructional Priorities

An elementary school master schedule reflects a school's values. If a mission for accelerating literacy in the early grades is highly valued, then that value will be evident in the master schedule's allotment of time, space, personnel, and resources. When "valued programs" are crafted in the master schedule, they can easily be monitored, evaluated, and adjusted as needed.

Increasing time for literacy instruction within the school day is critical for literacy acceleration to occur. Beyond increased time for literacy, systematic placement of ELGs and I/Es in the master schedule promotes early literacy acceleration, especially when the literacy instructional program is led by a highly effective LT with a primary focus on Tier 1 instruction. With an emphasis on accelerating literacy achievement in the early grades, the need for Tier 2 and Tier 3 services can be greatly reduced (Vaughn, Wanzek, Woodruff, & Linan-Thompson, 2007).

Beyond increasing time for literacy, schools must develop well-crafted master school schedules that provide time for all other programs. In the primary grades, if 180 minutes are given to literacy acceleration and 90 minutes to math and science, schools have 120–150 minutes remaining for I/E, homeroom, encore (arts and PE), lunch, recess and transitions. It is assumed that social studies in the primary grades will be integrated in the literacy block. For an example of a master schedule designed to accommodate ELGs and various interventions, and to provide extended planning time, see Figures 5.1, 5.5 and 7.1. Chapters 5 and 6 have specific information on designing a well-crafted master schedule that puts literacy first and also accommodates other instructional needs of students.

Developing OST Programs

Although not intended to make up for literacy instruction offered during the regular school hours, effective OST programs tend to be integrated into the overall literacy acceleration plan and targeted to students who need additional help (Cooper, Nye, Charlton, Lindsay, & Greathouse, 1996). Any literacy instruction that is a continuation of literacy learning during OST has the possibility of being successful. Examples of OST options include summer school, before and after school time, and at-home learning time. With consideration to cost factors, in this book we examine research-based options for increasing academic OST.

Evaluating the Program

For each student who has not reached proficiency in reading, a baseline is established and individual goals are developed based on skill needs. The goals for students who are not yet proficient readers are consistent with an acceleration mindset as defined earlier in this chapter. These goals are monitored frequently throughout the school year. As goals are met, new goals are established based on assessment data. If goals are not met, problem-solving occurs during LT meetings to determine the underlying cause or causes. Before changing interventions, it is important to clarify the specific intervention needed and to ensure fidelity of intervention implementation.

Explicit word-level instruction with explicit application to reading and writing must be observed during intervention time each day. Coordination between the reading instruction offered by the classroom teacher and by the interventionists also is important. The appropriateness and the level of the books the child is reading throughout the school day must also be monitored. For some students, literacy gains occur with adjustment of the current reading group. For others, an additional reading group could contribute to the desired accelerated outcomes. LT leaders with expertise in monitoring and using both formal and informal assessments are critical to the success of an accelerated literacy program.

Changing school culture is not easy. Understandably, school staff and leaders can become discouraged; therefore, it is important to break larger into smaller goals. When success is achieved, celebrate each small step. Both teachers and students need to be validated for their persistent efforts. Celebrating small successes also provides frequent and much needed encouragement and can contribute to a growth mindset (Dweck, n.d.), which includes the determination to persist and to work hard. Students who put forth extra effort need to experience frequent, incremental successes to maintain persistence. Particularly, children "who grow up in poverty face readiness and literacy lags that require extra efforts" (Canady, Canady, & Meek, 2017, p. 65). For example, students can be asked to write about and share what they are learning. When students return their books with parent signatures, they earn a small reward. When they meet larger reading goals, they then celebrate as a class such as by blasting off with rocket balloons! Each celebration also provides an opportunity to analyze and determine why we were successful, or if we were not successful, what adjustments we need to make.

The Schoolwide Literacy Initiatives Questionnaire

The Schoolwide Literacy Initiatives Questionnaire in Figure 1.2 can be helpful in observing and evaluating district, school, and classroom performance to maximize the likelihood of accelerated reading achievement occurring at an individual school.

Figure 1.2 Schoolwide Literacy Initiatives Questionnaire

FACTORS	TRADITIONAL APPROACH Focus: Status Quo Student Achievement	SYSTEMATIC APPROACH Focus: Accelerated Student Achievement
Student Literacy Expectations/Schoolwide Priorities and Goals (Introduction or Chapter 1)		
Literacy Expectations for Students What are our student literacy performance expectations?	• Our expectation is based on achieving on-grade level performance for each student.	• Readers who receive ELGs and Interventions are expected to progress at acceelerated rates (at least 6 years in 4 years). • Proficient readers are expected to progress at accelerated rates and/or beyond proficiency in enrichment areas (i.e., science, social studies).
Schoolwide Literacy Priorities/Goals What are our schoolwide literacy priorities and schoolwide goals?	• Literacy is not the priority in the master schedule; ELGs & I/Es are not in the master schedule. • We have not set accelerated schoolwide & grade level literacy goals at incremental times, PK-3.	• Literacy is the priority in the master schedule; ELGs and I/Es are in the master schedule. • We have set accelerated schoolwide & grade level literacy goals at incremental times, PK-3.
Commitment to Literacy Teams (Chapter 2)		
Community Organization/Culture Do we have a culture of collaboration? Are meetings focused on using data to increase student performance?	• A few teachers in isolated classrooms achieve excellent results each year. • Most teachers work alone or with a partner. • Core teachers and support teachers seldom co-teach or plan together.	• The concept of Professional Learning Communities (PLCs) is fully enacted schoolwide. • Extended planning meetings focus on student performance data; student work is analyzed to determine instructional priorities.
Literacy Teaming (LT) Are LTs in place and effective? Do they meet during extended common planning time and accomplish priorities?	• LTs are not in place or are not effective. • LTs do not meet during extended planning time to analyze data, flex groups, and plan instruction.	• A LT leader is appointed and LTs are functioning. • LTs meet during extended planning time to analyze data, flex groups, and plan instruction.
LT Professional Development (PD) To what degree is PD oriented toward achieving goals?	• PD is lacking or not central to important priorities and staff needs. • External PD lacks follow through and/or PD is not conducted at the school level.	• External PD is provided based on identified needs and includes quality follow through. • Most PDs are conducted at the school level.
Assessment (Chapter 3)		
Screening and Progress Monitoring	• Summative assessments may or may not occur. • Formative assessments do not occur or are not frequent (daily, weekly) and/or are not used to identify student needs, to flexibly group students, and/or to establish instructional priorities.	• Summative assessments are in place. • Formative assessments are performed daily or weekly and are used to identify student needs, to flexibly group students, and to establish instructional priorities.
Literacy Instruction (Chapter 4)		
Alignment of Curriculum with Standards and Assessments	• The curriculum is not aligned with standards and assessments at each grade level.	• The curriculum is aligned with standards and assessments at each grade level.
Literacy Block How many minutes are dedicated daily to research-based literacy elements? Do teachers provide support for student learning?	• The literacy block is less than 160 minutes. Students do not receive modeled/shared reading, ELGs, independent time or extra ELGs. • Teachers do not provide appropriate scaffolding.	• The literacy block is 160–180 minutes. Students receive modeled/shared reading, ELGs, independent time or extra ELGs/Interventions. • Teachers provide appropriate scaffolding from higher to lower levels of support.
ELG/Intervention Lessons For less proficient readers, how many minutes are dedicated to ELGs or interventions per week?	• Sufficient time is not spent in ELGs and Interventions. • LT members do not provide structured lessons focused on literacy goals.	• Sufficient time is spent in ELGs or interventions (at least 300 minutes weekly). • LT members provide structured lessons focused on literacy goals.
Enrichment For proficient readers, how much time is dedicated to enrichment per week? What are the results?	• Sufficient time is not spent in enrichment. • LT members do not provide structured units focused on essential enrichment questions. • Proficient readers do not progress to advanced levels in the enrichment areas.	• Sufficient time is spent in enrichment. • LT members provide structured units focused on essential enrichment questions. • Proficient readers progress to advanced levels in the enrichment areas.
Text Quality, Quantity, Appropriateness Are multiple types of quality texts of appropriate difficulty provided and utilized? Are they easily accessed?	• Students do not read multiple types of quality texts of appropriate difficulty. • Students do not spend time reading or are not held accountable for their reading. • Resources are not provided or are not easily accessed.	• Students read multiple types of quality texts of appropriate difficulty. • Students spend time reading texts and are held accountable for their reading. • Resources are provided and easily accessed.

Figure 1.2 Schoolwide Literacy Initiatives Questionnaire (*Continued*)

Flexible Grouping What are our ELG and I/E foci? Do they flex according to student needs?	• ELGs, I/Es do not have a specific focus based on assessed needs of students. • Students do not show mastery or they do not progress to other groups.	• ELGs and I/Es have a specific focus based on assessed needs of students. • As students show mastery, they progress to other groups.
Organizing and Scheduling (Chapters 5–7)		
Scheduling Priorities To what degree do we have a master schedule that supports our expectations/priorities/goals?	• We do not have a master schedule and/or • Instructional priorities are not fully represented in the master schedule.	• We have a master schedule that reflects instructional priorities. • The master schedule includes time for multiple levels of literacy instruction and support services.
Scheduled Planning Time Do LT members have common planning with grade level teachers? Do they have extended planning time during school time with the LT?	• LT members do not have common planning with grade level teachers on a weekly basis. • Extended planning time during the school day is not included in the master schedule.	• LT members have common planning with grade level teachers on a weekly basis. • LT members have extended planning time on a rotating basis during the school day to frame future instruction.
Parallel Block Scheduling Is PBS used optimally to reduce groups and to build student background knowledge?	• PBS is not used optimally to reduce groups and benefits are maximized such as technology is incorporated to build student background knowledge.	• PBS is used optimally to reduce groups and benefits are maximized such as technology is incorporated to build student background knowledge.
OST Programs (Chapter 8)		
OST Program Focus Is OST a continuation of assessment-based instruction from the regular school day or year?	• OST is not a continuation of instruction from the regular school day or year. • The OST program is not developed based on analysis of student assessment or other data.	• OST is a continuation of instruction from the regular school day or year. • The OST program is developed based on analysis of student assessment and other data.
Weighing OST Options	• OST decisions are not made based on weighing costs and benefits of various options.	• OST decisions are made based on weighing costs and benefits of various options.
How are OST choices made? Are school/community factors comprehensive? Are student needs prioritized?	• School feasibility and student needs are not addressed in developing optimal OST programs.	• School feasibility and student needs are addressed in developing optimal OST programs.
Program Evaluation (Chapter 9)		
Instructional Program Is the program evaluation data-driven? Does evaluation guide program improvement?	• Each element of the literacy program is not specifically evaluated. • Evaluation is not used systematically to improve the instructional program.	• Each element of the literacy program is specifically evaluated. • Evaluation guides program improvement throughout the school year.
Program Equity Are we disaggregating the data to be sure we are focused on serving all students? Are less proficient and proficient readers being maximally served?	• We are not disaggregating the data to be sure our focus is on serving all students. • Less proficient and proficient readers are not being maximally served.	• We are disaggregating the data to be sure our focus is on serving all students. • Less proficient and proficient readers are being maximally served.

Summary

Beyond the well-documented importance of early literacy intervention, in this chapter we quantified the need for accelerated reading growth, defined as at least doubled reading gains in PK–1 and at least 1.5 years of growth per year in Grades PK–3 on average until students reach proficiency or on- or beyond-grade level performance as readers. Aligned with this aim, we documented the necessity of scheduling time in the master schedule for literacy groups. We discussed how to ensure results by organizing trained LTs to provide responsive and intensive small-group instruction that is built into a master schedule. We also described and highlighted key instructional factors, such as using a multi-tiered response to intervention approach within the context of a LT concept, a more specific literacy application of the well-documented PLC concept.

Significant increases in time, in coordination, and in intensity of diagnostic literacy instruction are necessary. One without the other will not be sufficient in producing an accelerated rate of growth. This proposed Reading Acceleration Framework prompts educators to comprehensively evaluate and improve school factors, in order to progress toward the goal of accelerating student literacy performance.

Reflection

Reflect on the content from this chapter as you consider the concept of literacy acceleration.

1. To what extent is literacy acceleration (at least two-year gains in one school year for students who read below grade level in K-1 and 1.5-year gains across K-3) occurring at your school? Discuss reading achievement at each grade level.

2. How is early literacy acceleration reflected: In hiring decisions? In budgets? In training and developing personnel? In instructional conversations? In how we collaborate?

3. What could be accomplished if we were to transfer the extra $12,612 (Alonzo, 2020), the 2018 per pupil cost of providing a retained student an additional year of schooling, to providing extra early literacy intervention for a non-proficient reader? What gains do you think we would see in this student?

4. Reflect on this statement: Because high stakes testing begins in Grade 3 and continues each year through the upper grades, administrators often focus on showing current year test score gains over the previous year. How do staffing decisions prioritize upper elementary instruction in testing grades at the expense of high-quality instruction in the primary grades?

5. What short-term outcomes do you predict in literacy achievement when an administrator commits to reading acceleration, especially in K-1? What long-term outcomes do you predict?

Chapter 2

Benefits of Literacy Teams and Roles of the Literacy Team Leader

Regardless of a student's background or lack of educational attainment at the start of school, evidence shows that the most important factor in an individual student's achievement gains is quality instruction from a highly effective teacher (Hanushek, 2016, 2011; Sanders & Rivers, 1996). However, not all teachers are equally skilled (Allington, 2011; Pianta, Belsky, Houts, & Morrison, 2007). In fact, only 23% of Grade 1 teachers provide high-quality reading lessons that enable every student to complete that grade as a successful reader (Stuhlman & Pianta, 2009).

Translated to literacy, in the end, "enhanced reading proficiency rests largely on the capacity of classroom teachers to provide expert, exemplary reading instruction" (Allington, 2002, 2011). Literacy Teams (LTs) and LT leaders mitigate the lack of highly qualified literacy education currently available to students and help boost the skills of low-qualified or ineffective teachers.

Literacy Teams Defined

To fully utilize the instructional expertise in each building, we propose LTs whose members develop both the collective instructional capacity and the efficacy needed to provide research-based instruction in the early grades. Our proposal for LTs is supported by multiple data sources (Dewitt, 2019; Tucker, 2019; DuFour & Marzano, 2011; DuFour, 2004).

Building from the Professional Learning Community (PLC) model, LTs or "job-alike" teams, where members share a common job, "are typically most effective in improving learning for both the adults and students" (DuFour & Marzano, 2011, p. 71). LT members share the responsibility of delivering appropriate reading instruction to students in their assigned classrooms and are dedicated to the coordinated, systematic, and collective improvement of literacy by ensuring the ongoing, job-embedded learning for the adults who teach literacy. Effective teams in a PLC are characterized by interdependence, one or more common goals, and mutual accountability. Without one or more of these characteristics, a team is just a group of teachers that happens to meet together.

Interdependence and Mutual Accountability

LT members share responsibility for addressing four critical questions that drive their work: "What do students need to know and be able to do? How will we know when they have learned it? What will we do when they haven't learned it? What will we do when they already know it?" (DuFour, DuFour, Eaker, Many, & Mattos, 2016, p. 251). For these essential questions to drive the work of a collective community, educators reflect critically on these essential questions and the ideas behind them until they become deeply embedded in the school's culture (DuFour, 2004).

LTs, when specifically focused on essential questions, show improved teacher effectiveness (Graham, 2007). LT members also are mutually accountable for performance (DuFour & Marzano, 2011), which encourages them to work together for a purpose much larger than the results of the specific students assigned to their classroom or reading groups.

Common Literacy Goals

LTs remain on task by setting and sharing common learning goals that are immediately applicable to their classrooms (DuFour & Marzano, 2011). The LT leader helps the LT clarify purposes and priorities, and to focus on the tasks required to continuously improve performance. They bring expert knowledge of the curriculum, instruction, and assessment linked to their subject. For students who have not reached proficiency as readers, goals are accelerated, as previously described, and progress is monitored more frequently for lower than for higher readers.

In Chapter 4, student goals that promote literacy acceleration will be further discussed LT members can use the SMART acronym to establish their own goals based on various formative assessments.

A SMART goal is (DuFour, 2015; O'Neill & Conzemius, 2006, p.126):

♦ Strategic and specific – The team's goal aligns with the goals of the school or district.
♦ Measurable – The goal includes quantifiable terms.
♦ Attainable – The team believes the goal is achievable.
♦ Results oriented – The goal requires evidence of improved student learning.
♦ Time bound – The goal will be accomplished within a specific period of time.

For the LT to function successfully, team members, especially the LT leaders, must have extended planning time to review student goal attainment based on data, build lesson plans, and organize instruction initially within each classroom, but ultimately across grade-level classrooms.

Benefits of Literacy Teams

A study conducted by the National Commission on Teaching and America's Future (Fulton, Yoon, & Lee, 2005), described isolated teaching in stand-alone classrooms as the most persistent norm standing in the way of school improvement. In stark contrast, LTs offer numerous benefit over more fragmented models for accelerating literacy learning:

- Compensate for the variability that exists among teachers, which is the most critical school variable in accelerating literacy in the early grades;
- Provide accountability by having highly trained members work in classrooms a minimum of twice daily;
- Provide on-site, job-embedded staff development daily in classrooms and during extended planning sessions;
- Provide additional staffing that allows flexible, assessment-based skill groups to be served daily in multiple ways that no core teacher, working alone, can provide;
- Work primarily with groups in the core teacher's classroom (i.e., 'push in'), reducing the stigmatization of students and fragmentation of the schedule typically associated with 'pull out' traffic;
- Plan with core teachers and share responsibilities for literacy acceleration, thereby eliminating the loneliness and isolation teachers experience when working alone in a self-contained classroom; and
- Blend and coordinate all the services available in most elementary schools today rather than requiring multiple programs, such as SPED, Title I and RTI, operating as separate fiefdoms, with different personnel, rules, regulations and budgets.

Three primary benefits follow.

Highly Skilled Literacy Teachers and Equity

Today, whether or not a child is taught to read on time during the PK–3 years is "luck of the draw," or depends on the teacher a student is assigned. Researchers have continually documented wide variation among individual teacher performance, which impacts student achievement. Hanushek, Rivkin, and Jamison (1992) estimate that the difference between having a good and a bad teacher can exceed one grade-level equivalent in annual achievement growth. In a study of first and second grade twins, researchers concluded that high-quality teaching allows children to fulfill their genetic potential while low-quality teaching impedes it (Taylor, Roehrig, Hensler, Connor, & Schatschneider, 2010). Similarly, Sanders and Rivers (1996) found that students assigned to the most effective teachers for three years in a row performed 50 percentile points higher on a 100-point scale than comparable students assigned to the least effective teachers for three years in a row.

The variation in teaching quality is also related to broader issues of inequity in schools. The children who enter school behind and who most need high-quality teachers to help them catch up typically are assigned to lower-quality teachers with less experience, education, and skill than those who teach other children (Peske & Haycock, 2006; Barth, 2004). "Regardless of how teacher quality is measured, poor and minority children get fewer than their fair share of high-quality teachers" (Peske & Haycock, 2006, p. 2). Additionally, the less effective teachers tend to be assigned to schools that have fewer parent advocates. Taken together, this means that the students who most need accelerated literacy growth are most likely to attend schools with a disproportionately large number of unskilled teachers (Almy & Theokas, 2010). LTs help to mitigate these problems by providing all students with a highly skilled literacy instructor. To achieve high levels of literacy, then, we must build the individual and collective capacity of teachers to teach reading.

Embedded Professional Development

Coordinated, systematic, and collective efforts rather than a series of individual efforts are required to sustain substantive school, district, and national improvement in literacy learning. In the words of DuFour and Marzano (2011):

> developing the collective capacity of educators to function as members of a PLC is a concept based on the premise that if students are to learn at higher levels, processes must be in place to ensure the ongoing, job-embedded learning of the adults who serve them (p. 21).

Being part of a collaborative teacher team such as a PLC or an LT, a more specific version of a PLC, is related to student achievement (Ronfeldt, Farmer, McQueen, & Grissom, 2015). Reading teachers became more effective after participating in 30 or more hours of targeted professional development, in addition to classroom coaching (Scanlon, Gelzheiser, Vellutino, Schatschneider, & Sweeney, 2010; McGill-Franzen, Allington, Yokoi, & Brooks, 1999); after receiving the targeted training and support LT Leaders provide, as championed here, teachers were able to help at-risk readers become achieving readers. Embedded staff development or internal "in-house" modeling, as offered by LTs, tends to have a greater impact on classroom practice than externally-offered approaches. For example, in LT meetings, the LT leader can demonstrate how to analyze assessment results and then how to use these results to develop appropriate lessons. The LT leader also can model quality instruction to the entire classroom before small groups are formed and taught on a rotational basis by all LT members. LTs address the need for continuous (versus one-shot) professional development, and they help solidify everyone as a dedicated teaching team.

A lesson delivered multiple times to multiple groups tends to be of higher quality than a lesson taught only sporadically. Multiple deliveries allow the LT member to reflect and make improvements. Upon joining an LT, even if a particular member does not have specialized literacy expertise, with repeated delivery of similar lessons and LT feedback, a team member can specialize and develop expertise in teaching-specific skills and strategies.

Centralized Instructional Monitoring

An LT model offers a centralized means for delivering literacy instruction, which can be an important factor in monitoring, controlling, and evaluating the alignment and delivery of assessment and instruction. As compared to individual classroom teachers offering literacy instruction, with more centralized LTs, the span of control, or the number of LT members the LT leader supports, is reduced. When span of control is reduced, LT leaders are more likely to maintain positive coaching relationships and provide more specialized training and development.

The Role of the Literacy Team Leader

Within any school, the principal's identification and development of an LT leader is essential to the success of establishing and supporting effective literacy instruction. Preferably, an LT leader has classroom teaching experience, advanced coursework or specialized training in reading, administrative potential, and technology skills. The International Reading Association (2000) states that reading specialists must have expertise in diagnosis, assessment, and instruction, as well as leadership skills, to positively affect student achievement goals.

Consistent with the IRA position statement, but specific to the reading acceleration concept presented in this book, the LT leader has a critical role in developing and training LT members, in organizing assessment-based flexible Early Literacy Groups (ELGs), and in scheduling Intervention/Enrichment (I/E) periods. Suggestions for lesson planning and overseeing the organization of materials for ELGs I/Es is offered in Chapter 4.

LT leaders have the following responsibilities:

+ Train personnel and monitor the literacy program at a particular grade level;
+ Develop greater specialization of staff members, particularly Teacher Assistants (TAs) by allowing them to develop competencies and confidence in delivering instruction;
+ Schedule all involved staff members to meet for various planning times;
+ Share materials and lesson plans;
+ Monitor student progress and develop accountability procedures.

Developing and Training Literacy Teams

Supporting and advancing teachers' development is the primary role of an LT leader (Hartnett-Edwards, 2011), and developing and training LT members is central to this effort. On an ongoing basis, the LT leader reviews sample lesson plans, demonstrates how to implement them with students, co-teaches with LT members, and observes lessons taught by the LT members to ensure that targeted instruction is being implemented for each ELG group.

When organizing LTs, school administrators and teachers draw on available staff members. Suggestions for staffing LTs during ELG and I/E periods follow:

♦ LT Leaders and Title I teachers,
♦ classroom teachers,
♦ special education teachers,
♦ English Language Learner (ELL) teachers,
♦ Teacher Assistants (TAs),
♦ librarians and media specialists,
♦ computer lab personnel (if PBS is used to reduce the size of ELGs),
♦ gifted and talented teachers for enrichment,
♦ encore (P.E., art, music, dance, drama) teachers, possibly in enrichment, and
♦ highly trained retired teachers on a contractual basis.

Depending on expertise, some LT members are focused on providing ELGs at Grades PK–1; other LT members are focused on providing intervention or enrichment services, typically for Grades 2 and beyond.

LT members rotate among the ELGs when regrouping occurs (explained in the following section), so all students have access to highly qualified instructors and exposure to a variety of instructional styles. A work board can be a useful reference for both LT members and students. For example, the various ELGs are color-coded and student pictures are attached to the work board with Velcro, allowing students to move easily from one group to another.

The LT leader strategically assigns LT members to ELGs based on LT member training and complexity of the lesson type or goal. LT members are rotated based on expertise, allowing specialization in delivery of particular types of instructions or strategies. Furthermore, TAs, under the supervision of the classroom teacher and the LT leader, can be trained to implement and repeat particular types of selected instruction. For example, Ms. Greene, a Kindergarten teacher assistant, has been trained to implement a particular lesson plan focused on applied letter sound instruction. At the beginning of the year, kindergarteners were assessed, and a green group was established to focus on learning letter sounds and applying this learning to reading a book. Ms. Greene was assigned to this group until students achieved mastery of letter sounds as evidenced by keying on beginning sounds in books. At that time, Ms. Greene moved to the yellow group, which now needed to focus on applying letter sound instruction. Once students in the yellow group achieve mastery, perhaps the teacher assistant could transition to working with the red group.

Consider ways of protecting students in classrooms with less-skilled literacy teachers. For many students who need to be accelerated in their literacy skills, we cannot leave such a critical decision to chance. We contend that the skills and demonstrated results of individual teachers must be considered when staffing and organizing LTs. There is substantial evidence that a less-skilled literacy teacher in the primary grades can create conditions from which students never recover (Barth, 2004). Others have reported that at-risk primary grade students assigned to a less-skilled literacy teacher for two consecutive years are unlikely to ever realize their true academic potential (Bogner, Raphael, & Pressley, 2002). The provision of quality professional development helps teachers and students learn and succeed. This includes providing educators with mentoring support and high-quality professional development programs (Johnson & Rudolph, 2001). We know that schools may have limited control over personnel decisions, but surely we can expect certain at-risk groups to be protected by ascertaining that the talents and weaknesses of *all* primary teachers are shared equally among *all* students. A focus on collective instructional capacity, (DuFour et al., 2016) as advocated in the PLC research, is critical in successfully accelerating literacy gains in the early grades. It is essential for administrators and LT leaders to identify the most effective literacy teachers in the school based on reliable performance data – not just on perception or reputation. Decide how best to utilize these teachers to reach the most students and determine how the remaining teachers can best serve them.

Assessing and Flexibly Grouping Students

Working with classroom teachers and LT members, the LT leader ensures that students are grouped and regrouped based on formal and informal assessment results utilizing a coordinated assessment schedule, and that they receive instruction reflective of such assessments. Initially, students may be grouped based on the results of a formal reading assessment; as they progress, they can be regrouped based on how they perform on quick, frequent, and informal mastery checks. An informal reading inventory or a running record can be used, for example, to form small groups focusing primarily on the development of fluency and primary-level comprehension skills. As another example, a brief group-administered spelling assessment can be the primary assessment used to regroup students when word study is the focus.

The LT leader helps classroom teachers use these assessment results to plan groups responsive to individual learning needs. Groups are "flexed" as goals are mastered; that is, students can be moved from one group to another in response to formative assessment results. This kind of placement allows students to progress to the next level on any particular sequence of instruction. Students not making adequate progress must be monitored closely so appropriate changes can be made in materials, practice sessions, and individual tutoring to facilitate their success. For students repetitively not meeting ELG and Intervention goals, the LT leader conducts a more thorough reading assessment and writes a plan of action, including reading gaps to be addressed, when goals will be met, and who is responsible for meeting goals. Chapter 3 provides more specific information on the assessment role of the LT leader, and Chapters 5 and 6 include information on the scheduling of ELGs and I/E periods.

Coordinating Literacy Instruction and Resources

The LT leader's responsibility is to coordinate the acquisition of curriculum and intervention materials so all supports are aligned with the literacy goals and practices of a school. Important to a coordinated effort, as directed by an administrator, the LT leader organizes a literacy center to provide materials for the ELGs and literacy interventions. Instructional materials are organized based on the primary focus of differentiated ELG instruction. Materials can include adaptable lesson plans, with multiple copies of books and materials for implementing each lesson plan. A computerized spreadsheet allows teachers to sort literacy center resources by a variety of fields such as *title, reading level, theme,* or *instructional strategy sequence.* In Chapter 4, more details, including pictures, are provided for organizing and coordinating the use of instructional resources, and more information on planning and implementing an intensive lesson plan necessary to make accelerated progress will be described.

Funding Literacy Teams

In addition to local and state funding sources, schools can tap into federal special education funding. As suggested by Allington (2011), schools can allocate "up to 15% of the district's total budget for special education to support the RTI process" (p. 40). This money can be used to fund the three tiers of RTI intervention, which allows schools to focus on prevention, thus reducing the need for later reading interventions.

Title 1 funding also can be utilized to provide Tier 2 and Tier 3 support. The criteria for Title 1 funding depends on whether a school qualifies for schoolwide or targeted assistance. If funding issues remain, school leaders are encouraged to use the parallel block scheduling ideas suggested in Chapter 7.

Summary

In this chapter, we recommend that the school administrator develop an LT concept for delivery of small group instruction and intervention/enrichment groups. LTs provide highly skilled literacy teaching, influence instructional practices in classrooms, and allow for centralized monitoring of instruction. Built on the strong research foundation for developing highly functioning PLCs, LTs train and work together to achieve common literacy goals. The school administrator appoints an LT leader with responsibility and authority to lead the highly functioning LTs. In general, the LT leader's role is to develop and train the LT, to assess and flexibly group students based on data, and to coordinate literacy instruction and instructional resources.

Reflection

Reflect on the content from this chapter as you consider the concept of LTs.

1. What percentage of students enter your school scoring below literacy benchmarks?
2. How many support people do you have in the building, such as TAs, Title 1 teachers, retired teachers with limited schedules, special education teachers, and RTI teachers/support staff?
3. What is the quality of the individual teachers/support staff? How willing and able are they to teach reading based on quality assessment data – not just reputation? Is there a wide or narrow range of teachers who can teach literacy as described in this text?
4. Who can lead the LTs? A strong leader will be needed who is given authority to carry out decisions and is fully supported by administration.
5. How does the administrative leadership plan to address issues involving personnel who are not collaborating effectively with the LT or who are not effective LT members?
6. Does the school have a master schedule that allows LTs to function properly? If not, what changes need to be made?

Chapter 3

Systematic Literacy Assessment and Progress Monitoring

Achieving accelerated reading outcomes requires expert implementation of a systematic process for assessing and monitoring student reading progress to facilitate productive use of data-informed instruction. In this section, we share a systematic process for assessing – whether an individual student, a small group, a classroom, a grade level, a school, or a school district – in reading:

1. based on an understanding of characteristics of effective assessment, assessment types, and the cognitive model of assessment, select appropriate screening and diagnostic assessments as well as progress monitoring tools for use throughout the school year to provide responsive teaching for each student;
2. establish literacy assessment schedules and expectations;
3. train the Literacy Team (LT) to administer and score the selected reading assessments; and
4. interpret and report the assessment information on an ongoing basis.

In Chapter 4, we will use assessment information to group and regroup students, and to make instructional adjustments. For reading acceleration to become a reality, administrators and LT members must engage in a high level of collaboration throughout the assessment process.

Characteristics of Effective Literacy Assessment

Based on our review of the research literature as well as our experience with assessment systems in various school districts, in this section we establish literacy assessment as purposeful, comprehensive, balanced, and integrated. Types of assessments are discussed based on the purposes for giving them. We also emphasize the importance of efficiency while maintaining validity and reliability. With this foundation in place, we then provide a systematic process for assessing students and monitoring their progress.

Assessment as Purposeful, and Assessment Types

From a practical standpoint, an important distinction among assessments is the purposes for giving them. Based on their purposes, we review four types of reading assessment (screening, diagnostic, progress monitoring, and outcome-based).

Screening Assessments

Screening instruments aim to provide a broadly defined estimate of a student's overall achievement (Stahl, Flanigan, & McKenna, 2020). The screening assessment can be viewed as the preventative wide-angle camera lens that zooms out to provide a broader view of a student's reading ability as compared to the narrower zoom lens offered by a diagnostic assessment or progress monitoring tool. They are administered to identify students who are meeting or not meeting grade-level reading benchmarks. Those not meeting benchmarks are deemed more likely to develop reading problems unless they receive timely reading intervention.

The best screening assessments are not only highly predictive in identifying students who need intervention, but they also can be administered efficiently. Although no screening assessment can predict reading difficulties with 100% accuracy, 90% sensitivity and 80% specificity have been established as the expectations for an effective Response to Intervention (RTI) process (Jenkins & Johnson, 2008).

> Sensitivity and specificity are the two primary statistics used to gauge a screening assessment's accuracy in classifying students. Sensitivity gauges the screening assessment's ability to correctly identify the students who later will experience reading difficulties (i.e., true positives), while specificity indicates the screening assessment's ability to correctly identify those who will not have later reading difficulties (i.e., true negatives).

Accuracy in screening is important, because when screening mistakenly over-identifies students as at-risk (i.e., false positives), schools spend precious resources on students who do not need extra help. Furthermore, not identifying truly at-risk students who cannot succeed without additional help (i.e., false negatives) can be an even more serious problem (Jenkins & Johnson, 2008). Therefore, screening assessments should strive to identify at least 90% of the students who will later exhibit reading failure and 80% of students who are not at risk.

For students who read below grade level, screening assessments appropriate to the student's approximate reading level are more likely to provide useful information than grade-level assessments. Also, the use of multiple measures such as progress monitoring, dynamic or interactive assessment, and other follow-up instruments to identify and further assess a student's literacy proficiencies, can significantly increase the accuracy of the screening process (Compton, Fuchs, Fuchs, & Bryant, 2006) as well as more quickly assess the appropriate level of instruction for a student (Fuchs et al., 2007).

Diagnostic Assessments

Diagnostic assessments are administered once a screening assessment has been used to identify a reading difficulty (Walpole & McKenna, 2013). Typically, a diagnostic assessment is administered individually and provides more detailed information in a specific area than a screening assessment. As referred to previously, diagnostic assessments zoom in to provide specific information about a reading difficulty. For example, a screening instrument could be used to identify students across all Grade 1 classrooms who require further intervention in reading; an assessment of specific word features could be used to more specifically diagnose word features for study.

When used appropriately, easily administered screening and diagnostic instruments are important in forming small groups, planning instruction, and monitoring progress (Walpole & McKenna, 2013). Diagnostic assessments can contribute to the recommended RTI levels of 90% sensitivity and 80% specificity for screening students to identify them for reading intervention.

Progress Monitoring Tools

After using screening and/or diagnostic assessments to identify students who are reading below grade level, students are placed in groups and goals are set (further discussed in Chapter 4). Progress monitoring tools are quick, easily administered literacy checks that allow for frequent monitoring of progress toward specific literacy goals. Analyses from over 200 studies on the ongoing monitoring of student learning show that progress monitoring, when used to plan and deliver instruction, can improve learning and help teachers improve student outcomes (Fuchs & Fuchs, 2006; Black and William, 1998; Dexter & Hughes, n.d.).

Initial development of progress monitoring tools can be a daunting task; however, some progress monitoring tools are included with commercial assessment packages. A LT leader can develop or compile a series of simple and sequenced literacy checks. As an example, to monitor a small group's progress toward segmenting sounds, a highly skilled LT leader can administer a phoneme segmentation subtask from Tests of Phonological Awareness (Stahl et al., 2020) to weekly assess a child's ability to segment words into phoneme units. As another example, to monitor the progress of a small group with a goal of differentiating short vowels, the LT leader can develop a short 5- to 10-word spell check containing the short vowels studied during the week.

Progress monitoring is most efficiently administered in the context of small group lessons with an intent to minimize the interruption of instruction. As a result of our work in schools, we have developed a Small Group Observation Form for ongoing use in a small group as shown on Form 3.1.

This flexible small group observation form is a powerful tool for daily documentation of a wide variety of literacy behaviors – noting application of word-level, fluency, and comprehension strategies – as needed.

Form 3.1

Small Group Observation Form

Group _____, Week _____, Days 1-4, 6-9

Student	Dates	Notes	Comments
Group Comments:			

In a right-hand comment column, an LT member can reflect on each student's progress toward goal mastery and application over the course of the week. A group comment section is provided at the bottom of the form for reflecting on group reading behaviors and for predicting upcoming instructional needs. Progress monitoring tools such as this one are continuously adapted in response to day-to-day progress monitoring requirements.

Outcome-Based Assessments

With a focus on evaluating overall student achievement, outcome-based assessments help administrators and teachers evaluate an individual student's progress as a reader, and the degree to which classrooms, schools, and school districts achieved their reading goals by an established deadline. Most teachers and administrators have a basic understanding of how to assess and interpret outcome-based assessments to determine students' general mastery of learning (Stiggins, 2002). They regularly use end-of-unit or year paper-pencil tests to assign a reading grade, and they administer state-mandated assessments each school year as an overall measure of content attainment.

Another example of an outcome-based assessment is the National Assessment of Educational Progress (NAEP). The Reading section is used to determine a student's standing in reading as compared to grade-level peers, and provides a means for evaluating national trends in reading and for making comparisons across schools and school districts. However, these outcome-based assessments would not be appropriate for understanding how individual students read or for guiding reading instruction.

Assessment as Comprehensive, Balanced, and Integrated

A *comprehensive* literacy assessment system includes all of the essentials of effective literacy instruction. The "big 5" essential elements of effective reading instruction include: phonemic awareness, phonics, fluency, vocabulary, and comprehension (National Institute of Child Health and Human Development, 2000). Later, What Works Clearinghouse (WWC) and a panel of experts (Foorman et al., 2016) also examined rigorous research studies on foundational skills to support reading for understanding and drew similar conclusions to the NRP. The field of writing has not been subjected to the scrutiny of scientifically-based reading research as reading has, but is important to assess as well, to align with instruction. These essential literacy elements are further described in Chapter 4 on instruction. For purposes of assessment, here we establish that comprehensive literacy assessment includes these essential literacy elements.

Effective assessment also is *balanced* between summative and formative.

> *Summative assessment* describes outcome-based assessments used solely for the purpose of evaluating or arriving at an end result (DuFour, DuFour, Eaker, Many, & Mattos, 2016). The focus is the degree to which students have learned content by a deadline. Typically, they provide the basis for a grade, because students and teachers know the degree to which students have mastered content and where each student stands in the class. Summative assessments are important to understand and use; however, they do not provide guidance to inform instruction.
>
> *Formative assessment* is used to frame ongoing instruction based on student progress toward literacy proficiency. The focus of formative assessment is the degree to which each student is learning intended knowledge and skills. Formative grades are not weighted very heavily, because students are in the process of learning the content. The "heart of formative assessment" (Dufour & Marzano, 2011, p. 120) is the monitoring and tracking of student progress over time, providing collaborative teams with rich data for instructional decision-making.

When summative assessment receives too much weight, teachers cover content, give paper-pencil tests, and record grades, but their instruction is not informed by student learning needs. Students are not as likely to master content, because the teacher has not distinguished mastered from non-mastered content, or how students can best learn the content. When formative assessment is used without cycling back to summative, however, teachers and students learn specific skills and strategies, but information is lacking regarding transfer to general reading ability. For literacy acceleration to occur, summative (screeners and outcome-based assessments) and formative assessments (diagnostic assessments and progress monitoring tools) must be used strategically to guide need-based literacy instruction. The lower the reading level, the higher the demand for assessment precision, and the greater the need for frequent monitoring.

Furthermore, the balance of assessments between summative and formative is important to consider within specific instructional contexts. Within the instructional context of literacy, we describe the importance of assessing isolated skills as well as integrated skill performances. Lipson and Wixson (2013) further describe as follows:

> If the only form of assessment is testing that is focused on isolated skills, then students are likely to be attending to skill mastery at the expense of integrated skill performances. In contrast, if the only form of assessment is student self-reflection, then students are likely to become more responsible for their own learning but may miss some important skills and not progress as rapidly as needed to perform at desirable levels (p. 37).

Thus, a systematic literacy assessment process is comprehensive in that all the elements of literacy instruction are assessed. It also includes a balance of summative and formative assessments as represented by isolated skills as well as integrated skill performances.

Assessment as Valid and Reliable, yet Efficient

Focused on minimizing loss of precious instructional time, practitioners look for assessment systems that can be quickly administered, scored, and reported. This emphasis on quickness has led many school systems to seek computer-generated screening and progress monitoring instruments, such as Pearson's AIMSweb (www.aimsweb.com), because they are viewed as being quick, easy and cost-effective. Although these computer-generated assessments continue to evolve and are promising in their ability to quickly screen or check student ability or progress, several studies have shown issues with measurement and fairness, particularly for younger students and those who have not learned test taking or computer skills (Harold, 2016).

While efficiency is important to making sound assessment decisions, just as important are reliability, the consistency of results, and validity, the degree to which the test measures what it claims to measure and what the examiner intends to measure. The Center on Response to Intervention (www.rti4success.org) offers valuable tools for comparing screening, diagnostic, and progress monitoring tools based on factors such as reliability, validity, format (individual versus group), computer versus non-computer generated, and time to administer. Validity and reliability will be considered within our discussion of specific assessment instruments as well.

Selecting Appropriate Literacy Assessments

The first step in effective implementation of systematic literacy assessment, selecting appropriate literacy assessments, must be an orderly, strategic information gathering process. Though comprehension is the goal of reading, astute instructional leaders understand that comprehension inadequacy can stem from a variety of reading difficulties.

For a child who does not demonstrate reading proficiency by reading and comprehending on-grade level texts, Walpole and McKenna (2013), and subsequently Stahl et al. (2020), have proposed a cognitive model of reading assessment driven by three pathways of strategic questions to help practitioners use appropriate assessment tools to "dig down" to the source of a reading difficulty. For each pathway, the strategic pathways delineated in The Cognitive Model shown in Figure 3.1 can help practitioners select the specific assessment information needed to pinpoint a reading difficulty.

If reading comprehension is below grade level, then practitioners first focus on Pathway 1, difficulties with automatic word recognition. Fluency assessments are administered. If fluency assessments are non-proficient, then decoding and high-frequency words are assessed. Low scores with these phonics and word-level assessments can alert the LT to assess phonological

Figure 3.1 The Cognitive Model

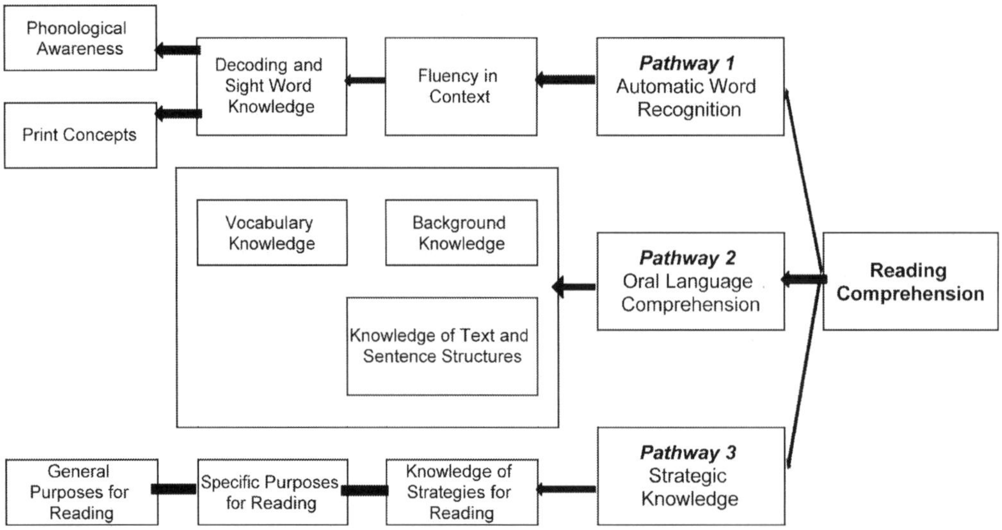

Source: **Used with Permission**. From *Assessment for Reading Instruction* (4th Edition) by Katherine A. Stahl, Kevin Flanigan, and Michael C. McKenna. Copyright 2020 by Guilford Press, 370 Seventh Avenue, New York, NY 10001. **All rights reserved**.

awareness and print concepts. In contrast, if a practitioner assesses fluency and the student is proficient, then the focus turns to Pathway 2, Language Comprehension. If assessment of language comprehension is non-proficient, then further assessment focuses within the language comprehension pathway; however, if language comprehension is proficient, then the assessment focus turns to Pathway 3, Strategic Knowledge.

Because emergent and beginning readers do not read texts conventionally, Walpole and McKenna (2013) suggest a modified two-part set of strategic questions. On Pathway 1, after assessing fluency in context and finding that a student is non-proficient, the LT asks, "Is the child learning the decoding skills and sight words that have been taught?" and then assesses decoding and sight word knowledge. If decoding and sight word knowledge are problematic, then the practitioner considers issues with phonological awareness and print concepts. If decoding and sight word knowledge are proficient, then difficulties with fluency are considered. In contrast, if fluency is assessed and not considered problematic, then Pathway 2, Listening Comprehension, becomes a focus area. When a teacher reads aloud, the reading barrier is removed, and a child should be able to more easily focus on a text's meaning. The LT asks, "Can the child comprehend on-grade level text read aloud by the teacher?" The teacher documents the child's responses to daily interactive read alouds to gauge whether or not comprehension is impeded by background knowledge, vocabulary, or lack of syntactic familiarity. With the cognitive model in mind, we turn our attention to assessment options.

Fluency in Context, Comprehension, and Vocabulary

Addressing questions about a student's reading abilities often starts with a sample of oral reading, which involves administering an Informal Reading Inventory (IRI) or a Running Record (RR) (Stahl et al., 2020). Walpole and

McKenna (2006) suggest using IRIs as screening instruments. For over 50 years, IRIs have been chosen for determining a child's reading levels: independent (the highest level a student can read without help), instructional (the highest level a student can read with instructional support), and frustrational (any level at which a student is likely to be frustrated, even with support).

Word Identification Fluency (WIF), the ability to identify words from graded lists with accuracy and automaticity, is a strong predictor of early reading ability (Schatschneider, 2006).

Oral Reading Fluency (ORF), the ability to orally read a passage with accuracy, automaticity, and prosody (prose-like), is often measured with an informal reading inventory or a running record. ORF has shown high correlation with overall reading comprehension (Fuchs, Fuchs, Hosp, & Jenkins, 2001) and has shown to be a significant factor in studies accounting for reading difficulty.

The most successful reading screeners at each grade level have used various combinations of Word Identification Fluency (WIF) and Oral Reading Fluency (ORF). Although screening assessments relying on WIF and ORF can contribute useful information about student performance, they do not account for all of the variation in reading performance–they are not likely to reach the recommended RTI levels of 90% sensitivity and 80% specificity–therefore, they will need to be used along with diagnostic assessments and progress monitoring tools specific to a reading focus area.

The IRI continues to be widely used in schools to assess WIF and ORF through sequenced grade-level word lists and passages (Walpole & McKenna, 2006). Typically, passages are followed by comprehension questions and sometimes they are followed by retelling prompts. Most IRIs provide conversion charts aligned to a refined primary text-level equivalency (e.g., Fountas & Pinnell, 2020) or a Lexile. IRI analysis can help practitioners identify appropriate progress monitoring tools to target specific unmastered skills or strategies. As a screener with follow-up diagnostic and progress monitoring tools, and with attention to consistency of administration and scoring, the IRI can be a very valid, reliable, and useful assessment of a student's reading level.

The Qualitative Reading Inventory, 6th Edition (Leslie & Caldwell, 2017), and the Basic Reading Inventory, 12th Edition (Johns, 2017) provide graded word lists in timed and untimed formats, which are helpful in differentiating automatic word recognition and decoding needs. They also contain leveled reading passages used in measuring ORF. Nilsson (2008) examined and compared the strengths, limitations, and unique characteristics of eight IRIs published between 2002 and 2008. Results suggest the IRIs range in technical rigor, with only one, Leslie and Caldwell's Qualitative Reading

Inventory, 4th Edition (2006), providing sufficient reliability data (based on comprehension scores) to support the use of alternate forms. Furthermore, Leslie and Caldwell (2006) examined consistency of instructional level based on the comprehension scores of each passage and reported the same instructional level on both passages 71% to 84% of the time.

Fountas and Pinnell's Benchmark Assessment, 3rd Edition (2017a), Beaver and Carter's Developmental Reading Assessment, 3rd Edition (DRA-3) (2019), and Richardson's Next Step Forward in Guided Reading (NSGR) Assessment (2016) are commonly used in the primary grades to measure ORF. Of note, DRA-3 offers an online version. Also of note, NSGR includes a classroom-based read aloud assessment. Although NSGR passages are quicker to administer than these IRI comparisons, graded word lists for measuring WIF are not included, and NSGR passages do not include a timed option. Perhaps the LT can compensate by using graded word lists from another assessment such as the QRI-6 and by timing passages at mid first-grade levels and beyond.

Whereas an IRI contains a specific set of leveled oral reading passages (and often a specific set of graded word lists), a RR is an informal set of procedures for marking and noting oral reading (Stahl et al., 2020). Because a RR can be used with any reading selection, it is a useful tool for informing instruction on an ongoing basis and for monitoring finer gradients of progress toward goals. A 50-Word Mini-Running Record Form is shown in Form 3.2 below.

This mini-RR form can be used, either with new and challenging text to aid in decision-making for the upcoming week or with familiar text students already have read to ensure mastery and to monitor application of taught reading strategies. We recommend using a form such as this one on a 5-day cycle during daily 1-hour Early Literacy Groups (ELGs) or Interventions; for daily 30-minute ELGs, this form can be used on a 10-day cycle. More extensive RRs also can be used to check fluency as well. Narrative and informational retelling, and vocabulary and comprehension questions can be used at regular intervals as part of an IRI or can follow a RR (Stahl et al., 2020).

Based on Serravallo's research (2015) on fiction and nonfiction comprehension, we have developed small group discussion forms to use when framing reading comprehension questions and documenting student responses. Form 3.3 offers a Small Group Discussion Form for Nonfiction Comprehension. Nonfiction comprehension question types focus on: main idea, key details, vocabulary, and text features.

In Form 3.4 the focus of the Small Group Discussion Form is Fiction Comprehension. Fiction comprehension questions focus on: plots and settings, characters, vocabulary and figurative language, and themes and ideas. Also based on Serravallo's (2015) components for teaching fiction and nonfiction comprehension, a colleague and I developed a Nonfiction Comprehension Scoring Guide as charted on Form 3.5.

Form 3.2

50-Word Running Records for a Small Group

Group ____, Week ____, Days 5, 10, Date __/__/__

Student	Notes									Comments

Group Comments:

Form 3.3

Nonfiction Comprehension Discussion Form

Names: _____   Nonfiction Unit: _____Book/Level: _____

Main Idea	Q1:	Q2:	Q3:
1.			
2.			
3.			
4.			
5.			
Key Details	Q1:	Q2:	Q3:
1.			
2.			
3.			
4.			
5.			
Vocabulary	Q1:	Q2:	Q3:
1.			
2.			
3.			
4.			
5.			
Text Features	Q1:	Q2:	Q3:
1.			
2.			
3.			
4.			
5.			

Form 3.4

Fiction Comprehension Discussion Form

Names: _____   Fiction Unit: _____Book/Level: _____

Plots & Settings	Q1:	Q2:	Q3:
1.			
2.			
3.			
4.			
5.			
Characters	Q1:	Q2:	Q3:
1.			
2.			
3.			
4.			
5.			
Vocabulary & Figurative Language	Q1:	Q2:	Q3:
1.			
2.			
3.			
4.			
5.			
Themes & Ideas	Q1:	Q2:	Q3:
1.			
2.			
3.			
4.			
5.			

Form 3.5

Nonfiction Comprehension Scoring Guide

Category	1- Beginner Level	2 - Intermediate Level	3 - Advanced Level
Main Idea	From selected text, can identify 1 simple, overarching idea (i.e., title as main idea). Might use text features and/or other support.	From selected text, can identify 2 main ideas. Each main idea might lack precision and/or the combination might not be comprehensive. Might use text features and/or other support.	From selected text, can identify at least 3 or all main ideas. Each main idea is accurate and the combination of main ideas is comprehensive. Does not use text features or other support.
Key Details (Supporting evidence)	From selected text, can identify 1 detail to support a main idea. Might require support.	From selected text, can identify 2 details to support each main idea. Might require support.	From selected text, can identify 3 or more or all key details for each main idea. Does not require support.
Vocabulary	With support, can get the "gist," of word/concept; meaning lacks precision. Might rely on pictures/other sources. Context is not clear.	Without support, can provide a simple definition of the word and/or simple explanation of a concept. Context might not be clear.	Without support or referring to a source for help, can fully define word and/or fully explain meaning of a concept, and can appropriately use in context.
Text Features	Can identify (i.e., locate) text features (i.e., table of contents, title, headings, picture captions, glossary, index) in book/article.	Can use text features to answer specific questions from book/article.	Can clearly explain information gained from text feature(s), even when information is not explicitly stated in book/article.

Scoring: Main Idea: _____   Key Details: _____   Vocabulary: _____   Text Features: _____   **TOTAL SCORE: _____**＊

＊Can score out of 4 points (0 = Cannot identify 1 = Can Identify) or out of 12 points (with a maximum of 3 points for each category).

Source: Carol E. Canady and Heather Payne (2020).

This scoring rubric can be used with any nonfiction text and similar to the nonfiction discussion form, assessed categories include: main idea, key details, vocabulary, and text features.

The Fiction Comprehension Scoring Guide is depicted in Form 3.6. This scoring rubric can be used with any fiction text. As with the fiction discussion form, assessed categories include: plots and settings, characters, vocabulary and figurative language, and themes and ideas. For each scoring category, the teacher can simply score ability or non-ability; or can use more precision, ranging from a beginner to an advanced level of comprehension.

To assess vocabulary, the Peabody Picture Vocabulary Test, 5th Edition (PPVT-5) (Dunn, 2019) and the Expressive Vocabulary Test, 3rd Edition (EVT-3) (Williams, 2019) can be used as screeners or as diagnostic assessments. Both are norm-referenced and individually administered paper-pencil or digital assessments. Based on words in Standard American English, PPVT-5 measures receptive vocabulary and EVT-3 measures expressive vocabulary and word retrieval. For both the PPVT-5 and the EVT-3, average completion time is 10-15 minutes. More informal, teacher-made vocabulary

Form 3.6

Fiction Comprehension Scoring Guide

Category	1- Beginner Level	2 - Intermediate Level	3 - Advanced Level
Plots and Settings	Can identify 1 problem from the story. Can identify 1 generic, but not specific setting.	Can identify 2 problems from the story (external vs. internal). Can identify 1 specific or 2 generic settings from the story.	Can identify 3 or more problems from the story. Can identify at least 2 specific settings from the story.
Characters	Can use a generic name (i.e. boy) when a specific name is given and/or can identify a single character trait. Cannot use a specific example or the example is not appropriate.	Can use a specific name (i.e., Orville Wright), when given, can identify a single character trait, and can appropriately use a specific example from the text.	Can use specific names, identify multiple character traits and, for each character trait, can appropriately use specific examples from the text.
Vocabulary and Figurative Language	With support, can get the "gist," of the word/figurative language, but the meaning lacks precision. Might use pictures or other resources to aid understanding. Context is not clear.	Without support, can provide a simple definition of the word and/or simple explanation of figurative language. Context might not be clear.	Without support or referring to a source for help, can fully define word and/or fully explain meaning of figurative language, and can appropriately use in context.
Themes and Ideas	Can provide a simple theme that is story specific.	Can provide a simple theme that is universal and/or 2 themes that are not universal.	Can provide multiple universal themes.

Scoring: Plot: _____   Character: _____   Vocabulary: _____   Themes/Ideas: _____   **TOTAL SCORE: _____***

*Can score out of 4 points (0 = Cannot identify 1 = Can Identify) or out of 12 points (with a maximum of 3 points for each category).

Source: Carol E. Canady and Heather Payne.

recognition tasks (Stahl & Bravo, 2010) can be used to ascertain student vocabulary knowledge related to an upcoming unit of study, to inform unit development; and if re-administered after the unit, these tasks also can be used to measure vocabulary growth. Vocabulary-focused reading follow-up questions also can be used as ongoing informal measures of vocabulary and to inform upcoming instruction.

Decoding and High-Frequency Words

Proficient reading requires automatic recognition of letter sounds and words. Most words can be decoded or sounded out because their beginning, middle, and ending follow common phonetic patterns of the English spelling system. Stahl et al., 2020 provide informative decoding and high frequency word screeners and diagnostic assessments such as an Informal Phonics Inventory, and an Informal Decoding Inventory, and The Z-Test. The 93-item Informal Phonics Inventory contains subtests for consonant sounds, consonant digraphs, beginning consonant blends, final consonant blends and -ng, short vowels in CVC words, words containing silent-e, long-vowel digraphs, dipthongs, and r-Controlled and l-Influenced vowels. Individual subtests or the entire inventory can be scored as needed to determine mastery, the need for review, or the need for systematic instruction. The 110-item Informal Decoding Inventory contains 20-item subtests for short vowels, consonant blends and digraphs, r-controlled vowel patterns, vowel-consonant-e, and vowel teams. Each 20-item subtest contains 10 actual words and 10 pseudowords. A 10-item subtest of actual multisyllabic words also is included. The Z-Test contains 37 pseudowords. All pseudowords start with the letter z and word features include a mix of short- and long-vowel patterns. For progress monitoring, The Z-Test can be timed.

Written assessments of spelling can provide useful insights for both reading and writing and can be administered in a group setting, making them efficient to administer. Bear, Invernizzi, Templeton, and Johnston's (2020) Primary Spelling Inventory (PSI) and Elementary Spelling Inventory (ESI), and Ganske's (2014) Developmental Spelling Analysis (DSA) are useful as screeners or diagnostic assessments, and can be adapted to the range of a particular grade level, classroom, or small group for progress monitoring as well. The screeners offer fewer items with a broad range of word features, from emergent to advanced stages of spelling development; the word feature inventories offer increased precision, with more items devoted to a narrow range of word features, as compared to the screeners. The Phonological Awareness Literacy Screening (PALS) website (www.pals.virginia.edu) and our publisher's website also include useful literacy checks such as checks of alphabet name, alphabet sounds, and spell checks of specific word features, which can be useful progress monitoring tools.

With decoding as a foundation for identifying new words, proficient readers develop the ability to recognize an increasing number of words by sight, including both regular and irregular words. Automatic recognition of high-frequency words, which occur most often in English text, is a priority for early readers. Traditionally, many schools and school systems have used Fry's 300 Instant Sight Words (1980) or Dolch's 220 (1936) high-frequency word lists to assess high-frequency words. Our analysis of the Dolch and Fry word lists found very few words on Dolch that do not also appear on Fry. Thus, by studying Fry's 300, plus a few unique Dolch words; both Dolch and Fry lists are accounted for. Stahl et al. (2020) assessment publication includes a 300-word Fry Sight-Word Inventory and Dolch Words Organized by Level. The Dolch levels range from Preprimer (before the beginning of Grade 1) to Grade 3. The leveling by grade level is useful; however, reading acceleration requires higher expectations for high-frequency word learning. For example, only 40 high-frequency words are presented at the Preprimer level. Other word lists can be useful, such as the 100 Most Frequent Words in Books for Beginning Readers (Bodrova, Leong, & Semenov, 1998), Richardson and Lewis's word lists by guided reading level (2018), and Orton Gillingham's (OG) (2020) word lists originating from Dolch, Fry, and high-frequency nouns. Dictated sentences and writing samples can be analyzed to confirm a student's word-level needs.

Schools and school systems will do well to do the following: use word lists from multiple well-recognized sources, develop rigorous standards for automaticity in reading and writing them, and coordinate high-frequency word instruction across both reading levels and grade levels. To achieve accelerated literacy gains, efficient and customized teaching of high-frequency words also is imperative, as further described in Chapter 4.

Phonological Awareness and Print Concepts

> *Phonological Awareness (PA)*, which involves the ability to hear spoken sounds, is an essential literacy skill. When students can blend, segment, and manipulate sounds at the level of the phoneme, the smallest unit of spoken sound, they are thought to have achieved *phonemic awareness*, the highest level of PA. For example, a child who has full phonemic awareness can blend the sounds /c/-/a/-/t/ to produce the word "cat," break apart the word "cat" into its three sounds, and change the /c/ to /m/ to produce the word "mat".

The Phonological Awareness Literacy Screening (PALS) (Invernizzi, Meier, & Juel, 2007; Invernizzi, Swank, & Juel, 2007; Invernizzi, Sullivan, Swank, & Meier, 2004) is a Pre-K through Grade 3 screening and progress monitoring system used to assess literacy fundamentals such as phonological awareness and alphabet knowledge. PALS 1-3, designed for Grades 1 through 3, primarily measures WIF and ORF. PALS-K, designed for Kindergarten, culminates with a Concept of Word (COW) subtest, which is a scaffolded translation of WIF and ORF for the emergent reader. In addition to assessing phonological awareness and alphabet knowledge, PALS Pre-K and PALS-K also assess earliest developing literacy skills such as letter sounds and print concepts. PALS users also can access a variety of informative progress monitoring tools or literacy checks for quickly checking reading progress. Reflective of effective classroom instruction, rather than relying primarily on auditory response, young children can use manipulatives to respond by marking or pointing to pictures and by pointing under words in actual books. PALS is being updated to more precisely screen for reading difficulties.

Stahl et al. (2020) provide a useful test of phonological awareness, including guidelines for administration, task descriptions, and mastery indicators. An important guideline for this test, and any test of phonological awareness, is oral performance without use of printed letters or words. For example, the blending task requires students to *listen* to words read in a secret code, and then put sounds together to decipher words. They also provide useful assessments of Concepts of Print such as a Checklist for Concepts of Print, a Concept of Word Scale (adapted from Gill, 2019), and Book-Handling Knowledge Guidelines. These assessments can be used in full to assess a particular student's reading needs, subtests can be used for progress monitoring of particular phonological awareness skills, or they can serve as models for in-house progress monitoring and adapted to meet ongoing instructional needs.

Knowledge of Reading Purposes and Strategic Knowledge

Teaching reading strategies can improve reading and studying abilities (Afferbach & Cho, 2009; Pressley & Woloshyn, 1995). According to Stahl et al. (2020), interviews and self-reports are the best ways to determine student strategy use while reading or studying. Alternatively, some students, while reading or studying, can think aloud or verbalize their thinking and strategy use, but most are not comfortable or their strategies are not developed to the level of maintaining optimal comprehension while reading and thinking aloud. Based on research distinguishing proficient and struggling readers in their knowledge of general and specific reading purposes and in strategic knowledge, Stahl et al. (2020) suggest several useful assessments such as a Purposes for Reading Interview (PRI), a Textbook Interview (TI), and an Index of Reading Awareness (IRA). The PRI contains seven student interview questions on perceptions about reading such as, "What makes someone a good reader?" (p. 232). The TI contains student interview questions specific to a particular fiction or nonfiction text selection not yet read. The IRA contains 20 multiple-choice questions with four subtests of five items each – gauging the need for instructional support in these areas: evaluation, planning, regulation, conditional knowledge, and can be administered in a group setting. Similar subtests or revised assessments can be used for needs-based reading purpose and strategy groups.

Affective Factors

A student's attitudes, interests, values, and self-concepts about reading influence motivation to read (Conradi, Jang, & McKenna, 2014). These affective dimensions are shaped by the people students hold in high regard, what they think about reading (Stahl et al., 2020); when LT members model a love for literacy, build relationships with students and their families, and show attentiveness to their reading interests, students are more motivated to read and to give their best efforts.

We encourage LT members to consider starting the school year or group with a brief and documented student discussion of favorite books, best places to read at home, best and worst reading experiences (and how to improve the worst ones). Giving a reading interest inventory can help boost student enthusiasm for reading, largely based on receiving input into the book selection process. For PreK–K students, we recommend that students circle pictures representing certain book topics. Reading interest inventories with pictures sometimes can be found in IRI or benchmark kits. For Grade 1 and beyond, students enjoy pretending to be the teacher and giving reading topics a grade, such as with the Tell Me What You Like! inventory (Stahl et al., 2020).

On an ongoing basis, LT members can ask students what they think about book selections and why they feel that way. A simple thumbs up-down or a book rating form such as Form 3.7 can go a long way in generating student enthusiasm for reading.

Form 3.7 Book Rating Form

Did You Like the Book?

1. Rate this book.

1 = Not good at all.					
2 = The book was OK.	1 ☆	2 ☆	3 ☆	4 ☆	5 ☆
3 = I liked the book.					
4 = I really liked the book.					
5 = I loved the book!					

2. Would you recommend this book to a friend? Why or why not?

_____

_____

_____

Students color stars to rate their books (one star gets the strongest disapproval and five stars get the strongest approval) and recommend books to their friends. Teachers receive insight about student reading interests. For students with negative attitudes, interests, values, and self-concepts about reading, more intensive use of affective assessment can be informative, such as those provided by Stahl et al. (2020). Involving families in reading with students at home can be important to reading feelings and behaviors as well, and is further discussed in Chapter 8.

Weighing Assessment Options

Educators must consider multiple factors when selecting appropriate reading assessments. We definitely encourage administrators and the LT to use assessment principles and the cognitive assessment model as a basis for decision-making. A new assessment also must be considered in relation to other assessments given. If another assessment is current and already provides much of the needed information, then perhaps it can be used.

Beyond that, we also recommend weighing practical costs and benefits. Benefits typically focus on how much and the type of information an assessment provides. Stahl et al. (2020) provide a useful shopper's guide for use when purchasing an IRI or Benchmark Kit. Purchasing considerations include, but are not limited to the presence of field-test data substantiating the reliability of assigned reading levels, questions specific to each passage, and multiple forms at each reading level. Cost can involve time to administer an assessment, especially any time taken from instruction, training needed to administer effectively, and sometimes the literal cost of purchasing the assessment.

For each of the three reading focus areas, at each grade level, what assessments could you give? Form 3.8 provides a form you can use as you consider appropriate assessments for each area. After completing the form, reflect on your school's or district's strengths and needs in terms of ability to provide needed assessments. Consider current assessments you use as well as new assessment possibilities and ability to purchase, administer, and train teachers to use them appropriately.

Establishing Assessment Schedules

Once assessments have been selected, an integrated selection process then starts with scheduling screening and progress monitoring before the start of the school year. Because of the importance of building relationships with students as well as understanding student feelings and interests related to reading, affective assessments are built into the schedule at the beginning of a 9-week period. An outcome-based assessment also is built into the schedule at the end of this 9-week period, to evaluate student progress. A sample 9-week assessment plan before the start of the school year is shown in Figure 3.2 below.

Form 3.8

Assessment Selections by Reading Focus

Grade:		
Reading Focus	**Screeners and Diagnostic Assessments**	**Literacy Checks**
Automatic Word Recognition		
Fluency in Context		
Decoding and High-Frequency Words		
Phonemic Awareness and Print Concepts		
Language Comprehension		
Background Knowledge		
Vocabulary Knowledge		
Knowledge of Text and Sentence Structures		
Strategic Knowledge		
Specific Purposes for Reading and Knowledge of Strategies for Reading		
General Purposes for Reading		

Figure 3.2 Sample 9-Week Assessment Plan

Days	Assessment Type	Assessment Recipients
1–5	Affective Assessment	Individual, Small, Whole, or Cohort Group
	Screening/Diagnostic Assessment	Individual, Small, Whole, or Cohort Group
6–10	Progress Monitoring	Individual or Small Group
11–15	Progress Monitoring	Individual or Small Group
16–20	Progress Monitoring	Individual or Small Group
21–25	Diagnostic Assessment	Individual, Small, Whole, or Cohort Group
26–30	Progress Monitoring	Individual or Small Group
31–35	Progress Monitoring	Individual or Small Group
36–40	Progress Monitoring	Individual or Small Group
41–45	Screening/Diagnostic and Outcome-Based Assessment	Individual, Small, Whole, or Cohort Group

Adapted by Canady, C. (2020) from Walpole, S. & McKenna, M. C. (2013). The Literacy Coach's Handbook (2nd Ed.). New York, NY: Guilford Press.

The scheduled screening and diagnostic assessments are focused on giving the same screening assessment across small groups of students, so students can be flexibly regrouped for small-group instruction. Screening, diagnostic assessments, and progress monitoring tools also can be given to individuals and groups of students as needs arise. To illustrate, when a reading group starts to lack homogeneity as evidenced by a student reading words and books with accuracy and faster than others, the teacher will want to assess the high flyer and possibly move the student to a higher group.

Setting Literacy Expectations

In order to interpret reading assessments and to identify students for ELGs and I/E periods, below-, on- and above-grade-level literacy expectations must be in place at each grade level. When expectations in all three areas – basic, proficient, and distinguished achievement – are emphasized by the LT rather than solely on-grade level expectations, logic follows that practitioners are more likely to focus on reaching higher levels of literacy achievement. As much as possible, national norms are used to set these expectations. National norms are available for instructional reading level and for other standardized reading assessments, but are not typical for informal assessments such as progress monitoring checks. For example, Fountas and Pinnell, developers of guided reading (2016), have established and maintained nationally normed instructional guided reading level expectations (2017), well-recognized in the field of reading, including a useful monthly progress monitoring chart accessible through their website. When national norms are not available, perhaps a literacy assessment can be aligned with normed reading level expectations.

Reading fluency begins to receive emphasis at a mid-first-grade reading level when students who have demonstrated accuracy need to progress from a choppy word-by-word to a more fluid reading style. Expectations can be set for fluency according to the four dimensions–expression and volume, phrasing, smoothness, and pace–found on a rubric such as the Multidimensional Fluency Scale (Stahl et al., 2020); however, these are qualitative measures. Beginning at a mid-first-grade reading level, grade level norms for reading rate can add precision and objectivity to measures of ORF, which also are used to obtain an overall reading level. Grade level norms for reading rate by Hasbrouck and Tindal (2017, 2006) are based on extensive studies of ORF.

If reading acceleration is to occur, appropriate word-level expectations also must be set. Acquisition of phonics and word study skills can be compared with benchmark standards. Spell checks and other informal sound and word-level data can be informally aligned based on analysis of text demands. Traditionally, by the end of Grade 2, students have been expected to master the reading of Fry's 300 Instant Sight Words (1980) or Dolch's Sight Word Lists (1936). Richardson and Lewis's (2018) Word Lists by reading level are aligned with guided reading level expectations. Following the logic of automaticity theorists (LaBerge & Samuels, 1974), to maintain comprehension, these high-frequency words must be recognized automatically, typically in one second or less.

To be on track with end-of-year reading level expectations, phonemic awareness expectations can be set for each grade level based on a normed PA assessment. Even if phonemic awareness is not set as an on-grade level Pre-K expectation, the percent of students who have achieved phonemic awareness can be tracked and continuous improvement goals can be set each year.

Training the Literacy Team to Administer and Score Assessments

LTs committed to reading acceleration also must be committed to becoming intimately familiar with their students as readers, which involves knowing how to administer and score assessments. Given the importance of efficiency while maintaining validity and reliability, LTs receive explicit training in how to administer and score each published assessment according to each assessment manual's protocol. After reviewing assessment protocol, trainees will need to observe administration of an assessment according to protocol and then engage in monitored practice, giving the assessment to multiple students of various reading abilities while supervised by the trainer. Trainees then receive specific feedback from the trainer on how the assessment was administered and scored, with attention to consistency across those administering and scoring the particular assessment.

The selected IRI is one published assessment essential for LT members to administer and score according to protocol, as its results will be combined with other information to form reading groups. Before training how to use a selected

IRI; however, basic ability to conduct an informal running record is paramount. Once able to conduct a running record, LT members have the basic tools for flexibly conducting any IRI. They only need to learn the protocol for the specific IRI.

Spelling inventories and checks also are important to administer and score correctly. Most are easily administered by simply calling out each spelling word, using it in a given sentence, and then repeating the word, but modeling, then offering monitored practice and feedback when administering to the intended audience can contribute to consistency. A trainer can demonstrate how to stretch out sounds to spell a practice item, and how to remove this support after assessment begins. Scoring specifics also are important to coordinate, such as whether or not letter reversals count as errors. When students read from word lists, a consistent time can be allotted for each word, such as one second, for example. As offered with some commercialized assessments, computers can ensure consistent timing of a word list presentation.

Also informative, yet not consistently practiced in many schools, the assessment administrator can record the student's actual response next to the expected response. As an example, if a student reads *though* instead of *through*, the assessment administrator would note this (i.e., THOUGH/through), so follow-up instruction can include how to distinguish between the words. As another example, when giving a letter-sound assessment, consistent notation and scoring must occur when a student adds a vowel to a consonant sound (says *muh* instead of /*m*/).

Interpreting Assessment Information

Once reading assessments have been administered and scored, an LT leader compiles the information at various levels – individual student, small group, classroom, grade level, school, and district wide – in a manner useful for decision making. A sample compilation of mid-year data from an IRI, a spelling screener, and a High-Frequency Words Assessment is shown in Figure 3.3.

Notice that scores in the areas of word recognition, fluency and comprehension can be compared for each student and across students and classrooms. Data can be sorted based on any of these categories. Primary and secondary sorts can help the LT base grouping decisions on multiple data sources and across classrooms if warranted. Also, if greater detail is required

Figure 3.3 Sample Mid-Year Data Analysis

	Word Rec		Fluency						Comprehension					
Student	Sight Words	Word Study	GR (Inst)	Tracking (0-6)	Accuracy %	Lit/Inf	Reading Rate	Fluency Rating	Retell Score	Comp Score	Comp Total	Comp out of	Comp %	Notes
Shane	26	10	C		90	L		2.5	3	3.5	6.5	9	72%	
Shana	35	5	C		90	L		2.5	5	4	9	9	100%	
Carter	35	11	D		94	I		3.5	3	5	8	10	80%	
Marquee	32	14	D		91	L		3	3.5	4.5	8	10	80%	
Weston	29	18	E		94	L		2.5	3.5	5	8.5	10	85%	
Brianna	32	18	F		95	I		2.5	3.5	3.5	7	10	70%	Failed GR-G b/c Comp
Kaylee	38	21	F		95	I		2	4	4	8	10	80%	

to pinpoint the instructional needs of a certain student or group, assessment subtest scores can be inserted into the spreadsheet and analyzed.

Once the LT leader compiles the data, it is shared with the LT. Guiding questions for use in a data meeting focused on analyzing multiple IRIs or RRs can be found in Form 3.9.

Form 3.9 Guiding Questions for IRI/RR Analysis

Sample Guiding Questions for IRI/Running Record Analysis

Instructions: Sort your classroom Running Records from low to high based on instructional reading level.

I.   **Word-Solving.**
   A. On your IRIs/RRs, highlight the strategies you noticed your students not using/using: pictures clues (PC) (yellow); letter-sound clues (LC) (orange); cross-checking (CC) (pink); self-monitoring (SM) (green); any other strategies (O) (blue).

	Non-Examples (Student)	Examples (Student)
PC		
LC		
CC		
SM		
O		

   B. For each item, what strategies can we use to help them move to the next level as word solvers?

PC	
LC	
CC	
SM	
O	

II.   **Fluency.**

   A. For RR, GR-A, GR-B, GR-C readers, compare how students are tracking print.

0 = As each word is spoken, the student gets off track.	1 = As each word is spoken, the student points to each word correctly.

0 - Non-Examples (Students)	1 - Examples (Students)

(Continued)

Form 3.9 (Continued)

B. What strategies can we use to help students move to the next level with accurate tracking of print?

C. Give examples of GR-D+ readers who are not/are reading in phrases or read slowly.

  1 = WXW (slow reading rate)   2 = 2–3 word phrases
  3 = longer phrases/smooth with rough spots 4 = smooth with few pauses

Examples of a 1 (Student)	Examples of a 2, 3, 4 (Student)

D. What strategies for reading in phrases can we use to help students move to the next level?

E. Give examples of GR-D+ readers who are not/are reading with expression.

1 = no expression 2 = some expression	3 = appropriate expression most of the time 4 = consistent appropriate expression

F. What strategies for reading with expression can we use to help them move to the next level?

III. Comprehension Retelling

A. For students who scored a 3 or less, mark an X and note learning needs.

Form 3.9 (Continued)

Literary Text

1-Recall few or no story elements (Literary)	4-Retells important story elements and events in
2-Retell basic story elements (chars) (L)	sequence (BME) (L)
3-Retells important story elements (L)	5-adds personal thinking.

Student	Characters	Story Elements	Sequence of Events	Personal Thinking	Look back?

Informational Text

1-Recall few or no information	4-Retells important information in sequence
2-Retell basic information (1–2 facts)	5-adds personal thinking
3-Retells important information (main idea/random facts)	

Student	Basic Facts (1–2)	Main Idea/Facts	Main Idea/Key Facts in Order	Personal Thinking	Look back?

B. For students who scored a 4 on retelling, explain the difference between average and higher level personal thinking at a few different reading levels. Also, how can we can prompt for personal thinking when we give a Running Record?

C. What strategies can we use to teach literary/informational retelling?

IV. Comprehension Questions.

A. Compare students who scored a 0 vs. .5 vs. 1 in the following areas.

Form 3.9 (Continued)

	0 Examples (Students)	.5 Examples (Students)	1 Examples (Students)
Vocabulary (V)			
Key Details (KD)			
Character Analysis (Fiction) (CA)			
Analyze Relationships - NF (AR)			
Infer (I)			
Main Idea/Summarize (MI/S)			
Evaluate (E)			

B. For each type of comprehension question address the following questions:

	What do students need to do to progress to the next level?	What strategies can we use to help them get there?
Vocabulary (V)		
Key Details (KD)		
Character Analysis (Fiction) (CA)		
Analyze Relationships-NF (AR)		
Infer (I)		
Main Idea/Summarize (MI/S)		
Evaluate (E)		

These guiding questions encourage the LT to become familiar with student use of word-solving, fluency, and comprehension strategies, which can help LT members plan and deliver responsive literacy instruction.

Furthermore, individual student data must be reported to parents. A sample ELG or Intervention Progress Letter can be found in Figure 3.4. This mastery-based information can be included in a report card, or reported separately in the form of a letter, as is the case here. Notice that this letter reports useful information, a child's reading level at the beginning and then at the end of the ELG or Intervention. Coupled with a leveled booklist or leveled books, the parents can use this information to support the school by reading appropriate books at home.

Figure 3.4 Sample ELG or Intervention Progress Letter

Date

Dear Parent or Guardian,

We are writing to report your child's progress in reading. Please see the chart below of your child's reading progress based on the school district's guided reading (GR) level expectations for each grade level.

Kindergarten	First	Second	Third	Fourth	Fifth
A B C D E	E F G H I J	J K L M N	N O P Q	Q R S T	T U V W

Your child's GR level from the beginning of the school year is highlighted in pink, and your child's current GR level is highlighted in yellow.

Thank you for contributing to your child's growth as a reader! We encourage you to read with your child each night and look forward to your child's continued reading success. Please feel free to contact us with questions or ideas on how we can support you and your child.

Sincerely,

The Literacy Team
Contact: _____

Summary

In this chapter, *Systematic Literacy Assessment and Progress Monitoring*, we emphasized that effective literacy assessments are purposeful, comprehensive, balanced, and integrated, as well as efficient, while maintaining validity and reliability. Within this context, we reviewed four types of reading assessment (screening, diagnostic, progress monitoring, and outcome-based) based on purposes for giving them. With these reading assessment principles in place, we were able to recommend a strategic assessment process beginning with selection of appropriate reading assessments based on a cognitive model of reading, affective factors, and factors involving cost-benefit analysis.

From there, we showed how assessments are scheduled, expectations are set, a trained LT administers and scores, the LT leader compiles and presents, and the LT interprets the assessment information. In Chapter 4, the strategic process continues as we use assessment data to form literacy groups, to establish goals, and to provide instruction with a focus on accelerating literacy progress.

Reflection

Reflect on the content from this chapter as you develop or fine-tune your system for assessing and monitoring literacy progress.

1. What is your school's or district's process for administering, compiling, interpreting, and reporting assessment results? To what degree are you using a strategic process similar to this

chapter? What is needed to be more strategic? Record responses and be sure to include:

a. What needs to be assessed, compiled, analyzed, and reported,

b. When and how often we will report data (include daily, weekly, every 3–4 weeks, not just 9-week and beginning, middle, end of year),

c. How information can be understood and accessed,

d. Overall strengths and needs.

2. Reflect on student observations shown in Forms 3.1 and 3.2. How can such assessments be used to focus on abilities in specific skill areas as well as overall reading abilities? How can it be used to enhance rather than detract from daily instruction?

3. Compare your school's quarterly assessment schedule to the one in this chapter. Determine whether or not revisions are warranted.

4. Reflect on literacy expectations for each assessment area. Are your literacy expectations aligned with one another and with a nationally normed assessment? Are literacy expectations communicated and coordinated across grade levels?

5. What are the literacy team's assessment training needs? What measures can the literacy team take to maintain consistency across administrators?

6. Reflect on meetings at your school where data is shared. What is working? What can be improved in order for data to be used to flexibly group students and to inform instructional decisions on an ongoing basis?

Chapter 4

Systematic Literacy Instruction for Accelerating Progress

As established in Chapter 1, the need for early literacy acceleration is clear. However, coordinated structural and instructional implementation efforts remain inconsistent across school systems (Gewertz, 2020a). Regarding instructional implementation, the focus of this chapter, although a multitude of programs, resources, and professional development options are available to school systems, this plethora of often-conflicting options can be incredibly difficult to navigate. Walpole and McKenna (2009) capture the essence of the instructional side of implementation difficulties as follows: "At best, these efforts may be overwhelming. At worst, they may yield an incoherent instructional patchwork. In fact, teachers may be suffering from an embarrassment of riches as they try to navigate their choices" (p. 1).

In this chapter, we strive to help administrators and Literacy Team (LT) leaders navigate their literacy choices. More specifically, we discuss the following key action steps for accelerating schoolwide literacy: (1) plan a comprehensive and multi-leveled literacy block as part of an overall master schedule and (2) plan Early Literacy Groups (ELGs), Interventions, and Enrichment units (I/Es) based on how literacy develops and identified student needs. As part of planning responsive ELGs and I/Es, we offer ideas for (a) organizing instructional resources, (b) grouping students flexibly into the pre-scheduled ELGs and I/Es based on assessed needs, and (c) planning lessons for each group based on literacy goals and expectations. Beginning with a sample structured literacy block, we aim to deliver explicit, systematic, sequential literacy instruction to maximize the likelihood of literacy acceleration for virtually all students.

Instruction in the Literacy Block

The literacy block provides a systematic structure for the delivery of literacy instruction at multiple levels. Highly effective teachers use direct instruction to introduce a new or unfamiliar concept and then gradually release responsibility as appropriate, with the goal of students reaching independence as learners.

Exemplary teachers naturally flow between *teacher-directed* and *student-participation* stances (Taylor, 2004)

During the *teacher-directed stance*, teachers provide high levels of support and direction, demonstrating important concepts and engaging students in shared activities. During the *student-participation stance*, teachers gradually release support and direction, offer opportunities for guided practice, and move students toward independence as learners.

To ensure that direct instruction and then a gradual release of responsibility occurs, they are systematically built into the literacy block schedule.

Building on Tyner's differentiated literacy block (2009) and based on other research studies (Shanahan, 2019a; Sisson & Sisson, 2016; Canady & Canady, 2012; Canady & Rettig, 2008; Alkin, 1992), we have developed a sample structured 165- to 180-minute literacy block.

Literacy Acceleration Highlights

With 90-minute literacy blocks representing a common 'average effort,' Shanahan (2019b) recommends 120–180 minutes, and encourages the high-end of that recommendation for schools and districts with more challenged students or for those seeking to increase reading achievement.

Our sample literacy block in Figure 4.1 shows an excellent example of the strategic planning of curriculum and instruction to provide multiple levels of teacher support and a variety of texts and text levels within a comprehensive literacy program.

Differentiated ELGs are shown, as well as an Intervention option as a modification of independent reading time (Canady & Canady, 2012). Of note, delivery of literacy in one large block of time is neither required nor preferred (Shanahan, 2019a). Strategic division of the literacy block could involve the LT flooding the classroom to provide a morning ELG and then returning to provide an afternoon ELG, for example.

Within each element of the comprehensive literacy block shown in Figure 4.1, teacher instructional support ranges from a high level (i.e., Modeled Reading and Writing) to little or no instructional support (i.e., Independent Reading and Writing) to meet the literacy and cognitive demands of the task and the multiple levels within a typical heterogeneous classroom. Each element contributes to a comprehensive literacy program.

Figure 4.1 Sample Differentiated Literacy Block (165–180 Minutes)

Extended Time	Instruction (Multiple Levels of Support)	Curriculum (Multiple Texts)	Text Level (Multiple Text Levels)
75–90 minutes	Modeled Reading	Quality fiction and non-fiction texts	Above grade-level
	Shared Reading	Text from Grade-Level Curriculum or Alternative Source	Grade-level and/or Instructional Level
	Writing	Quality Mentor texts to model writing genres, traits, and conventions; Student-Written Texts	Multiple Text Levels
60 minutes	ELGs offered by the Literacy Team	Goal-Focused Texts	Instructional Reading Level
30 minutes (Select one)	Individual/Partner Reading/Writing	Goal-Focused Texts	Independent Reading Level
	Interventions	Goal-Focused Texts	Instructional to Independent Reading Level

Adapted by Canady, C. E. (2020) from Tyner, B. (2009). Small Group Reading Instruction: A differentiated teaching model for beginning and struggling readers. (2ⁿᵈ Ed.). *International Reading Association.*

Modeled Reading and Writing

Although exemplary teachers naturally model effective reading and writing strategies throughout the day, a dedicated whole and cooperative group time for Modeled Reading and Writing is most appropriate (Tyner, 2009). The primary purpose of this time is to expand listening comprehension, and, as part of an integrated lesson, to explicitly teach higher-level concepts, vocabulary, and comprehension strategies (Shanahan, 2019b). The teacher often uses quality above-grade level fiction and non-fiction texts to read aloud to students. Because of the reduced content demands offered by their more readable texts (Beck & McKeown, 2007), emergent and beginning readers largely depend on their teachers to provide the higher-level content offered by read alouds. At times, books also are read aloud primarily for the purpose of exposing students to published or student-written models of excellent writing (i.e., Modeled Writing). Students use these models to develop ideas for their own writing.

Non-fiction read alouds especially are important, because they often contain rich vocabulary and concepts (Miksic, n.d.), such as in *Everything Spring* (Esbaum, 2010). The concept of Spring is described as follows: "Spring tiptoes in, stirring up earthly smells, coaxing color from the winter-brown woods" (p. 2). Although some words can be difficult for students to understand, exemplary teachers naturally explain how spring *tiptoes in* and how spring is *coaxing color from the winter-brown woods*; examples and non-examples of key vocabulary or of the concept of Spring are used to ensure student concept attainment.

Emergent and beginning readers also benefit phonologically from hearing read alouds focused on literacy concepts such as word play, rhyming, alphabet sounds, and word features (Kilpatrick, 2015; Yopp & Yopp, 2000, 2009). For example, in *The Hungry Thing* (Slepian & Seidler, 2001), The Hungry Thing visits a town and points to a sign around his neck. The sign says, "Feed Me." When the townspeople inquire about the food he would like to eat, The Hungry Thing responds with garbled beginning sounds, such as "schmancakes" for pancakes. Only a little boy can interpret his utterances. Books such as this one encourage students to practice playfully rhyming and manipulating speech sounds. In the pre-Kindergarten and primary grades, all types of read alouds – those focused on developing comprehension, content vocabulary, ideas for writing, and early reading concepts – are essential daily components of a comprehensive literacy program.

Shared Reading and Writing

Along with Modeled Reading and Writing, Shared Reading and Writing also are most appropriate during whole and cooperative group times (Tyner, 2009). During Shared Reading, the teacher uses text from a grade-level curriculum or alternative source for the primary purpose of addressing grade-level literacy standards. Both the teacher and students "share" the reading by having a copy of the grade-level text in front of them. In the early grades, teachers also use big books, projectable digital texts, or enlarged books placed under a document camera to share books, pointing under the words as they actively read together. During Shared Writing, the teacher and students write together. Both the teacher and the students view themselves as mutual composers of a shared written work. Especially in the pre-Kindergarten and primary grades, teachers use flip chart paper and sentence charts with sentence strips to write (and read) together.

Across all elementary grades, teachers display text digitally, on a document camera, or utilize individual text copies as they engage together in Shared Reading and Writing. Follow-up cooperative group and independent activities, especially hands-on ones, provide engagement and reinforce content learning.

Writing Instruction as Separate and Integrated

Dedicated time for specific writing instruction is necessary for growth. In a federal practice guide published by the Institute of Education Sciences (IES), a panel of researchers (Graham et al., 2012) recommends providing daily time for student writing. During this time, they also recommend teaching students the writing process and its use for a variety of purposes, and teaching students to become fluent writers. They explain that fluent writing is developed by providing instruction in handwriting, spelling, sentence construction, typing, and word processing.

Writing also is integrated throughout all of the literacy components (i.e., Modeled, Shared, Differentiated, and, Independent Writing) (Sisson & Sisson, 2016). As a follow-up to reading instruction, writing helps students process their reading. Synchronic with the blending task of reading, the segmenting task of writing dictated letters, words, and sentences also can help emergent and beginning readers learn to decode. Unlike reading that begins with text, a student's writing ends with differentiated text. To illustrate, while one student simply draws and labels a plant, a more advanced writer uses advanced vocabulary to trace the entire process of photosynthesis. Therefore, during our model of Differentiated Reading and Writing time, writing is an important component, but reading receives priority over writing, which is naturally differentiated.

Differentiated Reading and Writing

Differentiated reading and writing allows students who have different needs to receive and apply learning focused on specific literacy goals (i.e. needs-based instruction) (Tyner, 2009). Students receive differentiated reading and writing instruction in a homogeneous small group setting. Instruction may include phonological awareness, explicit phonics, word recognition, vocabulary, and reading practice for fluency and comprehension. Students receive systematic literacy instruction based on a specific literacy goal.

> *Systematic literacy* involves systematic and cumulative instruction (International Dyslexia Association [IDA], 2020). Systematic means the teacher follows a sequence from easiest to most difficult concepts and elements, and cumulative means current lesson concepts built from previous ones. Direct teaching of concepts with continuous teacher-student interaction is emphasized, and diagnostic teaching occurs within and apart from each lesson, with emphasis on adjusting instruction to help students progress with a specific goal as well as with overall reading abilities. Once students demonstrate accuracy, assessment of word reading and overall reading abilities includes measurement of automaticity, due to its association with comprehension.

Goal work is followed by goal-oriented application within an integrated lesson. Reading and writing applications are related to and reinforce the goal. A variety of texts are used strategically to maximize learning (Shanahan, 2019a), including concept books, predictable books, decodables, controlled vocabulary readers, and leveled readers, as well as digital texts.

Based on findings such as Taylor, Pearson, Clark, and Walpole's (2000) that the use of coaching during small group instruction was a distinguishing characteristic between effective and exemplary schools, the term *guided* connotes an educator's role in coaching students (Sisson & Sisson, 2016; Ford & Opitz, 2011), as they read at their own paces (Fountas & Pinnell, 2016; Tyner, 2009). Beginning readers read in a whisper or quiet voice as the teacher flexibly listens and provides individualized and collective corrective feedback in-the-moment, explicitly teaching and prompting students to apply decoding skills and reading strategies. Transitional and higher level readers silently read a designated small section of text, then the teacher engages them in oral or written discussion to process textual concepts and application of reading strategies, including word-level and comprehension strategies focused on deeper understanding. Teachers help students master specific goals with the ultimate goal being flexible application to a wide variety of increasingly demanding texts.

Independent Reading and Writing

Independent writing time can be beneficial as a follow-up to whole group Modeled or Shared Writing or small group differentiated instruction (Tyner, 2009). During Independent Reading, students read familiar instructional or independent level text by themselves or they partner with another student (i.e., partner reading).

This time can be very beneficial for students who have acquired basic decoding and sight word recognition to enable independence. Proficient readers and writers with stamina can read independently, with a partner, or engage in writing activities such as journal response writing as a follow-up to previous reading. For less proficient readers, however, independent reading may be less effective. Providing an additional teacher-directed lesson is a strategic modification to their reading block. Another option for independent practice, especially for less proficient readers and writers, involves use of technology software to target specific literacy skill needs.

Monitoring independent reading and writing time also is key to its effectiveness. We suggest developing accountability measures and support structures to increase the likelihood that this time is well-spent. Conferencing with students regularly about book selection and reading strategies increases accountability and creates an opportunity for teachers to build relationships with students around reading. Students also are held accountable by being assigned a task or a reading guide to complete and turn in. A possible support for work completion is to pair students who are not with influential peers who are effective time managers. As another support idea, teachers can audiotape students reading as the teacher listens and offers prompts, then the student or students can replay the recording during independent reading time. This option also offers students an extra opportunity to clarify reading follow-up assignments.

Defining Literacy Essentials

Literacy essentials are important to consider when planning instruction across the literacy block, and an understanding of the developmental path within each essential is critical for planning differentiated literacy instruction. Based on a rigorous review of scientifically-based research on preventing reading difficulties, the National Reading Panel (NRP; Snow, Burns, & Griffin, 1998) reported the following "big 5" essential elements of effective reading instruction: phonemic awareness, phonics, fluency, vocabulary, and comprehension. In 2000, the National Institute of Child Human Development (NICHD) thoroughly analyzed and expanded the work of the NRP, and confirmed NRP conclusions regarding essential elements. In 2016, What Works Clearinghouse (WWC) and a panel of experts (Foorman et al.) also examined rigorous research studies on foundational skills to support reading for understanding and drew similar conclusions to the NRP and the NICHD. They also rated the strength of the research evidence. In this section, we share this extensive NRP, NICHD, and WWC research, as well as other relevant research supporting each essential literacy element.

Phonological Awareness

Phonemic awareness is an essential reading foundation, because it is highly related to later success in reading and spelling, and can be successfully taught (NICHD, 2000). Consistent with the NICHD (2000), the WWC (Foorman et al., 2016) found strong research evidence for teaching phonemic awareness and matching oral sounds to written print.

> *Phonological Awareness* (PA) development involves identifying and manipulating smaller and smaller spoken sound units–words, syllables, onsets, (the beginning sounds in a word, such as the /c/ in *cat*) and rimes (the sounds in the middle and at the end of words, such as the /at/ in *cat*), and phonemes, the smallest unit of spoken sound.
>
> *Phonemic Awareness* is the highest level of PA. Students are thought to have achieved PA when they can identify phonemes, such as recognizing the word *ship* as having three phonemes (sh-i-p), and manipulate them to read and write (Yopp & Yopp, 2000).

Teaching students to recognize and manipulate speech sounds (PA) and to match those sounds to print (Phonics) is necessary in preparing them to read words and comprehend text.

Word Recognition

Students can learn to read efficiently by being explicitly taught a research-based phonics sequence based on how children learn to hear sounds and how they learn to read and write words (Blevins, 2019; NICHD, 2000; NRP, 1998).

> *Phonics* involves teaching students how letters are represented by spoken sounds and how to use this knowledge to read and write (NICHD, 2000).
>
> *Explicit* phonics instruction means the letter–sound relationship or phonics skill is directly introduced to students. For example, the teacher directly states to students that the /b/ sound is represented by the letter b.
>
> *Systematic* phonics instruction involves following a research-based sequence from easy to more complex skills, gradually introducing each new skill (Blevins, 2019).

Similarly, WWC (Foorman et al., 2016) found strong evidence for teaching students to decode words, analyze word parts, and write and recognize them.

While explicit and systematic instruction is recommended, Blevins (2016) also suggests that students receive opportunities to practice with teacher guidance using word awareness activities – such as word building and word sorts. He explains that this practice helps students become flexible in their knowledge of sound-spellings, and solidifies their learning. Readers can benefit from learning high frequency words, or words encountered frequently in text, as well. (NICHD, 2000). Analogy to known words can be used; however, this approach often is less efficient than teaching high frequency words within the context of an explicit and systematic phonics program (Walpole & McKenna, 2009).

Fluency

In 2000, the NICHD confirmed fluency as one of the five essentials of effective reading instruction.

> *Fluency* is the ability to read orally with sufficient accuracy and speed, and with appropriate expression. Methods to improve fluency have been found to support comprehension as well (Foorman et al., 2016; NICHD, 2000; NRP, 1998).
>
> Once students are able to read words with accuracy or correctness, and are able to read words automatically or fluidly and with expression that reflects meaning, they can focus their cognitive resources on comprehension (Rasinski, 2013).

Later, the WWC (Foorman et al., 2016) found moderate evidence for ensuring that students read connected text every day to support reading accuracy, fluency, and comprehension. Other reviews of research also have found fluency is an essential component for success in learning to read (Rasinski, Reutzel, Chard, & Linan-Thompson, 2011; Kunn & Stahl, 2003; Chard, Vaughn, & Tyler, 2002), and a prerequisite to more sophisticated levels of reading comprehension (Rasinski et al., 2011).

In a large-scale observational study of the reading instruction offered by over 100 1st and 2nd grade teachers, Foorman and others (2006) examined the role of reading volume in daily classroom reading lessons. They reported that time allocated to text reading was the key factor explaining variance in outcome measures, including word recognition, decoding, and reading comprehension. Other *time* factors (i.e., time spent on phonemic awareness, word recognition or decoding) were not as related to reading growth. These findings suggest that teachers design lessons such that student reading volume is expanded (Allington, 2014).

Based on 18 studies, one decade later Foorman and others (2016) found moderate evidence for their recommendation that teachers ensure student daily reading of connected text to support oral reading accuracy, reading comprehension, and word reading. Contributing factors, also recommended, included previewing words before reading connected text, receiving support or feedback from a more able reader when students experience difficulty identifying a word, and teaching self-monitoring strategies with emphasis on attending to textual meaning. Initial short-term intensive fluency interventions also have shown effectiveness (DiSalle & Rasinski, 2017).

Comprehension and Vocabulary

The NICHD (2000) confirmed that vocabulary should be taught both directly and indirectly.

> *Direct* teaching of vocabulary occurs apart from text. *Indirect* teaching of vocabulary is embedded or occurs within text-based lessons.

To assist with vocabulary development, they also recommended repetitive and multiple exposures to vocabulary words, and use of technology. All of these methods were suggested within the context of a multiple-strategy approach. Reciprocal teaching is one such approach focused on teaching the multiple strategies of predicting, clarifying, questioning, and summarizing within a single lesson (Oczkus, 2018). WWC (Foorman et al., 2016) also found minimal, but still significant evidence for teaching students academic language skills, including inferential and narrative language, and vocabulary knowledge.

Concerning reading comprehension, the NICHD (2000) also found that multiple techniques and systematic strategies are optimal to assist with recall of information, question generation, and information summarization.

> Comprehension strategies are sets of steps good readers use to make sense of their reading. Seven comprehension strategies were found effective in improving comprehension: monitoring comprehension, metacognition (or thinking about one's thinking), using graphic and semantic organizers, answering questions, generating questions, recognizing story structure, and summarizing (Adler, 2001).

They also emphasized the importance of teacher training on when and how to teach specific reading strategies. Similarly, the WWC found strong evidence for teaching students how to use comprehension strategies. They found moderate evidence for teaching students text structure to comprehend, learn, and remember content, and for establishing an engaging and motivating context for teaching reading comprehension. They found minimal evidence for engaging students in discussion of the text's meaning and selecting text to support comprehension (Shanahan, 2010).

Planning Early Literacy Groups (ELGs) and Interventions

Planning ELG instruction and intervention requires a coordinated effort by school administrators, LT leaders, and LT members as described in Chapter 2. Differentiated instruction and interventions are planned by organizing instructional resources, grouping students flexibly based on data, planning specific types of lessons based on goals, and selecting goals and planning lessons for specific student groups, including text selection.

Organizing Instructional Resources

Coordination of a literacy center, a central location for quality literacy resources (i.e., multiple-copy books, corresponding lessons and materials), is important to the implementation of responsive ELGs and I/E periods (Canady, 2012). For a direct connection between the literacy center and academic standards (Lance & Loertscher, 2001) and for easy access to resources (Duke, 2004), collaboration among library and media center personnel, teachers, and administrators is essential. Larger, more current, and high quality library collections also can contribute to higher student achievement (Lance, Rodney, & Hamilton-Pennell, 2005). The LT leader can ensure collaboration among teachers and their easy access to resources. These literacy resources can be organized and color coded according to the four types of ELG and intervention goals we discussed previously in this chapter as charted in Figure 4.2.

Figure 4.2 Organization of ELG Resources

Phonological Awareness (PA)	Word Recognition (WR)	Fluency (F)	Vocabulary and Comprehension (VC)
Organize PA concept, familiar, and predictable texts and materials by: • lesson type (PA), • PA goal, and • reading level. Note type of lesson (PA), PA goal(s), reading level, and themes on books and materials. Also, note word patterns (I see...) on familiar and predictable texts.	Organize decodable and high-frequency texts and materials by: • lesson type (WR), • text type (decodable, high-frequency), • WR goal, and • reading level. Note type of lesson (WR), text type, WR goal(s), reading level, and themes on books and materials.	Organize fluency texts (typically fiction with strong emotions) and materials by: • lesson type (F), • Fluency goal, and • reading level. Note type of lesson (F), fluency goal(s), and reading level, and themes on books and materials.	Organize Vocabulary and Comprehension texts (mostly nonfiction) and materials by: • lesson type (VC), • VC goal, and • reading level. Note lesson type (VC), VC goal(s), reading level, and themes on books and materials.

Phonological Awareness lessons, books, and materials (i.e., resources) with a primary focus on phonological awareness development are in red book baskets; Word Recognition resources are in yellow book baskets; Fluency resources are in green book baskets, and Comprehension and Vocabulary resources are in blue book baskets. A color-coded chart and signs are posted to explain the meaning of the colors and how the books are organized.

Books, lessons, and materials are selected and further developed. The literacy center is continually updated as curriculum is shared among LT members. A central database allows LT members to sort resources based on a variety of fields such as ELG goal, book title, author, reading level, phonological awareness focus, word feature, fluency focus, comprehension focus, theme, and academic standard. Resources, such as sample book lists, lessons, and activities for delivering instruction within each of the four types of ELG goals are provided on our website. These resources are useful to the delivery of goal-focused lessons in the provision of accelerated literacy instruction.

Flexibly Grouping Students Based on Data

ELG and Intervention instruction must be based on identified skill needs. Let's consider the following scenario: an ELG teacher is exemplary at teaching the planned content. Five students are in the ELG group.

Two students need to learn the content, but three students have already shown mastery. The teacher can provide the highest quality instruction available, but only two students are likely to benefit from the intervention. Thus, the importance of homogeneous grouping, especially in the early grades when readers are the most sensitive to the difficulty of books and materials.

Accelerated ELG and intervention groups also are flexible throughout the school year. By working with LT members, the LT leader ensures student grouping and regrouping based on appropriate assessments. Once students have been strategically assessed and the data have been reported and interpreted, the first task of the LT is to identify students for ELGs and Interventions, largely based on overall reading abilities. Figure 4.3 presents ELG options by grade and reading level for morning and afternoon, and an optional third ELG in Grades K-1.

We recommend that all Kindergarteners receive a morning and an afternoon ELG. For non-proficient Kindergarteners, we also recommend a partial or a full ELG. We recommend that all students in Grade 1 receive an ELG. Proficient Grade 1 readers also can receive a partial ELG (20 minutes) or monitored independent reading. Proficient readers are more likely to profit from independent time than less proficient readers (Scanlon, Anderson, & Sweeney, 2017). This independent work time is maximized when students are monitored by a teacher who holds them accountable such as by audiotaping their reading or by requiring students to complete and turn in responses to questions about their readings. Grade 1 non-proficient readers can receive 2 ELGs, 2 ELGs plus a partial ELG, or 3 ELGs focused on addressing skill needs.

Figure 4.4 presents options for high, moderate, and reduced ELG support, as students increase in reading level and develop independence as readers.

The three levels of ELG support range from the highest, with three ELGs, to the lowest, with one ELG and a monitored independent reading time.

Figure 4.3 ELG Options by Grade and Reading Level

Grade Level	Reading Level or Sum Score	Morning ELG (30 minutes)	Afternoon ELG (30 minutes)	Optional 3rd ELG (20-30 minutes)
K	>= Grade Level	ELG	ELG	
	< Grade Level	ELG	ELG	Partial or Full ELG
1	>= Grade Level	ELG	Partial ELG or Monitored Independent Reading (IR).	
	< Grade Level	ELG	ELG	Partial or Full ELG

Figure 4.4 Model for Gradual Reduction of ELG Support

Level of ELG Support	Morning ELG	Afternoon ELG	Optional 3rd ELG
High Support	ELG	ELG	ELG
	ELG	ELG	Partial ELG
Moderate Support	ELG	ELG	Monitored IR
	ELG	Partial ELG	Partial ELG
Reduced Support	ELG	Partial ELG	Monitored IR
	ELG	Monitored IR	Monitored IR

Figure 4.5 shows an I/E plan by grade level for proficient and non-proficient readers in Grades 2–3.

Proficient readers receive enrichment services; non-proficient readers receive intervention and have the option of receiving a second intervention or monitored independent reading time.

After students are identified for ELG and I/E services, the LT assigns students in flexible, need-based ELG or I/E groups based on identified skill needs, with consideration to overall reading abilities. Conceivably, two students who read at the same instructional reading level could have different instructional needs. Based on multiple data sources, perhaps one student needs to work on word recognition and another student needs to work on fluency, for example. Depending on various factors (i.e., grade level, reading level, skill needs, funding), a variety of flexible grouping options, including enrichment activities, also are available to students who read on or above grade level. Primary and secondary data sorts can be run to group students based on identified needs with consideration to reading level.

Planning Lessons for ELGs and Interventions

Based on assessment, the LT leader determines the type of literacy lessons that will be offered–phonological awareness, word recognition, fluency, or comprehension and vocabulary. Although lesson plans are designed with a primary focus of instruction based on assessed needs, emphasis is placed

Figure 4.5 Selection Process for I/E in Grades 2–3

Grade	Reading Level	Intervention/Enrichment	Optional 2nd Intervention
2	>= Grade Level	Enrichment	
	< Grade Level	Intervention	Intervention or Monitored IR
3	>= Grade Level	Enrichment	
	< Grade Level	Intervention	Intervention or Monitored IR

on integrating goal-based skills and strategies with authentic reading and writing tasks, using appropriate texts. Thus, essentials of effective literacy instruction are included in each daily or weekly lesson as needed. From there, the LT leader sets congruent goals and assessments and develops specific lesson plans, to include selecting appropriate text. In an attempt to progress at an accelerated rate, the diagnostic teacher uses a goal to focus instruction, but a goal is not to place a limit on student progress. As soon as a student shows mastery of a goal, instruction is to be elevated to the next level of student need.

ELG lesson templates, such as those found in Form 4.1 and Form 4.2, can be used as starting points for clarifying distinct goals for ELG groups with different literacy needs. Form 4.1 offers the structure for two 30-minute ELG lessons, each with a separate assessment-based goal.

Form 4.1

Two 30-minute ELGs, Two Goals

ELG 1 (30 minutes)	ELG 2 (30 minutes)
Goal Work (15 minutes)	
Goal 1[1] _____ ❑ Introduction and Demonstration ❑ Guided Practice leading to independence ❑ Goal 1 Assessment[3]	**Goal 2**[1] _____ ❑ Introduction and Demonstration ❑ Guided Practice leading to independence ❑ Goal 2 Assessment[3]
Reading and Writing Application (15 minutes)	
Goal 1 Application[2] ❑ New Book Reading (Day 1) ❑ Rereading (Day 2) ❑ Writing (as needed) ❑ Assessment of Application[3]	**Goal 2 Application**[2] ❑ New Book Reading (Day 1) ❑ Rereading (Day 2) ❑ Writing (as needed) ❑ Assessment of Application[3]
Take-Home Goal Practice with Book[4]	
Goal 1 Practice _____ Book from Rereading (2–3 books per week)	Goal 2 Practice _____ Book from Rereading (2–3 books per week)

[1] Goal 1 is based on assessment(s) used to identify student(s) as needing Goal 1; Goal 2 is based on assessment(s) used to identify student(s) as needing Goal 2.

[2] Goal 1 & 2 Applications are based on assessment of overall reading ability and are focused on goal.

[3] Assessment is goal and application based, embedded with daily instruction using Forms 3.1 and 3.2, and weekly.

[4] Goal practice and books are sent home in a take-home pouch and returned. Goal practice is previously-introduced, consistent, and engaging; the book has been introduced and reread.

In this sample ELG lesson, students are offered a higher level, transitioning to a lower level of support until independence is reached. During Goal Work, an LT member introduces the concept with a highly engaging activity and then demonstrates how to complete a task that reinforces the concept being learned. The take-home goal practice is demonstrated before being sent home. Then, students engage in Guided Practice leading to independence. During the 15-minute Reading and Writing Application, on Day 1, students engage in New Book Reading. On Day 2, students engage in Rereading. Depending on the type of lesson, goals, and student needs, Writing occurs daily, on Day 2 only, or is embedded into Goal Work.

Form 4.2 offers two 30-minute ELGs with the same components as Form 4.1; however, students focus on one instead of two goals.

The one goal is taught with double intensity over the course of the school day, typically on a short-term basis. The double intensity provides student groups with time and instruction to catch up on a needed skill or strategy, and is offered on a short-term basis, such as for three weeks or for one

Form 4.2

Two 30-minute ELGs, 1 Goal, Short-term/Double Intensity

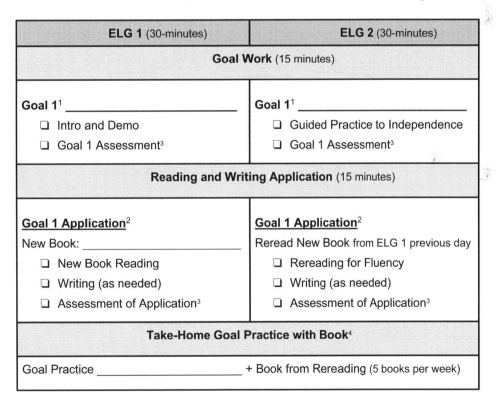

ELG 1 (30-minutes)	ELG 2 (30-minutes)
Goal Work (15 minutes)	
Goal 1[1] _____ ❑ Intro and Demo ❑ Goal 1 Assessment[3]	**Goal 1[1]** _____ ❑ Guided Practice to Independence ❑ Goal 1 Assessment[3]
Reading and Writing Application (15 minutes)	
Goal 1 Application[2] New Book: _____ ❑ New Book Reading ❑ Writing (as needed) ❑ Assessment of Application[3]	**Goal 1 Application**[2] Reread New Book from ELG 1 previous day ❑ Rereading for Fluency ❑ Writing (as needed) ❑ Assessment of Application[3]
Take-Home Goal Practice with Book[4]	
Goal Practice _____ + Book from Rereading (5 books per week)	

[1] Goal 1 is based on assessment(s) used to identify student(s) as needing Goal 1.
[2] Goal 1 Application is focused on overall reading ability and on Goal 1.
[3] Assessment is goal and application based, embedded with daily instruction using Forms 3.1 and 3.2, and weekly.
[4] Goal practice and books are sent home in a take-home pouch and returned. Goal practice is previously-introduced, consistent, and engaging; the book has been introduced and reread.

quarter of a school year, so students receive more than one lesson type and goal over the course of the school year. Because young readers often do not have reading stamina to manage two 30-minute ELGs or interventions, we suggest offering two split ELGs–with the first ELG occurring in the morning and the second ELG occurring in the afternoon.

With both plans, a previously-read book and goal practice is sent home each night in a take-home pouch. Small literacy-related rewards are earned weekly for completing goal practice and daily reading, and for returning books. The lessons are adaptable, depending on student needs as identified by regular progress monitoring checks. Based on accelerated growth models, student progress is monitored daily using an observation form such as Form 3.1 where the teacher flexibly records student observations related to the specific goal and its application. The teacher can use Form 3.2 weekly to monitor application and progress, conducting mini-running records as students are reading. At regular intervals, such as every 3–4 weeks, the weekly assessment is replaced by a more official measure of a student's reading ability.

As the number of LT members increases, collaborative team meetings become increasingly essential to coordinate instruction and to monitor progress toward exit goals. Groups have the option of flexing as often as every 6–7 days when all LT members meet grade-level core teachers for team planning during the extended planning time built into the master school schedule as illustrated in Chapter 5.

In the following sections, these lesson formats are applied to the four types of differentiated literacy instruction, and sequential goals and assessments are suggested. For each lesson type, lesson plans and resources are provided on the book's website.

Phonological Awareness (PA) Lessons

Emergent readers often engage in pretend reading, orally telling a story as they turn the pages in a book, attempting to match their words to the book's illustrations, with minimal consideration to print. To progress, they must develop the ability to hear spoken sounds (i.e., Phonological Awareness) (Foorman et al., 2016), and match those sounds to print (i.e., phonics, decoding). Students in PA-focused ELG groups might or might not know letter sounds. The distinguishing factor is that they cannot consistently apply sound knowledge such as hearing beginning sounds and blending, segmenting, and manipulating them.

PA Goal Work

Students can be identified for PA goals based on a PA assessment or check identifying sequenced PA skill needs. Inability to recognize and manipulate sounds would be indicators of the need to assess PA. Based on strong research support (Foorman et al., 2016), a sequence of PA goals are shown in Figure 4.6.

Figure 4.6 PA Goals

Phonological Awareness				
Alliteration and Rhyme Awareness	Word Awareness in Spoken Sentences	Syllable Awareness in Spoken Words	Onset-Rime Awareness in Spoken Words	Phonemic Awareness in Spoken Words

PA goals for ELG and intervention groups range from beginning sound and rhyme to phonemic awareness.

Rhyme awareness involves hearing the same sounds at the middle and at the end, such as in *bear* and *chair*.

Beginning sound awareness involves hearing similarities and differences among beginning sounds, such as recognizing that *bear* and *bat* sound the same at the beginning as represented by various pictures.

Word awareness involves hearing and identifying words in spoken sentences.

Syllable awareness involves blending, segmenting, and manipulating syllables in spoken multiple-syllable words.

Onset-rime awareness involves blending, segmenting, and manipulating the onset (or initial sound) and then the rime (the middle and ending sounds) in spoken two- and three-letter words.

Phonemic awareness involves blending, segmenting, and manipulating the spoken sounds in two- and three-letter words.

Rhyme and beginning sound awareness instruction often occurs during whole group time with interactive read alouds using beginning sound and rhyming books, along with beginning sound or rhyming follow-up activities. Based on assessed needs, rhyme or beginning sound awareness can become a goal during ELG or Intervention time as well. Teaching students to recognize and produce beginning sounds and rhymes often starts with comparing and playfully altering the beginning sounds in names such as *Mary, Mary, C-Cary, Cary, B-Berry Berry, Mary*! Instruction then progresses to determining whether or not two pictures sound the same at the beginning, or at the middle and end, if the goal is to rhyme. The teacher might ask students to put their thumbs up if two pictures sound the same at the beginning or thumbs down if they do not. Once this is accomplished, students progress to identifying two out of three picture cards. Beyond recognizing beginning sounds or rhymes, students need to produce them. For example, when the teacher reads the sentence from *Silly Sally* by Audrey Wood (1999), *Silly Sally went to town, walking backwards, up-side-_____*. The student learns to produce or fill in the rhyming word, *down*.

Word awareness instruction involves teaching students how words are combined to form a sentence (Foorman et al., 2016). Students are told that each word in a sentence has its own meaning. As the teacher says a sentence, the teacher and students count the number of words in the sentence. For example, if the teacher says: *The little girl ate an apple*, the correct response is that there are six words in the sentence. Beyond recognizing words in spoken sentences, students can be asked to track print in written sentences, an important foundational skill, but more related to language than to phonological awareness (Gillon, 2004). Students begin by cutting out words from a sentence strip where they see spaces, and pointing under each word as they say a sentence together.

Sample syllable, onset-rime, and phonemic awareness tasks to help students recognize and manipulate sounds are shown in Figure 4.7. In this chart, the PA tasks follow a sequence from easiest such as matching beginning sounds, to most difficult, deletion and substitution. As multi-sensory support for syllable awareness tasks, students and the teacher use a clapping sound or a pounding movement when they hear a syllable or beat in a pictured word card, and then they count the number of beats they heard before sorting the card by number of syllables. At more advanced levels, they delete or manipulate syllables in compound or other two-syllable words. Support to blend and segment sounds to read a word include using turtle-rabbit talk with puppets–the turtle talks slowly to stretch out sounds and the rabbit talks fast to blend sounds together. Another support involves the use of tokens and sound boxes, with each token and box representing one sound in a two- or three-letter word, or the use of elastic bands to stretch-and-say sounds.

Phonological Awareness (PA) Acceleration Highlight #1

Although PA instruction generally progresses from larger to smaller units of sound, children are not required to master one level before being exposed to higher levels of phonological awareness (Yopp & Yopp, 2009).

One such PA activity that exposes students to increased levels of PA within one lesson is Phoneme Puzzles (Richardson & Lewis, 2018). Students can start with multisyllable student names and then progress to multisyllable words from their reading.

1. With student input, the teacher writes a multisyllable word from a book preview, such as the word *hippopotamus*.
2. The teacher then cuts the word by syllables (i.e., hip/po/pot/a/mus) and asks students to reassemble the word.
3. The teacher further cuts the same word by onset and rime (i.e., h-ip/p-o/p-ot/a/m-us) and supports students as needed to reassemble the word.
4. For students who can do #3, then the teacher further cuts the same word by phoneme (i.e., h-i-p/p-o/p-o-t/a/m-u-s) and again supports students as needed to reassemble the word.

Figure 4.7 *Sample Phonological Awareness Tasks*

	Matching	Blending	Segmentation	Deletion	Substitution
Directions	"I'll say two words. Thumbs up if they sound the same at the beginning, Thumbs down if they do not."	"I'm the turtle. I say the words really s-l-ow. You're the rabbit. You say the words really fast!" to put all the sounds together.	"Now, I'm the rabbit. I say the words really fast! You're the turtle. You say the words really s-l-ow" to stretch out each sound.	"Say _____ (word) without /__/ (sound)."	"Let's change one word into another word! Say __ (word). Change /_/ (sound) in __ (word) to /_/ (sound)."
Syllable Awareness	*basket, button (yes)*	*/spi/-/der/ (spider)*	*monkey (/mon/-/key/)*	*popcorn* without *pop (corn).*	*/gup/ in guppy to /pup/ (puppy)*
Onset-rime Awareness	*bug, pig Repeat for sounds at end.*	*h-op (hop)*	*big (b-ig)*	*bed without /b/ (ed)*	*/r/ in rat to /m/ (mat)*
Phonemic Awareness	*cup, lip Repeat for sounds in middle and at end.*	*m-o-p (mop)*	*bus (b-u-s)*	*big without /bi/ (g)*	*/i/ in ship to /o/ (shop)*

Phonological Awareness (PA) Acceleration Highlight #2

Reading progress can be accelerated when teachers connect student ability to manipulate spoken sounds with their knowledge of letter-sound relations (Foorman et. al., 2016), connecting phonological awareness and word recognition as appropriate. Basically, although PA activities begin orally, progress can be accelerated when PA is integrated with Phonics. As an example, with mastery of key letter-sounds, students can be exposed to applying this sound knowledge, blending CVC words to read and segmenting them to write. If the task is too difficult, the teacher temporarily increases support according to the PA sequence.

PA Application

For emergent and beginning readers who have phonological awareness goals, brief excerpts from read alouds focused on language play, ABC, rhyming, and syllable awareness books can be used to introduce concepts in an engaging way. As students progress with their PA-related goals, multiple-copy familiar books such as nursery rhymes and predictable books can be useful for development of word awareness.

Concept of Word goals can range from accurate tracking of print, recognition of words within the context of a familiar passage, to word recognition in isolation after extensive work with the familiar passage (Blackwell-Bullock, Invernizzi, Drake, & Howell, 2009). Familiar reading passages such as nursery rhymes or poems are selected and often memorized, because when students expect to see specific letter sounds, words, phrases, and sentences in specific locations within the familiar passage, they receive the support needed to start making beginning sounds in words and recognizing words. As a follow-up writing activity, students can benefit from arranging and rearranging sentences from the passage. For more information on the development of Concept of Word (COW) and a useful developmental chart, refer to

Blackwell-Bullock et al. (2009). Use of Elkonian or sound boxes with chips representing sounds, then replaced by actual letter sounds and reading of decodable books can be useful for solidifying onset-rime and phonemic awareness. When speech is matched with print, however, this application overlaps with the word recognition lesson. The goals for each lesson contain gray shading to represent areas where lessons often overlap as appropriate for students.

Word Recognition (WR) Lessons

Students in Word Recognition ELGs are developing or have developed phonological awareness, are learning or have learned to match speech sounds to print, and are practicing how to decode phonetically regular words, but they need to become more automatic in reading words, and to build a store of frequently encountered (i.e., decodable) words, including those with irregularities easily recognized by sight. They also need to apply their word learning to accurately read books at their highest independent and instructional levels (i.e., fluency development) and to apply word knowledge and to develop fluency in writing sentences containing these words. Students can be identified for Word Recognition ELGs primarily based on spelling and sight word checks, with consideration to accuracy scores from running records. Similar to Forms 4.1 and 4.2, the Word Recognition ELG lesson focuses on decoding work, followed by application to decodable books or sight-word work with application to sight word books. The lesson is designed to be used flexibly, based on identified needs.

Sound and Word Recognition Goal Work

Sample goals for teaching Sound and Word Recognition are shown in Figure 4.8. These goals can be adjusted to fit any research-based sequence of instruction.

In this sample, sound and word recognition goals range from alphabet name and sound recognition to phonetically regular two- and three-letter short vowels to long vowels and beyond. As one example, students with Word Recognition goals need to distinguish short vowels (b*i*t) from long vowels (b*i*t*e*) with the Consonant-Vowel-Consonant-e pattern. Whether the

Figure 4.8 Sound and Word Recognition Goals

Letter & Sound Recognition	Word Recognition (Single-Syllable Words)						
ABC Name Recognition and ABC Sound Recognition	CV/VC and Same Vowel Word Families	Mixed Short Vowels (CVC)	Mixed Short Vowels with Ending Blends	Short vs. Long Vowels (CVCe)	Vowel Teams	R-Influenced Words	Diphthongs
		without/with Digraphs/Beginning Blends					
	High-Frequency Words						

primary focus is short or long vowels, blends (i.e., two letters containing two sounds as in <u>truck</u>), and digraphs (two letters containing one sound as in <u>check</u>), also can be included as appropriate.

Once students establish a decoding base, they can more readily distinguish regular and irregular high-frequency words; then, they can work on recognizing these words automatically, typically in a second or less. K-2 students usually are expected to master Fry's first 300 and Dolch's 200 words by the end of Grade 2 (Blevins, 2019). To support and accelerate this learning, we have organized Fry's first 300 and Dolch's 220 high-frequency words by phonics feature (see publisher's website) as much as feasible. We suggest that teachers introduce them manually then gradually build automaticity.

Sound and Word Recognition Acceleration Highlights

The number and difficulty of sounds and words compared, and the pacing in teaching them is important to accelerated literacy progress (Blevins, 2019). Letter sound and word learning can be accelerated by comparing two, three, or four distinct word features as appropriate. For example, instead of teaching the word *then* in isolation, based on reading errors, students can compare the error *then* with *than* from the text and based on a word reading or spell check, students can compare words with the same word feature (*bat, bet, bad, bed*).

Within the ELG, frequent word recognition checks help teachers determine whether students can benefit maximally from a slow, moderate, or fast instructional pace.

Word Recognition Application

A phonics sequence must be followed systematically and applied to authentic reading practice – using appropriate decodable books to introduce word features, then progressing to less controlled readers to reinforce concept attainment. For example, if the group is focused on learning nasal sounds produced with nose vibration such as /n/ in the word *sing*, then a decodable book such as *Sing Song Sid* by Margaret Allen (1999) provides appropriate application. Similarly, if a student is identified as trying to sound out every word, even words that cannot be fully sounded out, such as s-a-i-d, this student can benefit from texts containing high-frequency words such as *said*. As students recognize more words, they progress to less controlled texts.

Beyond decodable and high-frequency word books, readers in WR-focused ELGs must read a large volume, and a wide variety of books on their instructional and independent reading levels (Allington, 2014). Rather than remaining on the same book for multiple days, teachers must move beginning readers through a lot of beginning reader books (as many as 500-1000 books) for them to make even adequate, much less accelerated progress.

Students also need to learn to appropriately apply word-level strategies as they encounter new or difficult-to-decode words. As students read, the teacher offers appropriate prompts and corrective feedback to each student as needed (Blevins, 2019). Word-level verbal and picture prompts promote the application of sound-pattern meaning relationships and word-level strategies are taught as part of a multiple strategy approach. Teachers notice and document patterns across student readings. After students read, the teacher makes direct teaching points to the small group, with references to the book. Carefully chosen examples and nonexamples are used to compare known approaches with new or less known ones. Examples are focused on words as well as meaning. To achieve mastery, a review and repetition cycle also is included.

Fluency Lessons

Students in Fluency ELGs typically have adequate decoding skills with a range of vowel patterns in single-syllable words, but they lack automaticity in applying them to multisyllable words, and they lack fluency in connected text. While applying word recognition goals, accuracy can be developed, but for students with fluency goals, oral readings do not sound natural, or similar to oral communication. They need to build automaticity (i.e., flow and reading rate) and/or attend to prosody (i.e., prose-like, expressive reading). The specific need for fluency work can be measured with an IRI, with running records, and also with a literacy check such as the Multidimensional Fluency Scale (2020) as described in Chapter 3.

A Fluency ELG lesson is focused on fluency goal work and application to authentic texts. Comprehension also comes into play when working on fluency. While students tend to maintain a high level of engagement in learning these fluency strategies, flexibility is important to maintain with readers who show some reluctance, perhaps due to issues such as shyness or lack of interest in modulating one's voice. Essentially, short-term exposure to fluency strategies focused on fluid and expressive reading can provide a bridge between word recognition and comprehension for many students. Fluency work, however, should not prevent an inexpressive reader who demonstrates comprehension from receiving lessons with a primary focus on vocabulary and comprehension.

Fluency Goal Work

Goals for Fluency-focused ELGs are shown in Figure 4.9: Fluency Goals. Fluency goals typically focus on building automaticity, attending to prosody,

Figure 4.9 Fluency Goals

Fluency		
Accuracy	Automaticity	Prosody

or a fluency goal can be established in general based on the total score on the fluency check.

Individual fluency strategies are described in Opitz and Rasinski's (2008) *Goodbye Round Robin, Updated Edition: 25 Effective Oral Reading Strategies*. Building on their work, we suggest the use of a natural and progressive combination of individual fluency strategies similar to Figure 4.10 below.

Fluency Acceleration Highlights

Multiple fluency strategies, naturally flowing from one to another, can be much more powerful in accelerating literacy than one strategy used in isolation.

Figure 4.10 Progression for Teaching Fluency

Fluency Goals and Checks	Fluency Activities
Preparation for Fluency Instruction	**Comprehend Text and Key Vocabulary.** To comprehend the text and key vocabulary and in preparation for fluency instruction, teachers engage students in new book reading.
Accuracy based on Words Correct/Total Words Read	**Word-Solving Tips.** Teachers offer word-solving tips before, during, and after reading to help students develop accuracy. **Rereading.** Teachers offer rereading practice to help students develop accuracy and in preparation for further fluency instruction.
Phrasing and Smoothness based on Multidimensional Fluency Scale and Words Correct per Minute	**Attend to Natural Breaks.** To improve reading flow when reading in natural phrases rather than in a word-by-word style; students can be asked to read texts that are marked with natural breaks such as the following: *One day,/ a chick got away/ from its mother!*
	Attend to Reading Signals. To notice and adhere to "reading signals," punctuation marks and typographical signals such as bolded, italicized, and differently sized print, students engage in lessons focused on marking and reading these signals appropriately.
	Timed Repeated Reading. Students time and compare their initial and repeated readings, typically only an awareness of pace is needed.
Expression and Volume based on Multidimensional Fluency Scale	**Use Different Character Voices.** Students notice quotation marks or lack thereof and references to characters as signals to use different voices for different characters.
	Self-Evaluation and Audiotaped Reading. Students practice using fluency strategies. As they listen to their recording and reread, they track the text. At the end they self-evaluate fluency strengths and areas for future improvement (possible goals).
	Practice and Perform Reader's Theatre, leading to Performance Reading. In a group or an individual setting, students apply multiple fluency strategies while maintaining attention to text. The highest level of support is for readers to perform only one character part; this support gradually is reduced until the reader can perform all character parts.

As long as comprehension is not impeded, students can build auto-maticity by being taught to read in phrases rather than in a word-by-word style or by being taught to adjust their reading rate to the type of reading at hand. Students can develop prosody by being taught to attend to reading signals (i.e., punctuation, other typographical marks) and by being taught to modulate their voices, especially when read-ing the voices of different characters. Typically, these fluency strategies contribute to comprehension of the text. For example, meaning can be enhanced when a student consistently stops at a period instead of run-ning sentences together.

Fluency Application

Students with fluency goals benefit from fiction books with strong emo-tion such as the folktale of *How the Chick Tricked the Fox* (Kirby, 1996), where a chick must be convincing or the fox will eat him. Once students have attended to specific areas of the text, they can practice by audiotaping and evaluating themselves, by engaging in Reader's Theater with gradually removed support, and by engaging in Performance Reading.

Also, to encourage students to comprehend the text and its vocabulary before rereading and shifting their focus to fluency strategies, a variety of comprehension strategies can be taught; however, because a large major-ity of the emotive texts for these fluency goals are fiction, oral fiction retelling strategies tend to work well with this fluency-focused ELG. Dur-ing Fluency-based ELGs and interventions, we often use the Cover and Tell strategy (CT), simplified from Jan Richardson's (n.d.) Stop, Think, and Paraphrase (STP) strategy. Our CT strategy involves covering up a small section of print and then telling about the content before moving to the next portion of text. CT works well with both fiction and non-fiction content and can be flexibly used first with smaller portions and then with larger portions of text.

Comprehension and Vocabulary Lessons

Students in Comprehension and Vocabulary ELGs typically are instructional readers who are less impeded by the mechanics of learning to read than less mature readers. The instructional reader's ability to read silently, without whispering or even moving lips, marks a major shift from the beginning and transitional stages of "learning to read" to the instructional reading stage, otherwise known as "reading to learn." With comprehension less impeded, the primary focus becomes comprehension and vocabulary development in a variety of readable texts across a variety of genres.

Sample ELG Comprehension and Vocabulary goals shown in Figure 4.11 are based on Snow et al. (1998) and NICHD (2000) recommendations, Shana-han's 2010 federal practice guide, and Serravallo's research (2015).

Figure 4.11 Comprehension and Vocabulary ELG Goals

Vocabulary	
Word Study: Multisyllable Words	Academic and Content-Specific Vocabulary (i.e., Tier 2, Tier 3) from Reading
Comprehension: Fiction	**Comprehension: Nonfiction**
❏ Plot/Setting ❏ Character ❏ Figurative Language ❏ Themes/Ideas	❏ Main Idea ❏ Key Details ❏ Vocabulary (above) ❏ Text Features

Vocabulary goals allow for both direct and indirect teaching of vocabulary. Comprehension goals are established for teaching with both fiction and nonfiction text, and can be adapted to meet the needs of students. Students focus on one specific goal at a time within a particular genre such as using nonfiction text features to explain information from the text. Their comprehension goals gradually broaden, with the ultimate goal of flexibly applying a variety of comprehension strategies across a variety of texts.

Vocabulary Goal Work

In the Pre-Kindergarten and primary grades, vocabulary is important to teach as a natural part of whole group instruction. In her award-winning article, appropriately titled *Small Kids, Big Words*, Pappano (2008) describes a Kindergarten morning meeting on the topic of weather. When conversing with students, the teacher uses sophisticated vocabulary, but embeds definitions. Upon sharing, "I heard *thunder* outside my window" (p. 1), she explains,–"It was a *loud, crashing, booming sound*" (p. 1).

In the context of an ELG or Intervention lesson, before reading, important words and concepts are previewed. Kindergarteners observe insects and sort pictures of them in various ways, such as by ability to fly, before reading about them. Before reading about big machines used to fight fires, Grade 1 students preview meaningful sentences containing important vocabulary from the book.

Vocabulary Acceleration Highlight #1

Snow et al. (1998) suggest a more direct approach–sorting selected words into categories based on a common feature. She contends that by learning certain word meanings we get a multiplying effect. For example, if a student knows the meaning of *preschool*, he can determine many other word meanings, such as *predict, prevent, prefix, preview, and preface.*

The most widely accepted framework for deciding which vocabulary words to teach is Beck, Kucan, and McKeown's (2013) vocabulary tiers.

> **Definitions of Vocabulary Tiers**
>
> *Tier 1 words* are easier versions of Tier 2 words. Students typically learn them on their own by listening to adults, peers, and other sources of language in their environment. Typically, teachers do not need to teach these words.
> *Tier 2 words* are important to academic success. These words must be explicitly taught.
> *Tier 3 words* are technical in nature and can be specific to a particular content or field.

Kindergarten students might know the Tier 1 word *wet* or even *soaked*, but perhaps the Tier 2 word *drenched* would be taught, for example. In Grade 1, the word *compact* as in a compact or a small car could be Tier 2, but in the context of the Mayflower Compact or agreement, *compact* could be Tier 3, and important to teach within a social studies unit in the colonial period. Tier 2 abstract words frequently encountered when teaching reading such as the words *consonant* and *vowel* are important to teach, and Tier 2 action words frequently encountered in written directions and on standardized assessments such as the words *list*, *explain*, or *compare*, are conducive to teach as appropriate.

> ## Vocabulary Acceleration Highlight #2
>
> Learning easier words is not required before more difficult ones are taught, as long as overall concepts are understood (Beck et al., 2013). Once Kindergarten students understand the concept of saturation from conducting class water experiments, they can understand the word *saturated* without first being taught the easier word *soaked*.

Comprehension Application

For reading comprehension instruction, use of a variety of fiction and nonfiction texts are recommended (Shanahan, 2010). When selecting text for an ELG lesson with comprehension application, teachers select text to support their instructional purposes as related to identified student needs, and within the group's level of difficulty. They also look for text qualities such as rich content, strong organizational structure, and variation and richness of word choice and sentence structure.

In fiction texts, Serravallo (2015) suggests teaching these reading comprehension elements: plot and setting, inferencing and relationships among characters, vocabulary and figurative language, as well as themes and ideas.

Teaching themes and ideas involves interpreting central messages and lessons. For example, in *The Wolf's Chicken Stew* by Kasza (1996), higher-level discussion does not revolve around retelling a wolf's seemingly-beneficent behaviors in delivering scrumptious meals to a chicken. Through the wolf's inner thoughts, the author traces the wolf's ill motive of fattening the chicken to eat her for dinner. The wolf's intentions take a twist at the end, however. When he goes to collect his meal, his newfound relationships with the chicken and her baby chicks become more irresistible than the meal. General lessons derived from the book's central message enhance higher-level meanings.

When teaching reading comprehension in nonfiction text, Serravallo (2015) recommends that teachers focus on these elements: understanding the main ideas and key details as well as content vocabulary, and the ability to connect textual meaning and structure. Comprehension application with a focus on main ideas and key details starts with using graphic and linear organizers to web or list, and then sorting single words and phrases related to a main idea (Project Creating Independence Through Student-owned Strategies [CRISS], 2010). For example, dog breeds would branch off from or would be listed under the main idea of dogs. Graphic and linear organizers are responsive to student learning needs as well as textual demands. From there, students are introduced to a book about dogs and their breeds. During and after reading, the teacher models how to highlight examples of main ideas and details from the text.

When introducing text structure, or the way a piece of writing is organized, the teacher starts with simple sequential or descriptive structures. Typically, a sequential text structure is organized chronologically or in a problem-solution format. A descriptive text structure introduces the topic and then describes traits of the topic and details of the trait before introducing a new trait. For example, a book about alligators is likely to start with the alligator's physical appearance, and then describe the alligator as cold-blooded and details of cold-bloodedness, before describing the second trait involving how baby alligators are hatched or born. The astute student connects the picture of the alligator lying in the sun with its trait of being cold-blooded. Teaching text structures such as these can help students comprehend increasingly demanding texts.

Building on the work of Serravallo (2015), we have developed observation forms and scoring rubrics for documenting student comprehension of fiction and non-fiction texts and progress toward goals. Observations can occur within the context of a mini-conference or an ELG, an intervention, or an enrichment lesson. Sample observation forms and fiction and nonfiction scoring rubrics are provided in Chapter 3 and as forms on the publisher's website.

Comprehension Acceleration Highlight #1

To reiterate, multiple techniques and systematic strategies are optimal to help students comprehend at higher levels (NICHD, 2000) – and at accelerated rates.

Comprehension Acceleration Highlight #2

In their recent review, Neuman, Kaefer, and Pinkham (2014) reveal that rather than simply *activating* prior knowledge, formerly a common teacher protocol, teachers can accelerate reading comprehension by *building* background knowledge. Educational videos and online informational read alouds can be used to introduce a unit. Similar to the *before, during, after* format for planning a reading lesson, the *before, during, after* format is beneficial to use when planning a viewing lesson. We recommend that building background knowledge occur separate from ELG or intervention time, but as a collaborative technology lesson.

Planning Enrichment Units

The LT leader assigns students who are proficient in reading and in math to enrichment one of two options during a pre-scheduled I/E period. The goal of enrichment is for students who are proficient to progress to advanced proficiency in literacy and mathematics, or in science, social studies, and writing if these areas are assessed. This is accomplished by offering targeted enrichment units, usually 3–4 weeks in length, taught by a variety of qualified personnel. Although the primary discipline for a unit is science, social studies, or writing; multi-disciplinary standards such as English Language Arts, mathematics, and technology are included. During the units, students address essential questions related to high-interest topics.

A chart of enrichment unit links for various science, social studies, and writing topics can be accessed through this book's website. Since an I/E period typically is built into the master schedule at Grades 2–5, links to enrichment units are offered at these grade levels as well. Although grade level recommendations are made, teachers can adjust the appropriateness and level of difficulty to meet student needs.

Summary

Structured instructional strategies and practices are essential for providing accelerated literacy instruction. Instruction in the literacy block includes providing multiple levels of instructional support during modeled and shared whole group, differentiated small group, and independent reading and writing times. Literacy essentials are included during all parts of the literacy block. Specific to differentiated small group time, we recommend developing differentiated ELGs and Interventions, organizing instructional resources, flexibly grouping students into ELGs and Interventions based on assessments, and setting goals and planning integrated lessons based on assessed student needs. ELG and Intervention lesson types include: Phonological Awareness, Word Recognition, Fluency, and Comprehension and

Vocabulary. Integrated lessons emphasize goal work and appropriate goal-focused reading and writing application. Enrichment units also are planned and delivered to students who show proficiency in reading and math during an I/E period.

Reflection

Reflect on the content from this chapter as you consider how you will implement literacy instruction with a goal of accelerated literacy learning.

1. Reflect on the proposed literacy block. Consider the following:
   a. How much time is allocated for the literacy block and each literacy element?
   b. What is the instruction proposed for each literacy element?
   c. What is the research for the proposed literacy block?
   d. What are the specific strengths of the proposed literacy block?
   e. Are there any barriers? If so, how can they be overcome?
2. After reflecting on the proposed literacy block, its strengths, and possible barriers to implementation, plan your literacy block.
3. Based on the literacy block you plan to implement, what books and materials do you already own and what do you need? How can your books and materials be organized to promote easy access?
4. Reflect on the flexible grouping model we propose.
   a. What research supports the proposed flexible grouping model?
   b. What are the strengths?
   c. Are there any barriers? If so, how can they be overcome?
5. Develop your flexible grouping plan.
6. Reflect on the proposed ELG, I/E lessons.
   a. What is the research supporting these literacy lessons?
   b. What are the strengths?
   c. Are there any barriers? If so, how can they be overcome?
7. What types of literacy lessons do you already have and need to plan? Develop the needed literacy lessons.

Chapter 5

Walking Through a Potential Master Schedule

Building a data-driven master school schedule is critical in making literacy acceleration a reality. In this chapter, we identify guiding principles for building a master school schedule to prioritize literacy. Then we show two sample master schedules that incorporate these guiding principles. Building from the sample master schedules, we illustrate how to schedule Early Literacy Groups (ELGs), typically in Kindergarten and Grade 1, Intervention/Enrichment (I/E) periods, and encore (i.e., related arts) rotations. More information on the instruction and content of ELGs and I/E periods is provided in Chapter 4.

As previously introduced in Chapter 1 and further explained in Chapter 4, *Early Literacy Groups (ELGs)* are goal-oriented small groups instructed by LT members – classroom teachers, reading specialists, special education teachers, or teacher assistants, for example – who have been trained to instruct in specific skills. Students are rotated to instructors specifically trained in the skills and strategies students need.

The *I/E period* stands for *Intervention and Enrichment*. I/E provides goal-oriented intervention services for students who are not meeting proficiency goals in reading or mathematics and enrichment services for students who have met proficiency goals in these areas. Instruction in the Intervention period is similar to ELG instruction, except ELG serves all students and Intervention serves identified students. Also, Intervention time tends to be longer than ELG time. Assuming ELGs are in place in K–1 Grades, I/E periods of 35–50 minutes (depending on minutes in total school day) usually appear in the master schedule in Grades 2–5. In some schools Grade 2 ELGs are needed primarily for transfer students who have not had access to intensive, assessment-based instruction in Grades PK–1 or K–1. Enrichment is designed to provide students who have achieved proficiency in reading and mathematics with opportunities to deepen their thinking or learning on a particular topic related to a specific discipline. The goal of enrichment is to move students from proficiency to advanced proficiency in literacy and mathematics or in science, social studies, or writing, if these areas are assessed.

Guiding Principles for Crafting an Elementary School Master Schedule

In working with schools and school districts over the past 50 years, we have developed the following guiding principles for designing an elementary school master schedule: 1) Conceptualize the master schedule as a data-driven resource for utilizing time and resources based on student needs – not just determining when bells ring and people transition from one space to another; 2) strategically select and schedule staff based on data; 3) provide extended planning time for literacy teams; and 4) use school and student data to build a master schedule and supporting schedules around identified student needs.

Conceptualize the Master Schedule as a Resource

A master school schedule largely determines if the school day runs in a manner that is smooth and productive or fragmented and chaotic. When we say school day, we include all activities that occur during the school day – lunch, recess, homeroom, encore classes and all instruction. A good question to ask is: "How, daily, do we use data, time, personnel, space, and materials?" A master schedule can be designed to eliminate unproductive pockets of small time increments, provide integrated support for students, and clearly define the roles of all staff members.

Staff the Schedule Rather Than Continuing to Schedule Staff

Administrators each year tend to build the master schedule based on their current staff rather than the staff needed. Yet, informed decisions are based on data; therefore, scheduling the same staff every year is not fully productive. Instead, over time we suggest hiring and training the staff needed, with hiring decisions based on data-driven student needs and scheduling priorities. This means developing the master schedule early in the spring for the following school year.

A schedule built on identified student needs should be crafted before final budgets are approved and before staff notifications have to be communicated. This practice does not imply massive firings, but it may mean planning for specific types of staff development during the school year preceding implementation of a newly crafted master schedule. It also could mean asking human resources to transfer some staff members or involve the scheduling team in selecting key staff members needed in the new schedule based on data-driven student needs that change yearly.

Create Extended Planning Time for Literacy Teams

Based on data confirming that: 1) much variability exists among teachers; 2) the teacher is the most important school variable in determining if students learn to read on time; and 3) the Professional Learning Communities (PLC) data over two decades provide evidence that building on the collective capacity of teachers is more productive than depending on each teacher working alone, as a minimum we advocate for Literacy Teams (LTs) to be assigned to work with students in Grades PK–3. For LTs to function maximally, they must have a master school schedule that protects their daily and extended planning time.

Do we want to provide student tutorials, supports and opportunities for students to retake assessments? If so, do not leave these practices for each teacher to implement. We have found teachers willing to permit students to retake assessments, but they are not willing to spend time before or after school supervising the retakes. If a policy and a schedule are in place relative to when and where students may retake assessments, greater participation and support will follow. Supervision of such practices can be rotated among staff. One or two days each week may be scheduled for extra tutorials and assessment retakes during I/E periods, as shown in Figure 5.1.

We include I/E periods in most master schedules in Grades 2-5 only, because in PK through Grade 1, ELGs usually provide sufficient time for interventions; however, in higher need schools, both ELGs and I/Es may be needed at Grades K-1. In addition to I/E periods, some schools include at least one Independent Study and Support (I/S) period, typically managed by homeroom core teachers.

Use Student Data to Build Schedules Based on Identified Student Needs

All students do not have to have the same daily schedule; for example, some students may need to meet in ELGs twice daily, while some may need additional meetings. During the I/E period(s), do not simply focus on students needing specific skills interventions but also plan for those students who have demonstrated proficiency in math and literacy skills by providing enrichment units (see Chapter 4 for more information on Enrichment units and also see the book's website for information related to enrichment units), so those students who are proficient in math and literacy skills can use their skills to move toward or reach advanced proficiency. During the past decade, we fear emphasis on increasing achievement for the bottom 50% has resulted in academic stagnation for the top 50% of students who are unable to work independently (Jolly & Makel, 2010).

Figure 5.1 Canbee Elementary School

Master Schedule for Canbee Elementary School, Showing Blocks of Time when K-1 ELGs Meet and I/E Periods for Grades 2-5

	I	II	III	IV	V	VI	VII	VIII	IX
Pre-K		Literacy Groups			Recess/Lunch	↔	Literacy Groups		I/S
Kindergarten	HR Activities and Math		*Early Literacy Groups (ELGs)	↔	Recess/Lunch	↔	Encore/Plan	Repeat a.m. ELGs ↔	
Grade 1		*Early Literacy Groups (ELGs)	Math/Science		Lunch/Recess	Repeat a.m. ELGs		Encore/Plan	
Grade 2		Literacy ↔	Literacy/Social Studies	↔	I/E	Recess/Lunch	Math/Science	Encore/Plan	
Grade 3		Literacy	Literacy/Social Studies	↔	Encore/Plan	Lunch/Recess	Math/Science ↔		I/E
Grade 4		↔	I/E	Encore/Plan	↔		Recess/Lunch	↔	
Grade 5			***Encore/Plan	I/E			Lunch/Recess		
Lunch/Recess					PK, K, 1	2, 3	4, 5		
Encore/Plan		**Plan	Grade 5	Grade 4	Grade 3	Lunch	Grade K	Grade 1	Grade 2
LT-1		Grade 1	Grade K		Lunch	Grade 1	Grade K		
LT-2		Grades 2 and 3	I/E 4	I/E 5	I/E 2	Lunch	2-3	2-3	I/E 3
I/E			Grade 4	Grade 5	Grade 2	Lunch			Grade 3

*ELG = Early Literacy Group   HR = Homeroom Activities   I/E = Intervention/Enrichment Period   Sc/Ss = Science/Social Studies   LT = Literacy Team   I/S = Independent Study and additional Student Support

**Available to provide 75-90 minutes of Extended Plan Time on a 7- or 14-school day rotation.

***Encore vs. core refers to classes such as art, music, PE, media and dance. It is during these class periods that groups of teachers have common planning time. Encore classes are what some schools historically called specials.

Note 1: If a second Literacy Team (LT-2) can be staffed, those persons would work with students in grades 2-3 who still need ELGs. Often these groups would be transfer students who have missed the early literacy skills taught in grades K-1. The LT-2 team also teaches during the I/E periods in grades 2-5.

Note 2: For additional information on implementing an Intervention/Enrichment (I/E) period in an elementary school, see Canady, R. L. & Rettig, M. D. (2008), Chapter 4, *Elementary school scheduling: Enhancing Instruction for student achievement* , (pp. 93-125), (ISBN 978-1-59667-080-8); Routledge (Taylor and Francis).

Note 3: Grades 4 and 5 have three equal blocks scheduled which is helpful if teachers in those grades wish to departmentalize and/or cross grade levels for selected skill groups.

Note 4: Lunch periods may need to be adjusted based on numbers and when school begins each morning.

A Sample Master Schedule with Explanations
for Decision-Making

Based on the guiding principles identified in the previous section, in Figure 5.1, we show a sample master schedule titled, Canbee School Master Schedule.

The Canbee master schedule was developed based on data provided to us. At the time, the school had 730 students, 7 grade levels, including PK through Grade 5, except for Grades PK and Grade 1, six teachers at each grade level, and a teacher's assistant (TA) assigned to each Kindergarten teacher. In Kindergarten and Grade 1, blocks of time are scheduled for ELGs to meet twice daily. In Grades 2-5, I/E periods are scheduled. Lunch, recess, and encore periods are scheduled for each grade level, and extended encore periods can be scheduled on a rotational basis during periods one and two.

Because the Canbee School principal, with the support of K-1 Canbee teachers, scheduled in the master schedule blocks of time for ELGs to meet twice daily, the K-1 teachers stated they did not need scheduled I/E periods. In some schools, however, at least one I/E period is scheduled for all grades.

Because the Canbee teachers in Grades 4 and 5 were implementing departmentalization, they requested to have three shared blocks of equal time be scheduled in the master schedule. Based on multiple data sources from the past school year, it was obvious there were Canbee students who still needed ELGs in Grades 2 and 3. By making two assigned personnel changes, the principal was able to staff a second Literacy Team (LT-2), and that team worked primarily with students in Grades 2 and 3 and during I/E periods with students in Grades 4-5. During the early weeks of the school year, LT-2 members assist with assessments for determining students' initial assessment-based ELGs in Grades K-1.

It is important that all teachers who are assigned to a grade level have common planning time daily, and extended planning time on a rotating basis. At Canbee Elementary extended planning time can be scheduled on a 6-, 7-, 12-, or 14-day rotation.

In Figure 5.2, we show a 6-day rotation of encore classes that have been scheduled in the Canbee School master schedule during Encore/Plan periods.

Because all grade levels, except PK and Grade 1, have six sections, all encore groups follow a 6-day rotating cycle (i.e., school Day 1, 2, 3, 4, 5, and 6) throughout the school year. Grade 1 has seven sections, but each classroom has small numbers; therefore, the principal kept the 6-day rotation during the encore period, and students from all seven Grade 1 homerooms were assigned to six encore groups during that one time period. If the Grade 1 numbers had been larger, the principal may have assigned Grade 1 students to 3-day and 4-day encore rotating schedules since we have found 7-day rotating schedules to be difficult to implement. Three-day and 4-day encore schedules are shown as Figures 5.3 and 5.4.

Figure 5.2 Canbee Elementary School 6-Day Rotations for Encore/Plan Periods Shown in Master Schedule

6 Student Groups	Day 1	Day 2	Day 3	Day 4	Day 5	Day 6
1	P_1	D	L	P_1	M	A
2	P_2	A	D	P_2	L	M
3	M	P_1	A	D	P_1	L
4	L	P_2	M	A	P_2	D
5	D	M	P_1	L	A	P_1
6	A	L	P_2	M	D	P_2

P = Physical Education   C = Computer Lab   A = Art   L = Library/Media   D = Dance
M = Music   X = Break Aide or To Be   T = Theater   O = Other   S = Science
PS = PE Aide/Support   Determined (TBD)   S = STEAM   PA = Performing Arts   G = Guidance
A/M = Art or Music on   I/S = May be supervised   WW = Writer's   G/L = Guidance/Library   Dr = Drama
    a rotating basis   Independent Study   Workshop   on a rotating basis
WL = World Language   B = Band   Ch = Chorus

Figures 5.3 Canbee Elementary School 3-Day Rotations for Encore/Plan Periods Shown in Master Schedule

3 Student Groups	Day 1	Day 2	Day 3
1	P	A	M
2	A	M	P
3	M	P	A

P = Physical Education   C = Computer Lab   A = Art   L = Library/Media   D = Dance
M = Music   X = Break Aide or To Be   T = Theater   O = Other   S = Science
PS = PE Aide/Support   Determined (TBD)   S = STEAM   PA = Performing Arts   G = Guidance
A/M = Art or Music on   I/S = May be supervised   WW = Writer's   G/L = Guidance/Library   Dr = Drama
    a rotating basis   Independent Study   Workshop   on a rotating basis
WL = World Language   B = Band   Ch = Chorus

Note: If numbers permit, students in grades that have 4 sections can be assigned to three groups for the Encore/Plan period. This Encore plan time also can be used in the morning to provide extended planning time on a rotational basis. In some schools the extended planning time retains the PAM rotation with PE and Music changing groups during the block time and Art remaining in the full time block. When the PAM rotation occurs for double periods, the grade level teachers meeting for the double time do not meet during their single period for that one day, and that is when the PAM team members have their planning period for that day.

Figure 5.4 Canbee Elementary School 4 School-Day Rotations for Encore/Plan Periods Shown in Master Schedule

4 Student Groups	Day 1	Day 2	Day 3	Day 4
1	P	A	M	L
2	A	M	L	P
3	M	L	P	A
4	L	P	A	M

P = Physical Education   C = Computer Lab   A = Art   L = Library/Media   D = Dance
M = Music   X = Break Aide or To Be   T = Theater   O = Other   S = Science
PS = PE Aide/Support   Determined (TBD)   S = STEAM   PA = Performing Arts   G = Guidance
A/M = Art or Music on   I/S = May be supervised   WW = Writer's   G/L = Guidance/Library   Dr = Drama
  a rotating basis   Independent Study   Workshop   on a rotating basis
WL = World Language   B = Band   Ch = Chorus

Regardless of the number of days in the encore rotation, we emphasize a rotating school day cycle – not a Monday through Friday week-day rotation. When schools follow a rotating Monday through Friday week-day cycle, some classes receive more instructional time than other classes. Because schools have more holidays on Mondays and Fridays, students with encore classes scheduled on those days meet fewer classes of that encore subject during the school year. By following a school-day rotating cycle, assuming a 180-day school year, all students receive an equal number of classes of each encore subject.

By scheduling double ELG periods in Grades K-1, reading difficulties can be prevented, thus reducing the need for interventions in Grades 2-5. However, to maintain proficiency as students progress through school, additional small group literacy instructions during I/E and I/S periods (see Figures 5.1 and 5.5), can provide a safeguard for continued acceleration, and can serve transfer students who have not reached proficiency.

Another Sample PK–5 Master Schedule with Explanations by Grade Levels

In Figure 5.5 we show the master school schedule for Lake Elementary, a school with 412 students, 6 grade levels, three teachers at each grade level, and a TA assigned to each Kindergarten class.

Because the school is struggling to meet district and state accreditation requirements, ELGs are offered in Kindergarten and Grade 1 as well as I/E periods in Grades 2-5. Lunch, recess and encore periods are scheduled for each grade level, and extended encore periods can be scheduled during

Figure 5.5 Master Schedule for Lake Elementary School Illustrating ELGs Meeting in Reduced Groups Twice Daily

Master Schedule for Lake Elementary School Illustrating K-1 Early Literacy Groups (ELGs) Meeting in Reduced Groups Twice Daily for Three Kindergarten and Three Grade 1 Teachers, Including Completed Schedules for Grades K - 5

Kindergarten Teacher A	Homeroom Activities, Mathematics and Unit Time (50)	*ELGs (40)	Literacy (80 Minutes)		Recess/Lunch (40)	Encore/Plan (40)	Math/Science (40)	Literacy/Social Studies (80 Minutes)	Repeat ELGs (40)
Kindergarten Teacher B		Literacy (40)	ELGs (40)	Literacy (80 Minutes)	Recess/Lunch (40)	Encore/Plan (40)	Math/Science (40)	Repeat ELGs (40)	Literacy/Social Studies (80 Minutes) / Literacy (40)
Kindergarten Teacher C		Literacy (80 Minutes)	ELGs (40)	Literacy (40)	Recess/Lunch (40)	Encore/Plan (40)	Math/Science (40)	Repeat ELGs (40)	Literacy (40) / Literacy/ Ss (40)
Grade 1 Teacher A	HR	ELGs (40)	Literacy/Social Studies (80 Minutes)	Literacy (80 Minutes)	Lunch/Recess (40)	Math/Science (80 Minutes)	Repeat ELGs (40) / Repeat ELGs (40)	Repeat ELGs (40)	Literacy/ Ss (40)
Grade 1 Teacher B	HR	Literacy (80 Minutes)	ELGs (40)	Encore/Plan (40)	Lunch/Recess (40)	Math/Science (80 Minutes)	Literacy/Social Studies (80 Minutes)	Literacy/Social Studies (80 Minutes)	Repeat ELGs (40)
Grade 1 Teacher C	HR	Literacy (40)	ELGs (40)	Encore/Plan (40)	Lunch/Recess (40)	Math/Science (80 Minutes)	Repeat ELGs (40)	Literacy/Social Studies (80 Minutes)	Literacy (40)
Grade 2	HR	Literacy (80 Minutes)	Encore/Plan (40)	ELGs if needed (40)	Lunch/Recess (40)	I/E (40)	Math/Science/Social Studies (120 Minutes)		
Grade 3	HR	80 Minutes	I/S (40)	80 Minutes	Recess/Lunch (40)	80 Minutes	Encore/Plan (40)	I/E (40)	
Grade 4	HR	80 Minutes	OPEN: Could be 4th block. Could be extensive I/E for students.	80 Minutes	Lunch/Recess (40)	80 Minutes	Encore/Plan (40)		
Grade 5	HR	80 Minutes	Encore/Plan (40)	80 Minutes	Recess/Lunch (40)	Encore/Plan (40)	80 Minutes		
Encore: Music, Art, PE, Library, Computer Lab, Guidance	**Extended Plan Time	Grade 2	Grade 1	Lunch	Grade K	5	3	4	
LT-1	HR	Plan	K	K	L/P	L/P	K	K	K
LT-2	HR	1	1	Plan (1)	2	2	Lunch	1	1
I/E			5	2	2	3	3		3

*ELG = Early Literacy Group   HR = Homeroom Activities   I/E = Intervention/Enrichment Period   Sc/Ss = Science/Social Studies   LT = Literacy Team

I/S = Independent Study and additional Student Support

** = Available to provide 75-80 minutes of Extended Plan Time on a 7- or 14-school day rotation.

Note 1: Arrows (↕) indicate how groupings can occur across grade levels.

periods one and two. The school's master schedule also includes specific times for K-1 ELGs to meet.

Because LT members meet with multiple groups, they must be scheduled in the master schedule. As students experience accelerated growth, the names and numbers of ELGs change often. Those assignments are made during the extended planning periods that also are included in the master schedule. In the Lake schedule, extended planning time occurs as each grade level rotates during the first 80-minute block when the encore staff has extended time with their assigned students.

The master school schedule for Lake Elementary (Figure 5.5) was constructed for a school having 410 minutes each day and three core teachers at each grade level. Schools that do not have 410 minutes in their school day can modify Figure 5.5 by making one or more of the following changes:

- Reducing lunch time to 30 minutes and removing the recess break;
- Reducing the scheduled ELG time from 40 to 35 or even 30 minutes if all ELGs meet in the core teacher's classroom. However, if any ELGs require travel to another space for instruction, we recommend that the ELG period be no less than 35 minutes to allow for transitioning and getting students on task. If students must move to a distant space, a connected 1-hour ELG might be preferred.
- Reducing the 80-minute blocks to 75 minutes. It has been our experience that any activity of less than 25–35 minutes may not be worth the time it takes for elementary students to be re-grouped and/or relocated. If blocks are reduced, encore periods would need to be refigured.

Although we do not show transition time in our master schedule, we assume any change or regrouping of students will take a minimum of 3–4 minutes. In addition to the three core teachers assigned to each of the six grade levels, the Lake instructional staff includes the following:

- A LT leader with one TA assigned.
- Two Special Education (SPED) teachers not assigned to self-contained classrooms and an assigned TA for each.
- Two reduced-time contracted Title I reading instructors.
- Encore Team: one art, one music, and one physical education (PE) teacher.
- One media (library) teacher with an assigned TA.
- One technology teacher assigned to help students with computers not in the media center; in some schools this position might be a trained TA.
- One English Language Learner (ELL) teacher.
- One TA for each Kindergarten teacher.

Figure 5.6 Extended Planning Time Provided by Encore Team

School Day	Grade
1	K
2	1
3	2
4	3
5	4
6	5
7	Encore Team

Note: On the day teachers at a particular grade level have extended (double period) planning time, students at that grade level have extended Encore time. They do not receive the day's scheduled single-period Encore time. The Encore teachers receive the grade level single period that day for planning. For example, on Day 1 of the extended planning time, Kindergarten teachers have the extended time; on Day 2, Grade 1 teachers have the extended time.

If a reading buddy program is available for selected students, reading buddy tutors meet with their students during their students' independent reading time.

In the Lake Elementary master schedule, we have scheduled ten minutes at the beginning of the day to provide homeroom (HR) time connected to the morning's first activity, 40 minutes for lunch and recess, a 40-minute common grade level planning time when students are in encore (art, music and PE) classes, plus an additional 80-minute block of common grade level extended planning time that can be scheduled on a 6-, 7-, 12-, or 14-day rotating basis in the morning which we explain in Figure 5.6.

A School Day in Grades K–2

Providing sufficient instructional time is critical to accelerated early literacy instruction. Kindergarten and Grade 1 teachers at Lake Elementary have over 200 minutes scheduled daily for literacy instruction. Within these 200 minutes, K-1 teachers receive 60 minutes of support from LT members, which provides needed staff for ELGs to meet throughout the school year.

Because Kindergarten teachers typically prefer extended time with their whole group at the beginning of the school day, we have collapsed Kindergarten homeroom time into a 50-minute period. We suggest using this time for morning homeroom activities and for some math instruction.

During a split ELG block, one Title I teacher and one specially trained reading TA join the Kindergarten teacher and TA to provide morning and afternoon ELGs, typically in the teacher's classroom. With four LT members, four ELGs can be staffed. If space permits and if travel time and distance are not too great, one or two of the groups could leave the classroom for this particularly reduced 30-, 40-minute period of instruction. During the course of the school day, the LT staff of one Title I teacher and one TA serve all three Kindergarten teachers to staff morning and afternoon ELGs.

We recommend that instructors rotate among the ELGs throughout the year. By rotating, the instructors can specialize in selected areas of reading, thereby, becoming more competent and confident in their instruction. Students benefit from this enhanced instructor competency.

Following Kindergarten Teacher A's ELG period, Kindergarten Teacher A and her TA regroup the students for their 80-minute literacy block. Following the extended literacy block, all three Kindergarten teachers' students transition to recess and lunch. Hopefully, this is a duty-free time for the three teachers. Once Teacher A's students complete recess (about 10-15 minutes), they go to lunch. Following recess and lunch, Teacher A's, B's and C's students have an Encore period shown as Figure 5.3.

The Encore period is scheduled on a 3-day rotation, with one group of Kindergarteners going to PE, another group to art, and still another group to music. All groups follow a 3-day rotating school day cycle – not a week-day rotation – throughout the school year. As addressed previously, when schools follow a week-day rotating cycle, students receive an unequal number of instructional meetings, because schools have more holidays on Mondays and Fridays. By following our plan, detailed in Chapters 2 and 3, Canady and Rettig (2008), if the school has a 180-day school year, all students receive 60 days of music, 60 days of art and 60 days of PE. By scheduling the encore/planning time adjacent to the Kindergarten lunch/recess period, if Kindergarten teachers have a working lunch, then they could be given an 80-minute lunch/planning time at least once a week, or even daily. The same plan also is available for Grade 1 teachers except their encore/plan time precedes lunch/recess.

Following encore time, Kindergarten Teacher A is scheduled for a continuation of math and science instruction from the first morning period. As the school year progresses, Teacher A extends this afternoon 40-minute period into the following 80-minute literacy/social studies block. Teacher A ends the day with repeat ELG groups.

The Figure 5.5 schedule for Kindergarten Teachers B and C is very similar to Kindergarten Teacher A's schedule except their ELGs meet at different times; this spacing of ELGs is necessary so the Kindergarten Literacy Team (LT-1) can serve all three Kindergarten teachers and the multiple ELGs needed at the Kindergarten level. Using the same staffing for all ELGs at a particular grade level makes it easier for the LT leader to address responsibilities as described in Chapter 2.

Kindergarten Teachers B and C follow the same schedule as Teacher A during the first 50 minutes of the school day. They also have the same recess/lunch, encore/plan, and math/science periods. During several periods of the day, at least two of the Kindergarten teachers share the same literacy instructional time periods, which can be useful as students become more diverse in their instructional needs. As the year progresses, teachers may need to create some cross-room and cross-grade-level groupings for teaching specialties such as writing, fluency and/or comprehension strategies.

The schedule for Grade 1 teachers shown in Figure 5.5 is similar in that all three Grade 1 teachers share the same homeroom, encore/plan, lunch/recess and math/science periods of time. The reduced ELGs are served by each classroom core teacher, one of the special education teachers who has a primary teaching background, the SPED's assigned TA, and the remaining Title I teacher. Because in this school Grade 1 teachers do not have TAs, three support persons are assigned to work with each of the three Grade 1 teachers during their ELGs that meet in the morning and repeated in the afternoon.

A schedule for Grade 1, Teacher B, shown in Figure 5.5 is as follows: After 10 minutes of homeroom activities, Teacher B provides core instruction for students in an 80-minute literacy block. Appropriate activities for this block could be for students to engage in morning meetings, Read Alouds focused on comprehension and vocabulary with follow-up comprehension and vocabulary activities, a writing demonstration and/or independent reading and literacy stations for selected students.

Following Teacher B's morning literacy block, the LT staff assigned to Grade 1 ELGs joins Teacher B to instruct the four ELGs. The LT leader has previously worked with Teacher B during extended planning time to assign support staff to these ELGs. Students can be re-grouped for another 7- to 14-day cycle of instruction. Instructors rotate among the groups as deemed appropriate by Teacher B and the LT leader.

Following instruction of ELG groups in Grade 1, Teacher B's students go to their encore classes which follow the same type of 3 school-day rotations shown for Kindergarten students in Figure 5.3, except Grade 1 students attend encore classes at a different time period. While Grade 1 students are attending their encore classes, the three Grade 1 teachers have a common planning period. The support staff members for the ELGs also are available to meet with Grade 1 core teachers for planning instruction for ELG groups.

It also is important for the LT leader to be available to meet with teachers at each grade level to assist with ELG lesson planning. Because Grade 1 encore classes are scheduled before lunch/recess, Grade 1 teachers can have a daily 80-minute working lunch and planning period as described for the Kindergarten teaching staff. Following Encore time, Teacher B's students go to lunch, followed with 10-15 minutes of physical activity. By combining recess and lunch, instructional time is not infringed upon by having teachers enter and exit lunchrooms three-five minutes apart.

Following lunch/recess, all Grade 1 students are scheduled for 80 minutes of mathematics and science. As the school year progresses, some cross-classroom and cross-grade level groupings could occur. During this time, additional staff, such as the technology teacher and the computer assistant, are available to assist Grade 1 teachers in reducing instructional groups for math and science as illustrated in Chapter 7. In some schools, the major science concepts taught at Grade 1 can be integrated with the literacy instructional program; if so, the major portion of this 75- to 80-minute time period would be devoted to numeracy instruction. After the math/science block, all Grade 1 teachers are involved in a 120-minute (40 x 3) block of literacy-social studies instruction, including the second daily meeting of ELGs. Grade 1 Teachers A and C and their students follow the same schedule as Teacher B except their ELGs meet at different times. As explained earlier, such scheduling is necessary if all Grade 1 teachers share the same instructional support staff.

Grade 2 teachers and students have a similar schedule to Kindergarten and Grade 1, except only one ELG and one I/E period are scheduled for Grade 2. The assumption is that by Grade 2 fewer students need foundational reading skills.

Remember we recommend that the LT leader and his/her TA be assigned to work with the Grade 2 ELGs, assuming these are the students needing the most intensive literacy interventions to become proficient readers by the end of Grade 3. The Grade 2 schedule also has a 120-minute block of time for mathematics, science, and social studies. We suggest that teachers spend at least 60 minutes of this block with mathematics and alternate science and social studies units instead of splitting the block and trying to teach both science and social studies on the same day. Often science and mathematics can be integrated. High quality instruction in mathematics, science and social studies often involves projects and "hands on" activities; therefore, the longer blocks of time shown in Figures 5.1 and 5.5 for Grade 2 students should be helpful.

A School Day in Grades 3–5

Grade 3 students, as illustrated in Figure 5.5, following their homeroom time, have 80 minutes of core instruction, then 40 minutes for additional independent work or support time (I/S) for selected students who have been assessment-based grouped across Grade 3 classrooms for individual needs primarily in the areas of math and literacy. These groupings are very personalized. After the I/S period, Grade 3 students have another 80-minute block of time before going to recess/lunch. Following recess/lunch, Grade 3 students have another 80 minutes of core time, followed by a 40-minute encore/teacher planning period, with students following the 3 school-day rotation shown as Figure 5.3, and the day ends for Grade 3 students with a 40-minute I/E period.

The proposed Grade 3 schedule has several positives that should be noted. First, Grade 3 core time is not "choppy." By having three 80-minute blocks of time, teachers could departmentalize; however, departmentalization is unusual at Grade 3. By scheduling the blocks the same for each home-room teacher, regroupings across classrooms are possible. We also like the idea that there is a core time, then I/S, another core block, then recess/lunch, then core time, then an encore period, and then closing the day with an I/E period that could include homeroom activities, such as supervised home-work and projects, independent reading, re-taking assessments, additional intervention or enrichment activities shared across Grade 3 classrooms and/or a combination of these activities. Note that all three sections of Grade 3 share the same time periods and blocks of time, which makes cross class-room groupings possible.

Students and teachers in Grades 4 and 5 have a schedule similar to Grade 3. Following a 10-minute homeroom period, the schedule for both Grades 4 and 5 has three 80-minute blocks of time before their lunch/recess period is scheduled.

Grade 5 students have their 3 school-day rotations following their recess/lunch period which means those teachers also could have a com-bined common lunch/planning period of 80 minutes. The fourth 80-minute block of time for Grade 5 students comes at the end of the day. By having the four evenly distributed 80-minute time blocks, it would be easy to implement several forms of departmentalization often observed in these particular grade levels. For example, one block could be for Reading/Language Arts, one for mathematics, one for science and one for social studies. Because three of the 80-minute blocks are the same for both grades, teaching staff could become specialized; for example, the best teacher in science might teach science for both grades, and another teacher might teach social studies for both grades. This staffing arrangement could have special appeal for schools with only one or two core teachers at each grade level and in school districts that have accountability testing in science and social studies at both grade levels. (For details of additional models of departmentalization in elementary schools, see Chapter 5, Canady and Rettig (2008), pp. 127–142.

We have described how the proposed schedule could be implemented in most elementary schools; however, if there remains a significant number of students in Grades 4 and 5 not reading and writing at grade level and not demonstrating proficiency in literacy and math competencies compa-rable to those described in the common state standards and the common assessments designed to measure them, we recommend that one of the 80-minute blocks of time be utilized as described in the second block shown in Figure 5.5 schedule.

In some school schedules, we leave this block OPEN. By labeling it OPEN, we are suggesting it could be the fourth block in the schedule as described previously. It also could be an extensive I/E period for students needing interventions in reading, writing and mathematics. This intervention block of time could be critical for students before they enter Grade 6 with all the potential liabilities identified with the middle school years. This block can be very effective if students are engaged in personalized learning throughout the school year. During this block students performing at or above grade level in language arts and math would engage in both horizontal and vertical enrichment activities. Typically enrichment units primarily include content in science, social studies, research and writing; however, if encore personnel are available, additional units of art, music and PE could be included.

If it is decided that in Grades 4 and 5, 80 minutes will be given to I/E, it may be best to schedule Grades 4 and 5 for I/E during their last block of time in the afternoon. Although one period overlaps in that block, it would allow more support staff in the building to assist with the Grade 4 and 5 I/E activities. Also, it may be important to keep the three earlier scheduled 80-minute blocks parallel so staff members can cross grades if subject specialization is needed.

If one of the blocks is designated for I/E time, typically students would receive one daily block for language arts, one for mathematics, and one for science and social studies. The science and social studies block could be two single periods each day, but we do not recommend that plan because it creates an unbalanced workload for both students and teachers with no academic gains that we can document. The classes could meet for the entire 80 minutes on a Day 1, Day 2 (alternate day) basis, but, again, the workload remains a problem for both teachers and students.

We recommend that the school do 4.5 weeks of science and then 4.5 weeks of social studies for the full block throughout the year. Even better would be for teachers to plan eight to ten science units and an equal number of social studies units, based on common state standards on which students will be tested in their particular state or school district, and then teach a science unit and then a social studies unit. Possibly, two weeks before state or district testing, these classes could meet on an alternate day basis to review major concepts known to be emphasized on the approaching tests.

Scheduling Extended Planning Blocks

In Figures 5.1 and 5.5, we show elementary master schedules where the encore staff are free for double plan periods, which may be in the morning or at the close of the day (Canady & Rettig, 2008, pp.83–86). When such staffing and scheduling are possible, one group (usually a grade level or PLC group, such as grade level LTs) has extended time on a rotating basis as shown in Figure 5.6. The day the group gets the extended plan time, they do not get the single period of planning time. The encore team has their plan time during that single period.

This 7-day cycle is repeated throughout the school year. If Encore teachers do not want to be included in the extended planning cycle, then the school follows a 6-school-day cycle.

In the Figure 5.5 master schedule, the encore instructors have the first 80 minutes open for planning, but that time could become extended planning time for teachers and their supporting staff at each grade level. If the early literacy and I/E groupings are to be successful in accelerating student reading, writing and numeracy competencies, it is critical that adequate planning time be provided for the core teachers and their supporting team members. By assigning the encore staff planning time during the morning block, a 6-, 7-, 12- or 14-school-day rotation can be established. For example, on school Day 1, following homeroom time, all Kindergarten students would attend one of the three encore classes available to them. Because of their age, two of the encore teachers may want to provide two different activities during the 80 minutes, but the art teacher might welcome the full 80 minutes. If so, then the music and PE teachers would exchange students during the extended time. Encore teachers tend to prefer keeping older students for the full 75-80 minutes; for example, the PE teacher then would have time for students to engage in activities such as a volleyball game which may not occur during 40-minute classes.

While Kindergarten students are in encore activities for 75–80 minutes on Day 1 of the morning planning rotation, all Kindergarten teachers and their support staff for the ELGs meet with a focus on planning for the ELGs meeting for the following 12–14 school days. On the day of extended planning time, the teachers do not get their regularly scheduled encore time shown in the master schedule. The encore teachers then get that period for planning. On school Day 2, Grade 1 teachers have the morning extended planning time in exchange for their regular 40-minute period shown in the master schedule. On school Day 3, Grade 2 teachers exchange their regular planning period for extended time in the morning. The same occurs for Grade 3 teachers on school Day 4. On school Day 5, Grade 4 teachers have the extended time, and on school day six, Grade 5 teachers have extended planning time. On school Day 7, the encore team may have the extended time or the rotation cycle starts over with Kindergarten teachers having the longer time.

If the extended time is scheduled only for K-5 teachers and only school days are scheduled in the rotating cycle – not weekdays – and the school has a 180-day school year, teachers and support staff have the extended planning block for a total of 30 days. The extended rotation can be on a 6-, 7-, 12-, 14-day cycle, and it can occur in the morning or in the afternoon. For additional details and other variations of scheduling models designed to provide extended planning time, see Canady and Rettig (2008), pp. 54–57 and 83–88.

Scheduling Intervention/Enrichment Periods

Once a school's ELG sessions are scheduled for Grades PK–1, I/E periods can be scheduled for the remaining grades. There are multiple ways of scheduling I/E periods in the master schedule. In Chapter 6, we give four examples of scheduling I/E periods and offer pros and cons for each.

During the I/E periods, less proficient readers and mathematicians continue to receive reading and math interventions, while students who are proficient in those subjects receive enrichment. In the case where some students require intervention for one subject and enrichment for another, intervention takes precedence. If a large number of students qualify for both interventions and enrichment, an I/E period can be added for a particular grade level or an intervention can be scheduled for the first nine weeks and then an enrichment can be scheduled for the second nine weeks.

Duke and Varlas (2019) point out that, especially in high-poverty settings, science and social studies content is lacking in K-3. Then, when students progress to upper elementary and beyond, authors and texts assume students already know foundational academic concepts and vocabulary. Through enrichment, we strive to ensure that students learn needed social studies and science concepts and vocabulary.

Enrichment staff members must be strong in science and social studies curriculum. If core teachers are not available to teach enrichment units, school personnel should seek others, such as gifted and talented (TAG) teachers. In addition to using individual school staff, some schools include trained community members or trained and supervised college students.

Certain basic skills are needed for progressing through an enrichment unit. As an example, if using technology is required to complete the unit, it is assumed that students would have basic keyboarding skills, knowledge of how to use a computer, and how to navigate a website within the parameters set by the school system. Competencies with basic note-taking strategies, such as power thinking, concept mapping, or using column notes, would be helpful for students to master before being placed in enrichment units.

Summary

Historically, elementary schools have been organized and scheduled based on the long-held assumption that instructional quality is equal across all classrooms; but we know that assumption is false. There are alternatives that can help ameliorate staff differences. Those we recommend are the following: create LTs and provide extended planning time to allow for embedded staff development based on the PLC collective capacity and collective efficacy research; use data to build the master schedule based on student needs; provide multiple ways of obtaining assessment-based skill groups; and maximize the use of time, personnel, and other resources so the school day is not fragmented. When schools consider these options as they design their master schedule, a school's values are reflected, personnel conflicts are minimized, and instructional priorities are established.

Reflection

Reflect on the content from this chapter as you consider how you will implement literacy instruction with a goal of accelerated literacy learning.

1. Do the school administrators believe the research on the merits of building instructional capacity as contrasted with individual teachers working alone? Does the school's master schedule illustrate those beliefs? For example, does your master schedule include extended planning time for LTs on a rotational basis?

2. Does your school's master schedule reflect that the school values accelerated literacy instruction? How are staff utilized? Is time valued and protected? Materials?

3. What is meant by the term "teacher efficacy"? Why is it important? How do we know it is accepted and practiced in a school? What evidence exists that it is present at your school?

4. Does the school have quality and reliable assessments available for teachers? Is progressive monitoring in place? Are daily literacy lessons being framed based on data?

5. Do teachers have access to a wide variety of reading materials for learning to read (i.e., predictable books, decodable books, controlled vocabulary books) as well as higher-level authentic reading materials? Do students have access to books they can read? Are books and corresponding materials categorized and easily obtained?

6. Are TAs trained to teach specific skills that students will need to master? Are the TAs rotated to strategically teach these skills to various groups throughout the school year?

Chapter 6

Collecting Data and Designing a Master Schedule to Prioritize Literacy Acceleration

Designing a well-crafted master schedule is a critical administrative function. A school's schedule reflects instructional priorities by illustrating how time and multiple resources are used every school day and by clarifying roles and scheduling support staff; it also can reduce potential conflicts among staff. We start with guiding principles for developing a comprehensive master schedule. We then illustrate how to use key data to develop a data-driven master school schedule with literacy acceleration as priority.

Developing a Data-Driven Master Schedule Draft

Data collection is the first step of the administrative team in preparing a master schedule that provides blocks of time for ELGs, encore, and at least one Intervention/Enrichment (I/E) period. To begin, complete the tasks listed on the Master Schedule Planning Worksheet shown in Form 6.1.

> Encore in some schools is called Specials and Related Arts in other schools. These classes often include: art, music, PE, theater, guidance, Science Technology Engineering Math (STEM), dance, media.

The form is a planning worksheet to collect and organize data for building the master schedule. Form 6.1 also is available on this book's website and can be downloaded and printed.

Calculating Total Minutes in the School Day

When calculating total minutes in the school day, total minutes represent the contracted minutes available for planned instruction and all activities, including time for homeroom, recess, and lunch.

Based on our consulting experiences, we have found that most elementary schools have 390 – 420+ minutes in the school day. To achieve literacy acceleration in the primary grades, at least 180 minutes of daily literacy instruction must be included in the master schedule. Teachers must meet

Form 6.1 Master Schedule Planning Worksheet

Form 6.1

Elementary/Middle School Schedule Planning Worksheet

Name of School: _____

Principal: _____

Phone Numbers: _____

Email: _____

	Total # of base Teachers by grade level	Total # of Teacher Aides by grade level	Total # of Students by grade level	Total # of Title I Teachers assigned to school	Total # of Special Ed Teachers	Total # of Special Ed Aides	Total # of Music Teachers	Total # of Art Teachers	Total # of PE Teachers	Total # of Media Personnel	Total # of Technology Teachers or Aides	Total # of other Encore Teachers
Pre-K												
K												
1												
2												
3												
4												
5												
6												
7												
8												
Totals												

4th GRADE: Give details about any departmentalization that takes place in 4th grade. List subjects taught by each teacher and any other important details.

5th GRADE: Give details about any departmentalization that takes place in 5th grade. List subjects taught by each teacher and any other important details.

If a middle school, is Grade 6 organized differently from Grades 7-8? _____ If so, explain: _____

Does your Media Specialist serve specific classes based on need?

Total population K-5? _____ 6-8 _____ other _____

Is the school Title 1? _____   Are any of your staff members part time? If so, describe below.

Do Pre-K students go to art, music, or PE? _____

Do Students have a required number of minutes of PE instruction per day, week, or year? _____

If so, explain: _____

(Continued)

Form 6.1 Master Schedule Planning Worksheet (Continued)

Are you concerned about both reading and math achievement in the school? If so, explain:

Except for secretarial, custodial, and maintenance staff, provide a list and description of any staff members in your school not listed previously.

Describe below the exact time students are ready to begin instruction and the exact time instruction must end, such as instruction begins after breakfast, after the morning announcements, homeroom, pledge and moment of silence. Instruction ends at the end of the day when students must prepare to load buses.

Describe below how many groups will be scheduled for lunch by grade level. Describe how lunch groups are currently supervised so that teachers get the mandatory Duty Free lunch. How long do you allow for each class or group to complete lunch? How many students can be seated in the lunchroom at any given time? Do you have single serving lines or multiple serving lines?

How many computer labs are in the school? Please list how many working computers are in each lab. Explain how computer labs are managed. Technology Teachers _____, Technology Aides _____, Classroom Teachers _____

Describe below any unusual circumstances related to scheduling that may apply to your school that have not been mentioned above.

Describe the current schedule at this school. Are there any major issues with scheduling in the school that you would like to be addressed, such as common planning time or structured intervention time? If so, describe:

daily with Tier 1 groups for a minimum of 90 minutes of core time. Furthermore, the master schedule must include 60-90 minutes per day for assessment-based ELGs (totaling 300 minutes weekly, minus transition time). It is preferable that ELGs meet twice a day, morning and afternoon, for at least 30 minutes each period.

Some students will require even more time devoted to building word knowledge and fluency (Hayes & Flanigan, 2014; Mesmer, Mesmer, & Jones, 2014). That additional time can occur during an I/E period included in the master schedule, and for some, additional time may be needed during the summer months (Chapter 8 of this text; Canady, Canady, & Meek, 2017). Most I/E periods consist of 30–45 minutes per day, providing an additional 150–225 minutes weekly of instructional interventions and support. The goal is to sustain concentrated instructional time and attention long enough for acceleration to occur, which typically is at least three years. Transfer students often also need this time until "catch up" can occur. If students are labeled as failing before acceleration can be accomplished, they often are placed in intervention programs with less than promising results, as discussed in other sections of this document.

Ascertaining Minimum Minutes for all Subjects and Programs

The minimum required minutes for all subjects should be calculated. These minutes can be flexibly scheduled with a variety of combinations over the course of a day, week, semester, or school year. For example, a science unit could be taught during the first quarter and then a social studies unit could be taught second quarter. This scenario reduces fragmentation of the school day and reduces the number of teacher preparations. With fewer preparations, the likelihood of high quality lesson plans is increased. Some key state and local considerations are as follows: Has the state or district mandated any minimum required minutes for certain subjects? If so, how much flexibility does each school have in meeting those requirements? Be certain that the calculation meets or exceeds minimum requirements.

Other key considerations include: Is the school required to offer 40 minutes of daily RTI time on a schoolwide basis? Can this requirement be met as a weekly average? Is 30 minutes of daily physical activity required? If so, must this activity be instructed by a certified physical education teacher? Can recess minutes count? Can the requirement be met as a weekly average of 150 minutes?

Such absolutes, when *not* expressed as averages, can reduce scheduling flexibility, making it difficult to develop a master schedule that reflects priorities. Such absolutes also force the master schedule to be very fragmented, often with pockets of potentially wasted time periods. Rather, school and district administrators must review school, district, local, and state policies and strive to develop a master schedule based on averages in a school-day cycle.

Developing and Ranking Priorities

The master schedule is optimal only when it is used as a tool for accomplishing priorities. The purpose of this book is to promote literacy as the top priority in the elementary school master schedule. That would mean, for example, the following priorities in order:

1. Provide extended literacy time with ELGs scheduled in the master schedule.
2. Include extended common planning time for Literacy Teams (LTs) on a rotational basis.
3. Implement a progress monitoring system that can frame instruction on a continuous basis.
4. Provide time for relevant, quality Professional Development (PD) primarily at the school and classroom levels.
5. Schedule I/E periods by individual grade levels.

When determining priorities, it is important to remember that the top schools in the world place a priority on data-driven planning time (Sahlberg, 2011; Tucker, 2019).

First, we suggest that the master schedule design team review the scheduling priorities we have listed and add any that might be unique to their particular school; then the scheduling team should ask all staff members to rank order the priorities and ultimately the top three or four priorities should emerge. Some typical scheduling priorities are listed below:

1. Extended Literacy time (determine the total number of daily and weekly minutes desired).
2. Extended mathematics time (determine the total number of daily and weekly minutes desired).
3. Grade level planning time or team planning time if working in Professional Learning Communities (PLCs). Cross-grade planning time by subject (possibly only cross-grade literacy planning time).
4. Encore daily rotations; use school-day rotations vs. week-day rotations as described in Canady and Rettig (2008), Chapter 3.
5. Extended planning periods on selected rotations, illustrated in Figures 5.1 and 5.5 of this text.
6. Lunch periods (contract minutes required and when lunch minutes must occur if there are forced limitations because multiple schools are sharing the same building or lunch facility).
7. Departmentalization (determine grades and staffing).
8. Bus schedules related to early or late arrivals and dismissals. Can any changes be made?

When experiencing difficulty including all desired priorities in the master schedule, administrators must consider a fundamental principle of scheduling: *it is difficult, if not impossible, to add something to a master schedule without removing something*; therefore, establishing priorities early in the scheduling process is critical. There are limitations as to what a master schedule can include in one particular time period or year, and priorities can vary from year to year. It is important to establish and rank schoolwide priorities before building the master schedule. We typically can build a master schedule with extended literacy time by eliminating what we refer to in our consulting work as "piddle time," or small time increments that tend to be used unproductively. For example, if a student has an encore class for 45 minutes and then returns to the classroom for only 15 minutes before exiting for lunch, the 15 minutes represent time that can be used more productively when combined with other small time increments.

"Givens" are minutes in the school day over which school administrators have limited or no control, and typically are determined by rank ordering priorities. Examples are scheduling blocks of time to accommodate departmentalization, scheduling I/E periods for single or multiple grade levels, and scheduling extended teacher planning time on a rotating basis. If multiple "desired givens" are wanted in the master schedule, such information needs to be known early in the master schedule building process, and priorities need to be determined. For example: Is daily common planning time for core teachers at each grade level the first priority? Are certain support teachers needed to meet with them? Is having ELGs meeting morning and afternoon daily the first priority? Does the school have sufficiently trained staff to offer two daily ELG meetings? Is the second priority providing all LTs and related core teachers extended planning time on a rotational basis?

Building Rotations Needed for Encore Teachers

Build encore rotations around school days, not week days. Typically, encore/plan schedules are built on calendar-week-day-rotations, but such scheduling has inherent problems because in most school calendars, more holidays occur on Mondays and Fridays than on other days. When Encore classes are built around calendar week days, classes meet an uneven number of days in a school year; for example, if schools have more holidays on Mondays and Fridays than other week days and a music class meets on either a Monday or Friday, those students receive fewer minutes of music instruction during a school year than if that class met on a Tuesday, Wednesday, or Thursday. If encore classes are scheduled on a school-day rotation, such as Day 1, 2, or 3, as shown in Figures 5.2, 5.3, and 5.4, classes meet an equal number of days during the school year. (For additional information on building encore schedules, see Canady and Rettig (2008), Chapter 3.)

Determining Placement of ELG and I/E Periods in Master Schedule

The I/E period is a time designed to provide (1) intervention services for students with Individualized Education Plans (IEPs) and/or students who are not meeting proficiency goals in reading or mathematics and (2) enrichment services for students who do not have an IEP and have met proficiency goals in reading and mathematics. Interventions are data driven, based on individual, assessment-based needs. The I/E period(s) also can provide extended time to provide student support in completing homework assignments, retaking assessments, and completing assignments as a result of absences. In some schools, two or more I/E periods may be needed to accommodate the multiple needs of students.

We now illustrate four master school schedules with I/E periods placed at each grade level and at multi-grade levels. Arguments can be made for all of these combinations. In large schools, it probably is best to schedule I/E periods by individual grades to give all support personnel in the building, such as special education, talented and gifted (TAG), ELL and enrichment teachers opportunities to address student needs throughout the school day. In smaller schools, scheduling the I/E period to serve two or more grade levels may be needed to have sufficient staff to provide the intervention and enrichment services needed. In the following schedule, shown as Figure 6.1, we illustrate a master schedule with the I/E period placed separately for each grade level. Note that in the Carlyn schedule shown as Figure 6.1, the I/E periods for Grades 4 and 5 have been placed in the master schedule to protect three blocks of time, which can be very helpful if the teachers in those grades wish to departmentalize as illustrated in Chapter 5 of Canady and Rettig (2008).

In Figure 6.2 we illustrate a master elementary school schedule with the I/E period scheduled with two-grade combinations, consisting of K-1, 2-3 and 4-5 Grades. Some small schools may prefer or need this combination. By placing the grades together, as shown, we have increased the chances that students can be grouped across these two particular grades in providing intervention and enrichment services. Also, note the three blocks of time have been protected in Grade 5, the grade most likely to departmentalize.

In Figure 6.3 shown below, we illustrate three-grade combinations, a plan most likely to be preferred in small schools. In Figure 6.3 the three grades placed together represent what schools typically think of as primary and upper elementary. Again note that Grades 4 and 5 have shared blocks of time.

In Figure 6.4, we show a master schedule designed with one schoolwide I/E period. One schoolwide I/E period is easy to schedule and to manage; however, having just one I/E period in the master schedule makes it difficult for support personnel to provide services to all students. In some schools, however, it may be necessary because of limited staffing.

In Figure 6.4, we have scheduled the schoolwide I/E period before lunch periods begin; however, we have worked with schools who prefer having the common I/E period at the end of the day. The argument given for the last period of the day is that parents often remove students early for various appointments such as dentists, music and dance lessons, and early holiday trips. The preference is for students to miss I/E time rather than core time; however, we have been told that both students and staff are too tired to have the I/E period at the end of the day. When there is dissension over the placement of I/E periods, perhaps the period should be rotated each quarter, such as the first period of the day, then before and after lunch periods, and also at the end of the day!

Figure 6.1 Carlyn Elementary School Schedule with I/E Periods Scheduled by Individual Grades

Carlyn Elementary School Schedule with I/E Periods Scheduled by Individual Grades

Periods →	I	II	III	IV	V	VI	VII	VIII	IX
Kindergarten	HR	Reading/Language Arts/Social Studies *ELGs		←→	Recess/Lunch	Math/Science ←→	Encore/Plan	I/E	Math/Science
Grade 1	HR	Reading/Language Arts/Social Studies ELGs		←→	Recess/Lunch	Math/Science	I/E	Encore/Plan	Math/Science
Grade 2	HR	Reading/Language Arts/Social Studies ELGs		←→	I/E	Recess/Lunch	Math/Science ←→	Math/Science	Encore/Plan
Grade 3	HR	Reading/Language Arts/Social Studies ELGs		←→	Encore/Plan	Lunch/Recess	Math/Science	Math/Science	I/E
Grade 4	HR	←→	I/E	Encore/Plan	←→	Lunch/Recess		←→	
Grade 5	HR	←→	Encore/Plan	I/E			Recess/Lunch		
Encore/Plan	HR	**Extended Plan Time	Grade 5	Grade 4	Grade 3	Lunch	Grade K	Grade 1	Grade 2
LT-1	HR	Grade 1		Grade K			Grade 1		Grade K
LT-2	HR	Grades 2 and 3	I/E 4	I/E 5	I/E 2	Lunch	IE 1	IE K	I/E 3
I/E	HR		Grade 4	Grade 5	Grade 2	Lunch	Grade 1	Grade K	Grade 3
Lunch/Recess					K-1	2-3	4-5		

*ELG = Early Literacy Group   HR = Homeroom Activities   I/E = Intervention/Enrichment Period   Sc/Ss = Science/Social Studies   LT = Literacy Team   I/S = Independent Study and additional Student Support

** Available to provide 75-90 minutes of Extended Planning Time on a 6- 12-school-day rotation.

Note 1: For additional information on implementing an Intervention/Enrichment (I/E) period in an elementary school, see Canady, R. L. & Rettig, M. D. (2008), Chapter 4, *Elementary school scheduling: Enhancing Instruction for student achievement*, (pp. 93-125), Taylor and Francis, Inc.

Note 2: Lunch periods may need to be adjusted depending on when the school day begins.

Figure 6.2 Carlyn Elementary School Schedule with I/E Periods Scheduled by Grades K-1, 2-3, and 4-5

Carlyn Elementary School Schedule with I/E Periods Scheduled by Grades K-1, 2-3, and 4-5

Periods →	HR	I	II	III	IV	V	VI	VII	VIII	IX
Kindergarten	HR	Reading/Language Arts/Social Studies *ELGs	←→			Recess/Lunch	Sc/SS	Encore/Plan	I/E	I/S
Grade 1	HR	Reading/Language Arts/Social Studies ELGs			←→	Lunch/Recess	Math/Science	Math/Science	I/E	Encore/Plan
Grade 2	HR	Reading/Language Arts/Social Studies				Encore/Plan	Recess/Lunch	Math/Science	Math/Science	I/E
Grade 3	HR	Reading/Language Arts/Social Studies			Encore/Plan		Lunch/Recess	Math/Science	Math/Science	I/E
Grade 4	HR	←→			I/E			Recess/Lunch	Encore/Plan	←→
Grade 5	HR			Encore/Plan	I/E			Lunch/Recess		←→
Encore/Plan	HR	**Extended Plan Time		Grade 5	Grade 3	Grade 2		Grade K	Grade 4	Grade 1
LT-1	HR	Grade 1			Grade K			Grade 1	Grade K	
LT-2	HR	Grades 2 and 3			I/E 4 and 5		Lunch		I/E K, 1	I/E 2, 3
**I/E	HR				Grades 4, 5		Lunch		Grades K, 1	Grades 2, 3
Lunch/Recess						K-1	2-3	4-5		

*ELG = Early Literacy Group   HR = Homeroom Activities   I/E = Intervention/Enrichment Studies   Sc/Ss = Science/Social Studies   LT = Literacy Team   I/S = Independent Study and additional Support

** Available to provide 75-90 minutes of Extended Planning Time on a 6- or 12-school day rotation.

Note 1: For additional information on implementing an Intervention/Enrichment (I/E) period in an elementary school, see Canady, R. L. & Rettig, M. D. (2008), Chapter 4, Elementary school scheduling: Enhancing Instruction for student achievement, (pp. 93-125), Taylor and Francis, Inc.

Note 2: Lunch periods may need to be adjusted depending on when the school day begins.

Figure 6.3 Carlyn Elementary School Schedule with I/E Periods Scheduled by Grades K-2, 3-5

Carlyn Elementary School Schedule with I/E Periods Scheduled by Grades K-2, 3-5

Periods →	I	II	III	IV	V	VI	VII	VIII	IX
Kindergarten	HR	Reading/Language Arts/Math *ELGs			Lunch/Recess	Sc/SS	I/E	Encore/Plan	Sc/SS
Grade 1	HR	Reading/Language Arts/Social Studies ELGs		Encore/Plan	Recess/Lunch	Literacy	I/E	Math/Science	←
Grade 2	HR	Reading/Language Arts/Social Studies			Encore/Plan	Lunch/Recess	I/E	Math/Science	←
Grade 3	HR	Reading/Language Arts/Social Studies		I/E	Literacy	Recess/Lunch	Encore/Plan	Math/Science	
Grade 4	HR	←		I/E		←	Lunch/Recess	Encore/Plan	←
Grade 5	HR		Encore/Plan	I/E			Recess/Lunch		
Encore/Plan	HR	** Extended Plan Time	Grade 5	Grade 1	Grade 2	Lunch	Grade 3	Grade K	Grade 4
LT-1	HR			Grade K	Lunch	Grade 1		Grade K	
LT-2	HR	Grades 2 and 3		I/E 3, 4, 5		Lunch	OPEN	OPEN	I/E 3
** I/E				Grades 3, 4, 5		Lunch	Grades K, 1, 2		
Lunch/Recess					K-1	2-3	4-5		

*ELG = Early Literacy Group   HR = Homeroom Activites   I/E = Intervention/Enrichment Period   Sc/Ss = Science/Social Studies   LT = Literacy Team   I/S = Independent Study and additional Student Support

** Available to provide 75-90 minutes of Extended Planning Time on a 6- or 12-school day rotation.

Note 1: For additional information on implementing an Intervention/Enrichment (I/E) period in an elementary school, see Canady, R. L. & Rettig, M. D. (2008). Chapter 4, Elementary school scheduling: Enhancing Instruction for student achievement, (pp. 93-125), Taylor and Francis, Inc.

Note 2: Lunch periods may need to be adjusted depending on when the school day begins.

Figure 6.4 Carlyn Elementary School Schedule with One I/E Period Scheduled for Entire School

Carlyn Elementary School Schedule with One I/E Period Scheduled for Entire School

Periods →	I	II	III	IV	V	VI	VII	VIII	IX
Kindergarten	HR *ELGs ↔	Reading/Language Arts/Social Studies	↔	I/E	Lunch/Recess	Math/Science		Encore/Plan	I/S ELGs
Grade 1	HR ↔	Reading/Language Arts/Social Studies ELGs	↔	I/E	Recess/Lunch	Literacy ELGs	Encore/Plan	Math/Science	Math/Science
Grade 2	HR ↔	Reading/Language Arts/Social Studies	↔	I/E	Encore/Plan	Lunch/Recess	ELGs if needed	Math/Science ↔	Math/Science
Grade 3	HR ↔	Reading/Language Arts/Social Studies	↔	I/E	Literacy	Recess/Lunch	Math/Science		Encore/Plan
Grade 4	HR ↔		Encore/Plan	I/E	↔			↔	
Grade 5	HR	Encore/Plan		I/E		↔			
Encore/Plan	**Extended Plan Time	Grade 5	Grade 4	**	Grade 2	Lunch	Grade 1	Grade K	Grade 3
LT-1	HR	Grade 1		Grade K	Lunch	Grade 1	Grade 1	Grade K	
LT-2	HR	Grades 2 and 3	2-3	I/E K-5	3	Lunch	2	2-3	2
I/E	HR			K-5		Lunch			
Lunch/Recess					K-1	2-3	4-5		

*ELG = Early Literacy Group   HR = Homeroom Activities   I/E = Intervention/Enrichment Period   Sc/Ss = Science/Social Studies   I/S = Independent Study and additional Student Support

**Available to provide 75-90 minutes of Extended Planning Time on a 6- 12-school-day rotation.

LT = Literacy Team

Note 1: For additional information on implementing an Intervention/Enrichment (I/E) period in an elementary school, see Canady, R. L. & Rettig, M. D. (2008). Chapter 4, *Elementary school scheduling: Enhancing Instruction for student achievement*, (pp. 93-125), Taylor and Francis, Inc.

Note 2: Lunch periods may need to be adjusted depending on when the school day begins.

Organizing and Staffing Within the I/E Period

In Figure 6.5, we give an example of a structured I/E period with routine activities occurring for specific periods of time; for example, one teacher, deemed the best at teaching the various genres of writing, instructs a group of students for 15+ days focusing on writing a persuasive document; then works with another group for 15+ days, and continues throughout the year until all students have had quality teaching for writing major genres.

Figure 6.5 Sample Structure of I/E Period for Grades 3-5

A Sample Structure of an Intervention/Enrichment (I/E) Period for Grades 4-5 with 6 Core Teachers and 140 students		
Groups	Activity	Staff
26 Students	Writing Lab	1 Core Teacher
26 Students	Science and Social Studies Enrichment Units	Library/Media Specialist with TAG Teacher, if available OR 1 Core Teacher
18 Students	Special Services	2 SPED Teachers & SPED Aide
34 Students	Math Interventions	2 Core Teachers with 1 Aide & Computer Lab
36 Students	Reading Interventions	2 Core Teachers, 1 Reading Specialist (Title I), 1 Aide

A Sample Structure of an Intervention/Enrichment (I/E) Period for Grade 3 with 3 Core Teachers and 62 Students		
Groups	Activity	Staff
24 Students	Social Studies Enrichment and Science Enrichment Units	One Core Teacher, Library/Media Specialist or TAG teacher, if available
	Writing Lab	One Core Teacher, when not working with Reading Intervention
9 Students	Special Services	1 SPED Teacher, 1 SPED Aide, ESL Teacher, Speech/Language Teacher
11 Students	Math Interventions	1 Core Teacher, and 1 Computer Lab with Aide
18 Students	Reading Interventions	Title I Reading Specialist, 1 Core Teacher, 1 SPED Aide, if needed

In the 6.5 model, students are assigned time with a writing teacher, and at various times during the year they complete enrichment units which have been designed with content from social studies and science. During the same period of time, some students are receiving assessment-based support in mathematics and literacy, while those with IEPs meet for their services. In schools with IEP students following the cycle of pre-teaching, co-teaching, and re-teaching model, students receive pre-teaching and re-teaching with their assigned special education teacher during the I/E period which meets daily. In Chapter 7 we show schedules illustrating the special education teacher's role in the co-teaching cycle. Schools having large numbers of students needing interventions may need to schedule two I/E periods so more students have access to quality writing instruction and selected enrichment units.

As shown in Figure 6.5, structuring the I/E time can make it easy to manage, because of the model's predictability and the fact that the model capitalizes on teacher strengths. Other scheduling models related to implementing Response to Intervention (RTI) policies include two approaches Rettig and Canady (2012) describe for organizing I/E periods, labeled the Centers Approach and the Re-grouping Approach.

- In the Centers Approach (1) individual classroom teachers provide enrichment centers or activities for Tier 1 students; (2) classroom teachers then pull small groups of students from centers to provide Tier 2, moderate, short-term interventions; (3) clinical specialists pull out or push in for additional Tier 2 interventions; and (4) other service personnel provide Tier 3 (intense, long-term) interventions either as pull-outs or push-ins in place of Tier 2 services during I/E time or in addition to Tier 2 services as a second intervention.

- In the Re-grouping Approach (1) classes are re-grouped across a team or grade level to form groups; (2) proficient students in reading and mathematics are provided enrichment by one or more classroom teachers or other personnel such as TAG teachers, or encore teachers; (3) Tier 2 students are provided interventions by other classroom teachers or special service providers; and (4) Tier 3 students are provided interventions by clinical specialists either in place of Tier 2 during I/E time or in addition to Tier 2 as a second pull-out service.

If the Tier 1 program, including ELGs and sometimes I/E periods, is implemented with fidelity and by highly trained teachers, virtually all students should be expected to reach successful levels of competency (Shapiro, n.d.). We contend that it is important for schools to maintain a quality Tier 1 program that includes ELGs to give acceleration a chance to occur. For children who enter school with low levels of literacy skills, if acceleration never occurs, then Tier 1 instruction cannot meet its expectations.

Determining Support Personnel Limitations, Minimizing Shared Staff

It is important to consider limitations that may apply to particular staff. For example:

♦ Can a Teacher Assistant (TA) supervise students using computers without a certified teacher being present?

♦ Must the speech therapist be present in the school only on Mondays?

♦ Must a designated TA work with only one specific child because of the way the IEP was written? Can the IEP be changed?

♦ Can a special education TA supervise the use of computers with a group of students that includes both identified and unidentified special education students?

♦ Are some teacher assistants assigned only to specific students? If so, are they permitted to work with other students in small groups if their assigned student is in the group?

♦ Are TAs permitted to monitor groups of students engaged in independent reading? May they instruct a small literacy group under the direction of a LT leader or core teacher?

♦ Can any shared staff members be placed on a Day 1, Day 2 schedule or quarter-on, quarter-off vs. changing schools daily?

Sometimes staff members are shared across multiple schools in a district. Shared staff related to daily operation of the school can present a major scheduling problem. For example, it is difficult for an art or PE teacher assigned to a school for part of a day to be included in the encore rotation. When making hiring decisions, consider ways to minimize shared staff. A school schedule can be improved when a shared staff member can be shared with one school on Day 1 and another school on Day 2 or possibly quarter-on, quarter-off, or by semesters. A staff member, such as a psychologist or speech therapist can be scheduled on a partial day basis because those persons are not included in daily encore/plan periods.

When encore teachers are assigned to a school less than a full-day, it is difficult to build a master schedule that has teacher planning time at the same time each school day. In addition, instructional time is lost when encore teachers must travel from school to school on a school day, and such scheduling increases costs of providing encore teachers.

Deciding on Grade-Level Departmentalization

Determine if departmentalization, where teachers focus on teaching fewer subject areas, should be implemented at any grade levels. For example, after reviewing longitudinal data, such as yearly test scores, lesson plans, and teacher observations, perhaps one teacher is identified as strong in

English and social studies, but mathematics and science represent weaker areas; however, another teacher has an opposite profile. Then, in this scenario, pairing these two teachers and allowing them to departmentalize can improve the quality of instruction students receive at a particular grade level.

If departmentalization is wanted, identify demonstrated teacher strengths at each grade level based on data as previously determined. Chapter 5 of Canady and Rettig (2008) offers multiple examples of various departmentalization plans for Grades 3–5. Once departmentalization at selected grade levels is determined, it is important to build blocks of time in the master schedule for those grade levels. It also is desirable that at least two of the time blocks be of equal length; it's even better if three blocks can be of equal length as shown in Chapter 5, Figures 5.1 and 5.5.

Calculating Number of Students Needing I/E

Figure the number of students requiring interventions at each grade level. Although these numbers change throughout the school year, having such numbers during the initial stages of building the master schedule is helpful in determining if it is best to have a single I/E period per grade level or to have a combination of grade levels for I/E periods as shown in Figures 6.1–6.4. Knowing these numbers also helps determine teacher strengths needed to best accommodate student needs, which is a factor in deciding the placement and combination of I/E periods. During early designing stages of the master schedule, percentages of students needing interventions can be used until actual names of students are available.

Considering Grouping Patterns When Assigning Homerooms

Consider grouping patterns needed in delivering quality literacy and math instruction, such as skill-based groupings, total heterogeneous or controlled heterogeneous groupings. If primary teachers are expected to accelerate early literacy skills of students, they must be provided schedules that give them periods of time when small, assessment-based literacy groups are possible. If this scheduling does not occur, and teachers have a wide range of groups in their classrooms, no group is likely to receive the amount of directed instruction required to accelerate the acquisition of literacy skills; therefore, in several of our scheduling models, we have used the principles of *controlled heterogeneous literacy and math groupings*. Some have called similar groupings "clusters." Controlled heterogeneity still provides a "mix" of students, but the range of the mix is reduced. See Canady and Rettig (2008) for information on controlled heterogeneous grouping patterns, Chapter 6, pp.152–156 and Chapter 8. Also see examples of schedules in Chapter 7 of this book illustrating selected periods in the master schedule where reduced groups are scheduled based on principles of controlled heterogeneity.

Scrutinizing Master Schedule Drafts

Checking master schedule drafts is an important step. When a proposed master schedule for the current school year is drafted, scrutinize the schedule to determine whether or not it can be improved. Check to be sure literacy priorities are represented in the schedule. For example, are ELG times in the master schedule coordinated with LT schedules? Check for fragmented minutes in the master schedule and eliminate them. For example, look for small pockets of time or less than 15-20 minutes that often are not used productively.

Summary

Creating an optimal master schedule can be challenging, and multiple factors must be addressed when creating one. For example, educators show their commitment to accelerated literacy gains by including accelerated literacy time in the master schedule – such as by allocating sufficient time for literacy in the school day, by creating specific times for ELGs and I/E periods to meet, by tapping the collective capacity of personnel, and by using progress monitoring data to determine goals and to flexibly group students throughout the school year. After making decisions such as these, a master schedule can be drafted that best supports literacy acceleration.

Reflection

Reflect on the content from this chapter as you consider how you will design a master schedule with a goal of accelerated literacy learning.

1. Does your school have a master schedule illustrating that accelerating literacy in the early grades is highly valued? If not, who is responsible for designing such a schedule? What changes need to occur?

2. Does your master schedule include extended planning time at least every 7-14 school days for individual grade levels? If not, what changes need to occur? Who is responsible for making such a change?

3. If you do not have a highly trained LT leader who is provided time to coach LT members, are there teachers in Grades PK–1 who have the expertise to provide the needed leadership? Are there any administrators? Title I teachers?

4. Describe all the data management systems present in your school. Are they effective and easy to use? What changes, if any, need to be made? Who needs to be involved in making such changes?

5. Determine how data are or are not framing daily and long-term instruction in your school. What changes need to be considered? Who needs to be involved in making such changes? How are "needed scheduling changes" addressed in your school?

Chapter 7

Utilizing Parallel Block Scheduling to Provide Reduced Groups

As established in previous chapters, (1) children entering school with limited literacy skills often continue to have reading problems in later grades unless reading acceleration occurs in the early grades (Hernandez, 2011; Annie E. Casey, 2010; Stanovich, 1986); (2) reading acceleration means that we must double or triple rates of reading growth in Grades PK–1; and/or by the end of Grade 3, we must obtain six years of growth in a 4- to 5-year span; and (3) accelerated rates of growth are critical for virtually all students who enter school with limited literacy skills (Allington, 2011).

In Chapter 5, we demonstrated how to provide time for schoolwide reading acceleration by building extended literacy blocks into a school's master schedule. Structuring time within the literacy block increases the likelihood that teachers will provide the level of instructional intensity needed to achieve reading acceleration. We illustrated how to structure time within the literacy block for Early Literacy Groups (ELGs) and recommended "flooding" the classroom for staffing ELGs.

Building on this thinking, in this chapter we demonstrate how Parallel Block Scheduling (PBS) can be utilized to reduce class size during extended literacy blocks. PBS represents an alternative to "flooding" the classroom for structuring time within the literacy block. PBS facilitates the creation of small, flexible groupings so that assessment-based literacy instruction can occur. Group size is reduced in classrooms by allowing students to engage in technology applications. Flooding the classroom requires a larger and more highly trained Literacy Team (LT) than PBS. To illustrate, with 20 students in a classroom, four LT members, including the classroom teacher, would be required to achieve ELG instruction with an average of five students in a group. With PBS, only one LT member for each classroom and one technology teacher or Teacher Assistant (TA) are needed to supervise students assigned to work with computers. The computer group is composed of approximately one-half of the students from two classrooms which typically would consist of a combined total of 20–25 students.

With young students, maintaining focus on a small group lesson, often with auditory emphasis, and managing a classroom at the same time is difficult and exhausting. As a result, teachers may cope with the situation by gradually reducing the amount of small group instructional time any group receives over the course of a school year. The schedules we propose in this chapter provide teachers with another strategic plan for providing small, assessment-based groups without having to manage the remainder of the class simultaneously.

Requirements for Parallel Block Scheduling

To make reading a priority in the master schedule by using principles of PBS, the following commitments from school leaders are essential:

+ Build into the master schedule extended blocks of literacy time at various grade levels.
+ Provide access to the technology lab or computers parallel to the extended literacy periods.
+ Use trained support personnel to provide reduced groups for literacy instruction.
+ Reduce the number of students traditionally pulled from core instruction for various types of remediation.
+ Form assessment-based literacy groups so that each classroom teacher is responsible for no more than two or three literacy groups at any given time; consider using the concepts of controlled heterogeneous grouping to provide such groupings.
+ With most IEP students, implement a pre-teach, co-teach, re-teach instructional format, especially in the upper grades for literacy and mathematics instruction.

Building Extended Blocks of Time in the Master Schedule

With literacy blocks built into the master schedule as illustrated in Figures 5.1, 5.5, and 7.1, the school day is less fragmented, and support personnel can become integral partners in the literacy program. When literacy blocks are not identified in the master schedule, support personnel can experience conflict in becoming literacy partners. Furthermore, we contend that all shared spaces, personnel, and equipment need to be included in the school's master schedule.

Providing Access to Technology Parallel to the Literacy Block

If literacy blocks are built into the master schedule with the intention of reducing the size of ELGs, technology must be available and scheduled parallel with the literacy blocks. When using PBS, about one-half of one teacher's class, or one or two of that teacher's literacy groups, is scheduled parallel to another teacher's literacy group(s), and the two different classroom groups are scheduled to be working with computer content parallel to the reduced teacher-directed ELGs. The two groups from each of the two core literacy teachers form the technology group (usually 20–25 students), leaving two classroom teachers with approximately one-half of their class, or hopefully, no more than two or three literacy groups with each teacher. With one group of 10–12 students remaining with each of the two classroom teachers, one support person, usually a Title I, RTI, special education teacher or a TA who has been trained in teaching specific skills for emergent and beginning readers, comes into each of the two classrooms to teach with each of the two core teachers, thus increasing the possibility of providing groups of 3–5 students, a size we try to maintain until students are advanced beginning readers, when groups of 5–8 may be permissible.

In Figure 7.1 we give an example of an elementary school master schedule with literacy blocks of time built in, which means highly trained LT members can schedule their time twice daily without conflicts and confusion. Also, by having the literacy blocks built into Austin Elementary School's master schedule, the time and activities that occur within those blocks can be monitored, evaluated and modified when needed. For schools that have PK classes, such as Austin Elementary, in Figure 7.2 we illustrate a PK literacy block that is included in the master schedule, and as arrows show, after giving ELG grouping preference, students can be re-grouped for multiple literacy activities within the block.

Illustrated in Figure 7.3 is an example of how the principles of PBS can be combined with technology to provide three Grade 1 teachers whole group time, and reduced group time, without having to manage the remaining students in seatwork or centers. In Union Elementary School, this block of time is repeated twice daily, and a support person, shown with a checkmark (√), co-teaches with the regular teacher during reduced group time, so group size for all emergent readers is between 3 and 5.

At Union Elementary, most of the LT instructors are Title I, RTI, English Language Learners (ELL), Talented and Gifted (TAG) teachers and TAs who have been trained to deliver several of the skills almost all students need in the early stages of learning to read. Also, in the early grades, Union special education teachers or special education TAs, who have been trained in primary literacy instruction by the LT leader, are part of the early LT. Because the school has a large IEP population, the school is using over 12% of its special education budget to improve Tier 1 literacy instruction for all students in an attempt to reduce the number of students eventually who need Tier 2 and Tier 3 services. At Union Elementary, a special education TA supervises students using computers for several of the grade levels; the school's Title I, TAG and RTI personnel work primarily with the upper grades and during Intervention/Enrichment (I/E) periods.

Figure 7.1 Austin ES Master Schedule

Figure 7.1   Master Schedule for Austin Elementary School, Illustrating Blocks of Time When the Literacy Teams are Available to Co-teach with Core Teachers in Grades K-2

	I	II	III	IV	V	VI	VII	VIII	IX
Pre-K				Recess/Lunch					
Kindergarten	Math/Literacy			Recess/Lunch			Encore/Plan	Repeat a.m. ELGs LT-1	
Grade 1		*ELGs/Literacy LT-1			Recess/Lunch	Repeat a.m. ELGs LT-1		Encore/Plan	Sc./SS
Grade 2		*ELGs/Literacy LT-2	Math/Science		Lunch/Recess	Encore/Plan	Repeat a.m. ELGs LT-2		Sc./SS
Grade 3	Reading/Language Arts			Encore/Plan	Lunch/Recess	ELGs, if needed LT-2	Math/Science/Social Studies		
Grade 4			Encore/Plan	Recess/Lunch					I/E
Grade 5			I/E	Lunch/Recess					Encore/Plan
I/E			5			3			4
LT-1		1	K	K		1	1	K	K
LT-2		2	5(I/E)	Plan		3 (I/E)	2	2	4 (I/E)
Lunch/Recess				PK, 4, 5	K, 1, 2, 3				
Encore	**Extended PLAN Time		4	3	Lunch	2	K	1	5

*ELG = Early Literacy Group   HR = Homeroom Activities   I/E = Intervention/Enrichment Period   Sc/Ss = Science/Social Studies   LT = Literacy Team   I/S = Independent Study   PS = Personal Support

**Plan: Available to provide 75-90 minutes of planning time for each grade level on a 7- or 8-day rotation. See details in Chapter 8 and pp. 83-86 (Canady and Rettig, 2008).

Note 1: Periods are 45-50 minutes, depending on the number of minutes in the school day.

Note 2: For additional information on implementing an Intervention/Enrichment (I/E) period in an elementary school, see Canady, R. L. & Rettig, M. D. (2008), Chapter 4, *Elementary school scheduling: Enhancing Instruction for student achievement.*, (pp. 93-125), Larchmont, NY: Eye on Education. (ISBN 978-1-59667-080-8); also see Routledge (Taylor and Francis). Also see: www.robertlynncanady.com

Note 3: Lunch periods may need adjustment, depending when school begins in the morning.

Note 4: Arrows (↕) indicate how groupings can occur across grade levels.

Note 5: Having two parallel blocks for grade 3 and three parallel blocks for grades 4 and 5 helps with departmentalization as well as accommodating principles of parallel block scheduling (PBS).

Figure 7.2 Austin ES Suggested Schedule for PK Group 120-minute Block

PK Group of 60 Students, Three Teachers and Four Teacher Assistants (TA)

Periods ➝	1	2	3	4
Teacher A and TAs 1 and 2: Guided Reading and Early Literacy Groups (ELGs) of 3-5	*1, 2	*3, 4	*5, 6	*7, 8
Teacher B: Station 1: Interactive Writing/Read Alouds	3, 4 ↕	5, 6 ↕	7, 8 ↕	1, 2 ↕
Teacher C and TA-3: Station 2: PA and Read Alouds with Application/ Literacy	5, 6 ↕	7, 8 ↕	1, 2 ↕	3, 4 ↕
TA-4: Station 3: (Choices: Restaurant, Doctor Office, Writing, CL and Recess)	7, 8	1, 2	3, 4	5, 6

*Groups 1- 8 represent various groups of the 60 PK students enrolled in Austin Elementary School. Teacher A, with TAs 1 and 2, determine the changing composition of groups throughout the school year as they flexibly alter their student groups of 3-5, based on students' mastering appropriate literacy content. The arrows indicate the changing membership of the remaining groups when students are not with Teacher A and TAs 1 and 2.

Descriptions (AM/PM):

Guided Reading AM - Word Study and New Book Reading. Guided Reading PM - Rereading for Fluency/Concept of Word (COW) and Sentence Making (Writing).

Station 1: Interactive Writing AM - Engage in teacher and student writing to process Read Aloud from previous day. Read Aloud with Application, PM - Comprehension/Vocabulary-Related Read Aloud, Comp/Vocab follow-up Activity.

Station 2: PA Read Aloud with Application AM - Phonological Awareness (PA) Focus (ABC, Rhyming Book, etc.), PA follow-up Activity.

Station 3: (AM with TA-3/PM with TA-4) - Free Choice Activity. PM - Writing (Includes Drawing, Painting, Art) to process free-choice activity

TA = Teacher Assistant; they are T-1, T-2, T-3 and T-4   CL = Computer Lab   PA = Phonological Awareness

Note 1: Students at Station 1 are taught by Teacher B because focus needs to be on developing vocabulary and thinking/predicting skills.

Note 2: Each period should be at least 25-30 minutes. The block is scheduled for morning and afternoon sessions in full-day PK programs.

In Figure 7.4, we illustrate a PBS model with four teachers assigned to the grade level. In Figure 7.5, we illustrate a scheduling model with two teachers each assigned to Grades 2 and 3 working in a four-period PBS schedule and sharing the same time blocks and extension staff. The Figure 7.5 schedule also would allow a school with four teachers assigned to a grade level to departmentalize by having two of them teach mathematics and science and the other two teach ELA and social studies.

In Figure 7.6, we illustrate how an elementary master schedule can be designed to provide teachers with reduced groups, four periods each day without having to manage the remaining students in the classroom. Again, the principles of PBS were employed. In the Union schedule, three teachers were assigned to Grade 4 and three to Grade 5; however, in reviewing the skills and interests of the six teachers, it was determined that three of the teachers were best prepared to teach the language arts, reading and social studies content and that the other three teachers were best suited for the math, science block.

Because the quality of the teacher is a critical variable in student achievement, it was decided to schedule two teams based on their strongest skills; while one team works with Grade 4 students, the other team instructs students in Grade 5, and then the teams switch grade level groups. Because

Figure 7.3 Three-Period PBS Union Elementary

Teachers	Period X	Period Y	Period Z
Teacher A	Whole Group 1, 4	Reduced Group 1 √	Reduced Group 4 √
Teacher B	Reduced Group 5 √	Whole Group 2, 5	Reduced Group 2 √
Teacher C	Reduced Group 3 √	Reduced Group 6 √	Whole Group 3, 6
Extension staff, including CLTs and support personnel	2, 6	3, 4	1, 5

Code Explanations:

√ = A support teacher (i.e., Title I, RTI or SPED) serves as a co-teacher with the reduced (R) groups.

R = Reduced groups, typically the focus is on reading and math instruction.

Extension staff could be Title I, SPED, TAG, ELL, TA, RTI, reading specialists, an assigned teacher, and/or CLTs.

SPED = Special Education Teachers; Title I = Title I Reading and/or Retired Teachers hired for specific time periods;

RTI = Response to Intervention (RTI) Resource Teachers; ELL = English Language Learner

TAG = Talented and Gifted Teachers; TA = Teacher Assistant; CLTs = Computer Lab Technicians

morning time was preferred by both teams, they reverse morning and afternoon grade levels on a rotational basis, such as every nine weeks; however, I/E, lunch, and Encore/Plan periods remain the same throughout the year.

The schedules illustrated for Figures 7.6 and 7.7 could operate in the Austin Elementary Master Schedule, shown as Figure 7.1, because the principal knew how to adjust the master schedule to accommodate the new staffing arrangement. The morning block could consist of periods I, II and V. When the teams changed grade levels, the afternoon block could consist of periods, VI, VII and VIII. Another plan could be to switch Encore time for Grades 3 and 4, and move Grade 4 lunch period to period V; then the morning block for Grades 4 and 5 could consist of periods I, II, and III, which most teachers would prefer.

In Figure 7.6, the R/LA/SS team schedule is shown. In Figure 7.7, the Math/Science (M/Sc) team schedule is shown.

Figure 7.4 Union ES Four-Period PBS Grade 3

Teachers	Period W	Period X	Period Y	Period Z
Teacher A **R/LA/Ss**	Whole Group 1, 5		Reduced Group 1 √	Reduced Group 5
Teacher B **R/LA/Ss**	Whole Group 2, 6		Reduced Group 6	Reduced Group 2 √
Teacher C **R/LA/Ss**	Reduced Group 3 √	Reduced Group 7	Whole Group 3, 7	
Teacher D **R/LA/Ss**	Reduced Group 8	Reduced Group 4 √	Whole Group 4, 8	
Extension Staff*	4, 7	3, 8	2, 5	1, 6

* Code explanations are given at the end of Figure 7.3.

Note 1: Periods W, X, Y, and Z can be any four periods in the master schedule; however, it is best if at least two of the periods are together. In grades 2-3, each period should be at least 30-40 minutes, and this four-period block should be scheduled twice daily.

In the Austin Elementary School math blocks shown in Figures 7.8 and 7.9, the special education co-teacher, shown with a check (√), meets daily with all IEP students scheduled in this math block during the school's I/E period, and teaches the concepts that those students will be taught a few days later when joining the other group shown in the schedules. Then the special education support teacher co-teaches during the reduced group periods as shown with a check (√); following co-teaching, the special education co-teacher (√) re-teaches during the next day's I/E period. This cycle of pre-teaching, co-teaching and then re-teaching keeps IEP students in the core curriculum which, with support, is very important if they must be tested along with general education students.

In Figure 7.9, we show a four-teacher model and an 8-school-day rotation.

The Figure 7.9 schedule provides four days of whole group instruction, with groups formed by combining two sub-groups, and four days of reduced groups where we suggest two teachers be available as shown with check marks. Often the support teachers in Figures 7.8 and 7.9 will be special education teachers if most of the special education students having IEPs are placed in the various groups. Depending on the state

Figure 7.5 Union ES Four-Period PBS Grade 2–3

Teachers	Period W	Period X	Period Y	Period Z
Teacher A R/LA/Ss Grade 2	Whole Group 1, 5		Reduced Group 1 √	Reduced Group 5
Teacher B R/LA/Ss Grade 2	Whole Group 2, 6		Reduced Group 6	Reduced Group 2 √
Teacher C R/LA/Ss Grade 3	Reduced Group 3 √	Reduced Group 7	Whole Group 3, 7	
Teacher D R/LA/Ss Grade 3	Reduced Group 8	Reduced Group 4 √	Whole Group 4, 8	
Extension Staff*	4, 7	3, 8	2, 5	1, 6

* Code explanations are given at the end of Figure 7.3.

Note 1: Periods W, X, Y, and Z can be any four periods in the master schedule; however, it is best if at least two of the periods are together. In Grades 2–3, each period should be at least 30–40 minutes, and this four-period block should be scheduled twice daily.

and/or school district in which students live, if students' IEPs require them to take accountability tests, then it is critical that those IEP students receive grade level instruction on which they will be tested. That is why we recommend that special education teachers most able to provide competent math instruction become members of the school's concept/mastery math team.

It is important to note that the special education co-teacher in the math groups meets with all student client groups daily during the school's I/E period and pre-teaches the concepts that those students will be taught a few days later when joining the other groups shown in the schedule. Then the special education support teacher co-teaches during the reduced group periods as shown in Figures 7.8 and 7.9; following co-teaching, the special education co-teacher (√) re-teaches during the next day's I/E period.

In subjects such as mathematics, it is critical that we build interventions throughout the course which we show in Figures 7.8–7.10. The interventions

Figure 7.6 Union ES Three-period PBS Grades 4–5 R.LA.SS

Teachers	Period X	Period Y	Period Z
Teacher A **R/LA/Ss**	Whole Group 1, 4	Reduced Group 1 √	Reduced Group 4 √
Teacher B **R/LA/Ss**	Reduced Group 5 √	Whole Group 2, 5	Reduced Group 2 √
Teacher C **R/LA/Ss**	Reduced Group 3 √	Reduced Group 6 √	Whole Group 3, 6
Extension Staff*	2, 6	3, 4	1, 5

*Code explanations are given at the end of Figure 7.3.

Note 1: Periods X, Y, and Z can be any three periods in the master schedule; however, it is best if at least two of the periods are together. Periods should be between 35–45 minutes, depending on grade level and number of minutes in the school day; the blocks of time should be embedded in the school's master schedule. The R/LA/Ss team works three periods opposite the Math/Science (M/Sc) team. When one team is working with students in grade 4, and other team is working with students in grade 5.

need to occur very close to the identification of student needs. If students do not understand something being taught in October and the teacher moves on, because of the sequential nature of mathematics, "the hole gets deeper," and for those students the achievement gap widens.

Although not as powerful in obtaining results, the simplest math concept-mastery scheduling model (Canady & Rettig, 2008), Chapter 8, is the one illustrated in Figure 7.10 (Canady & Rettig, 2008, p.253), where we show a concept-mastery model that might be scheduled for four teachers in Grades 3, 4, or 5. Of course, the number of teachers may vary, and the number of days designated for teaching, intervention and horizontal enrichment also may vary.

The math concept-mastery models described in this chapter use the concept groups to make certain all students have access to the full math curriculum and mastery groups to provide support to students needing extra time and instruction to master the concepts. Schools must raise the bar for students for whom low expectations traditionally have been set. If schools, however, do not have a plan for helping these students attain higher levels of mastery, both students and schools will experience failure (Canady & Rettig, 2008).

Figure 7.7 Three Period PBS Austin ES Grades 4-5

Teachers	Period X	Period Y	Period Z
Teacher A **Math/Science**	Whole Group 1, 4	Reduced Group 1 √	Reduced Group 4 √
Teacher B **Math/Science**	Reduced Group 5 √	Whole Group 2, 5	Reduced Group 2 √
Teacher C **Math/Science**	Reduced Group 3 √	Reduced Group 6 √	Whole Group 3, 6
Extension Staff*	2, 6	3, 4	1, 5

* Code explanations are given at the end of Figure 7.3.

Note 1: Periods X, Y, and Z can be any three periods in the master schedule; however, it is best if at least two of the periods are together. Periods should be between 35-45 minutes depending on grade level and number of minutes in the school day. This 4-way parallel block requires a minimum of two 135-140 minute blocks of time be included in the master schedule.

The major goals and benefits of the concept-mastery models of instruction in mathematics are as follows:

♦ To increase the odds that all students, except those most severely challenged, have access to the full grade-level curriculum, which we call concept groups. With accountability testing at multiple grade levels, and with most states adopting a common math curriculum, higher levels of mastery for students is a critical issue. Schools must find ways to give all students access to the full curriculum on which they are being tested, and to help students experiencing difficulty to obtain higher levels of mastery.

♦ To provide extended learning time within the school's master schedule for struggling students and enrichment for those students who have achieved proficiency.

♦ To allow opportunities for teachers on the team to group and regroup on a temporary basis to help a greater number of students reach mastery on the critical concepts and topics identified at each grade level.

♦ To organize intervention services as integral parts of the instructional schedule. In the concept-mastery models, teachers of supplemental and enrichment programs become valuable assets during

Figure 7.8 60- to 90-Minute Math Concept Progress Model 6-Day Rotation

School Days ▶	1 M	2 T	3 W	4 R	5 F	6 M
Teacher A	1, 4	1, 4	1 √	4	1 √	4
Teacher B	5	2 √	2, 5	2, 5	5	2 √
Teacher C	3 √	6	6	3 √	3, 6	3, 6
CL with Computer Lab Technician (CLT)	2, 6	3, 5	3, 4	1, 6	2, 4	1, 5

Note 1: Teachers A, B and C could represent three teachers at individual Grades 3, 4, 5, 6, 7 or 8 in a large elementary or middle school. They also could represent a Math Team that serves students at three or four grade levels during different blocks of time designated in the master schedule.
CL = Computer Lab for additional intervention and enrichment based on individual assessment data.

Concept Group= Two Controlled Heterogeneous Groups (e.g. 1, 4)

Progress Group = One Performance-based Group (e.g. 5), subject to change based on mastery of standards. Note: Some call these groups mastery groups.

A, B, C = Teachers

√ = Co-Teacher; e.g., math specialists, SPED or RTI Teachers

mastery groupings. The services of support teachers must be built into the master schedule so they do not fragment core instructional time. One way to maximize support services is to rotate the number of I/E days and periods with various grade levels.

♦ To improve the success rate for students assigned to heterogeneous classes by reducing the practice of comparison grading; standard-based grading is critical for these models to be successful.

♦ To provide a mix of heterogeneous and homogeneous groupings in mathematics that is instructionally practical, politically acceptable, and supported by research (Canady & Rettig, 2008; Slavin, 1986, 1987, pp. 244–245; 250–252).

♦ Major issues related to successful implementation of the concept-mastery math models of instruction are as follows:

♦ The models require collaboration among teachers; therefore, teachers must have common planning time to design curriculum, assessments, interventions and enrichment activities, and to construct various

Figure 7.9 60- to 90-Minute Math Concept Progress Model 8-Day Rotation Four Teachers

School Days								
School Days →	1 M	2 T	3 W	4 R	5 F	6 M	7 T	8 W
Teacher A	1, 5	1, 5	1 √	5	1, 5	1, 5	1 √	5
Teacher B	2 √	6	2, 6	2, 6	2 √	6	2, 6	2, 6
Teacher C	3, 7	3, 7	7	3 √	3, 7	3, 7	7	3 √
Teacher D	8	4 √	4, 8	4, 8	8	4 √	4, 8	4, 8
CL with Computer Lab Technician (CLT)	4, 6	2, 8	3, 5	1, 7	4, 6	2, 8	3, 5	1, 7

Note 1: Teachers A, B and C could represent four teachers at individual Grades 3, 4, 5, 6, 7 or 8 in a large elementary or middle school. They also could represent a Math Team that serves students at three or four grade levels during different blocks of time designated in the master schedule.

CL = Computer Lab for additional intervention and enrichment based on individual assessment data.

Concept Group= Two Controlled Heterogeneous Groups (e.g. 1, 5)

Progress Group = One Performance-based Group (e.g. 7), subject to change based on mastery of standard(s). Note: Some call these groups mastery groups.

A, B, C, D = Teachers

√ = Co-Teacher; e.g., math specialists, SPED or RTI Teachers

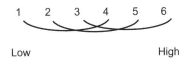

compositions of mastery groups. Schools that do not provide adequate planning time for these critical activities risk failure.

♦ For the mastery groups to function properly, teachers must diagnose what individual students and groups need during the mastery sessions. To be most effective, mastery groups need to be highly personalized. It is critical that the mastery groups do not deteriorate into "slow," "average," and "fast" groups or into study halls.

♦ For maximum results, mastery groups need to be highly personalized and instruction be data-driven by quality diagnostic assessments (Canady & Rettig, 2008, p. 245).

Figure 7.10 *Concept Mastery Math Team Schedule Grade 3*

	18 Days	5 Days	18 Days	5 Days	18 Days	5 Days	18 Days	5 Days	18 Days	5 Days	18 Days	5 Days	18 Days	5 Days	18 Days	5 Days
Teacher 3A	Concept Class Math 3, Part 1	Mastery Class: Interventions and Enrichment	Concept Class Math 3, Part 2	Mastery Class: Interventions and Enrichment	Concept Class Math 3, Part 3	Mastery Class: Interventions and Enrichment	Concept Class Math 3, Part 4	Mastery Class: Interventions and Enrichment	Concept Class Math 3, Part 5	Mastery Class: Interventions and Enrichment	Concept Class Math 3, Part 6	Mastery Class: Interventions and Enrichment	Concept Class Math 3, Part 7	Mastery Class: Interventions and Enrichment	Concept Class Math 3, Part 8	Mastery Class: Interventions and Enrichment
Teacher 3B	Concept Class Math 3, Part 1		Concept Class Math 3, Part 2		Concept Class Math 3, Part 3		Concept Class Math 3, Part 4		Concept Class Math 3, Part 5		Concept Class Math 3, Part 6		Concept Class Math 3, Part 7		Concept Class Math 3, Part 8	
Teacher 3C	Concept Class Math 3, Part 1		Concept Class Math 3, Part 2		Concept Class Math 3, Part 3		Concept Class Math 3, Part 4		Concept Class Math 3, Part 5		Concept Class Math 3, Part 6		Concept Class Math 3, Part 7		Concept Class Math 3, Part 8	
Teacher 3D	Concept Class Math 3, Part 1		Concept Class Math 3, Part 2		Concept Class Math 3, Part 3		Concept Class Math 3, Part 4		Concept Class Math 3, Part 5		Concept Class Math 3, Part 6		Concept Class Math 3, Part 7		Concept Class Math 3, Part 8	

Note: For additional information on establishing "controlled heterogeneous" groupings, see Chapter 6, pages 152-156 of Canady and Rettig (2008). For more information on Concept/Mastery math models, see Chapter 8, particularly pages 238-260 of Canady and Rettig (2008). For suggestions teaching mathematics in the elementary grades, see Chapter 11 of Canady and Rettig (2008). Multiple examples of completed elementary school master schedules illustrating various placements of Intervention/Enrichment (I/E) periods and, literacy and math blocks, are shown in this text, including Lake Elementary (Figure 5.1), Austin Elementary (Figure 7.1); Canady and Canady (2012), and Chapters 2 and 3, Canady and Rettig (2008).

Summary

Providing teachers with schedules that allow them to create assessment-based, multiple-sized groups throughout a school year is essential for accelerating student literacy and math gains. To maximize the possibility of students becoming proficient readers, assessment-based groupings and re-groupings are essential, and teachers must have scheduling structures that permit multiple-sized groupings to occur.

Schools also vary in resources available to them, which includes the number of staff members who can serve on LTs. PBS can help teachers form flexible groups and also provide students with blended learning through the use of technology.

One factor that distinguishes this book from others on improving early literacy gains is we focus on scheduling structures that provide teachers with multiple ways for creating groupings, along with daily and extended planning time to plan for the constant group changes students need during the early stages of literacy growth. Without a well-crafted master schedule, teachers working alone are limited in providing the optimal working conditions for accelerating math and literacy gains during the early school years.

Reflection

Reflect on the content from this chapter as you consider how you could use parallel block scheduling to develop a master schedule focused on accelerated literacy learning.

1. Does your school have quality software for students to view when working with computers during the literacy and math blocks? If not, who can be responsible for acquiring and managing such materials?
2. Does your school have a person or persons who can work with students using computers while core teachers are working with small literacy and math groups?
3. During various times in the school year, can students view online videos to build background knowledge and accompanying vocabulary on upcoming social studies and science content?
4. Does your school have resources to provide students with both horizontal and vertical enrichment? Horizontal enrichment is valuable in providing students with depth of learning, which increases retention levels. Project-based activities can be useful here.
5. Does your school's master schedule include structured time for students who require extra support throughout the school year to become proficient in math and literacy?
6. Does your school's master schedule include adequate time for assessing, communicating, and planning for student supports throughout the school year? If not, what needs to occur and who is responsible for making the changes? Each teacher working alone cannot provide sufficient student supports needed in most schools.

Chapter 8

Accelerating Literacy Through Out-of-School-Time Options

Literacy acceleration is most likely to occur when a student's enriched literacy learning environment extends beyond the regular school day or year. In this chapter, we describe research-based, educator-led literacy initiatives to capitalize on out-of-school-time (OST) options – summer school, before/after school and weekend time, and online distance or at-home learning. We start by discussing research on the effects of OST programs. Building on this research base, we then describe promising OST options, with consideration to the level of intensity and components necessary to significantly impact literacy learning. Many promising OST initiatives stem from our own practices or from consulting relationships with school and Literacy Team (LT) leaders across the country where we have participated in or observed OST practices in action. Some were inspired from discussion with other school and LT leaders or from our professional reading. Unprecedented school closings as a result of the COVID-19 pandemic also have led us to discover at-home learning options. We intend for the OST options described in this chapter to serve as a stimulus for discussion as school and LT leaders develop effective, yet affordable initiatives for extending literacy acceleration beyond the school day or year, which are unique to the needs of their schools and school systems.

Research on OST Options

Although not intended to make up for the literacy instruction offered during the regular school day or year, effective OST options can provide valuable time for accelerating literacy learning. Potential outcomes are maximized when we allow OST research to guide the design process.

The Cooper et al. (1996) research synthesis of 39 studies, 13 of which were included in his meta-analysis, on the effects of summer vacation on standardized achievement tests found that students' test scores were at least one month lower from Spring, before, to Fall, after the summer months. Differences were subdivided by skill area. Skills involving factual and procedural knowledge such as math computation and spelling were found to decline more than conceptual knowledge such as math concepts, math problem solving and reading comprehension. These studies supported Cooper and Sweller's (1987) suggestion that without practice, facts and procedural skills are more easily forgotten than conceptual knowledge.

Remedial programs showed more positive effects on math than on reading, as expected, since reading difficulties can require more time to remediate. A 2019 analysis of test data from a federal longitudinal study and the adaptive Measures of Academic Progress show reading gaps stayed constant during both school years and summers. Although overall reading gaps during the school year are consistent with those during the summer months, these studies document reading gaps at both low and high poverty schools, and highlight the need for reading and mathematics practice when school is not in session.

A 2000 research synthesis reported by Cooper, Charlton, Valentine, Muhlenbruck, and Borman used both meta-analytic and narrative procedures to integrate the results of 93 summer school evaluations. Results revealed that summer programs focusing on remedial, accelerated, or enriched learning made a difference in student learning. Remedial programs realized larger positive effects when the program was relatively small and when instruction was individualized. Thus, the size of the small group is important, and homogeneous grouping based on identified needs seems to enhance the potential for academic gains. Summer programs also had more positive effects for early primary and secondary than for late primary grades. When resources are limited, these data can help practitioners prioritize summer program resources.

Although students from all demographics showed gains, students from middle-income homes showed larger effects than students from lower-income homes (Cooper et al., 2000). Requiring parent involvement also was related to more effective programs. Perhaps comprehensive OST program plans can involve increased schoolwide as well as individualized family outreach efforts.

To determine the effectiveness of summer school programs since the 2000 Cooper et al. studies, in 2011 the RAND Corporation identified 13 experimental or quasi-experimental studies of nine voluntary, mandatory, and at-home summer school programs, and found similar effect sizes to Cooper et al. They concluded that "many types of summer learning programs have the potential to reduce summer learning losses, but they are not guaranteed to do so" (p. 28). With a focus on how summer programs can be implemented to impact student achievement, researchers from The RAND Corporation (2011) also conducted site visits in five cities and interviewed 60 summer school leaders. Site visits and interviewees were selected based on long-standing history of offering summer school as well as innovative aspects of the program. Analysis of observation and interview data revealed that practices associated with improved outcomes included small class sizes, individualized instruction, parental involvement, and maximized program duration and student attendance.

Allington and McGill-Franzen (2012) reported cumulative reading losses of two or more years for children in Grades 1–9 from low-income families during the summers when school is not in session. Proponents of the 'faucet theory' attribute this literacy gap to the differential input the two groups receive during summer months (McDaniel, McLeod, Carter, & Robinson, 2017). According to the faucet theory, resources provided by schools flow for all children when school is in session; however, in the summer, the faucet is turned off for students from low-income families when educational resources and support are no longer available. Summer learning loss data should provide a strong argument for increasing students access to summer as well as year-round OST options, including both in-person and online resources.

In a 2006 meta-analysis of OST program effects for at-risk students, Lauer, Akiba, and Wilkerson found mixed results. To clarify the OST program impacts, their synthesis examined 35 OST research studies meeting inclusion criteria on OST programs for helping at-risk students specific to reading and mathematics. Meta-analyses found small, but significant positive effects of OST programs on both reading and mathematics student achievement and larger positive effects for programs with specific characteristics such as tutoring in reading. Similar to previous findings, OST programs with a focus in reading and mathematics show larger positive effects with smaller group sizes. Whether the program took place after school or during the summer did not make a difference in effectiveness. This important finding allows us to apply many conclusions from summer school research to OST programs in general.

Concerning before- and after-school programs, a 2005 study showed that 20% of K-8 students participate (Carver & Iruka, 2006); however, the focus is not necessarily academic. Rather than simply adding time, these programs must be "carefully orchestrated to facilitate learning" (Beckett et al., 2009, p. 6). Findings from the evaluation of Enhanced Academic Instruction in After School Programs (Beckett et al., 2009; Black, Doolittle, Zhu, Unterman, & Grossman, 2008) shed some light on what works. Math and reading curricula from the regular school day were adapted for after-school settings. Students who received an average of 57 hours of enhanced math instruction showed modest, but significant gains in math achievement after one year as compared to students who received the regular after-school program. The enhanced after-school reading intervention did not show significant gains. Results suggest that "OST instruction can improve student achievement when delivered in a structured, focused format with adequate dosage" (Beckett et al., 2009, p. 6).

In a systematic review of 126 rigorous studies examining the effectiveness of various education technology interventions, Computer-Assisted Learning (CAL) programs rose to the top for improving academic achievement (Oreopoulos, 2020). CAL is defined as student software used to learn reading, math, and other skills. Oreopoulos (2020) states that almost all of the 30 studies of CAL programs they examined showed positive effects, with some "impressively large" (p. 20).

Figure 8.1 Reading Software Reports and Findings

Reading Software	Report	Findings
Earobics (PK-3)	https://ies.ed.gov/ncee/wwc/EvidenceSnapshot/158	Positive effects for Alphabetics. Potentially positive effects for Reading Fluency.
Lexia Reading (PK-Adult)	https://eric.ed.gov/?id=ED505846	Potentially positive effects for Comprehension
Success Maker (K-8)	https://files.eric.ed.gov/fulltext/ED561238.pdf	No discernable positive effects on Fluency or Comprehension.

Based on multiple controlled studies, ASSISTments showed academic gains over different grades (Oreopoulos, 2020). This free online platform allows teachers to assign homework and assess student progress remotely. Students also receive immediate feedback. Kahn Academy, featuring a library of courses across subjects and levels, and the Intelligent Tutoring System for the Text Structure Strategy (ITSS), which teaches text structure, showed significant gains with middle school students. For beginning reading, Earobics, Lexia Reading, and Success Maker have met What Works Clearinghouse's evidence standards and have shown positive results in certain areas of reading as charted in Figure 8.1.

On March 26, 2020, NCEE called for nominations of rigorous research that evaluates the effectiveness of specific distance education practices or products on student outcomes. These studies on the effectiveness of distance learning can be viewed on the What Works Clearinghouse (WWC) website. Regardless of the quality of video content, CAL programs have been found less effective than face-to-face instruction; however, they can provide useful supplemental instruction. More information about possible uses of these software programs is discussed in the next section under Option 4.

OST Program Recommendations

A federal practice guide on structuring OST (Beckett et al., 2009) supports much of the previous research findings and offers these recommendations:

1. Align the OST program academically with the school day.
2. Maximize student participation and attendance.
3. Adapt instruction to individual and small group needs.
4. Provide engaging learning experiences.
5. Assess program performance and use the results to improve program quality.

The first two recommendations are about OST program design (Beckett et al., 2009). Alignment of the OST program (with state and local standards, the school curriculum, and learning initiatives) and pacing of instruction are important. Fulfilling the needs and expectations of parents and students also weighs in. The LT leader or another central leader coordinates communication. Teacher-student relationships continue or new LT members are meaningfully debriefed on previous assessments and strategies used with students. Assessment information from the regular school day or year is used to form groups and to develop instructional goals and learning objectives, which also build on instruction from the regular school day or year. As part of the OST design process, parents are surveyed to learn about their needs and preferences. Awareness of the OST program is promoted within the school and to parents. Attendance data are analyzed, and parent contacts are made in an effort to overcome participation barriers.

The third and fourth recommendations (i.e., adapt instruction to individual and small group needs, provide engaging learning experiences) focus on the instruction provided in the OST program (Beckett et al., 2009). Teachers assess and document student literacy progress and use it to design instruction. Teachers are attuned to difficulty and pacing of lessons and the most appropriate skills to teach. Students are not simply taken through a series of rote literacy drills, but are engaged in high-interest, integrated literacy activities. The last recommendation involving assessment of program performance and use of the results to improve program quality (Beckett et al., 2009) is addressed in Chapter 9 along with overall program evaluation.

The amount of time required for acceleration to occur depends on various factors such as class size, instructional quality, instructional differentiation, and student age. Under the best conditions of an individualized one-on-one tutoring situation with a high-quality instructor and curriculum, 20 hours were required to make a significant difference (Vaughn, Linan-Thompson, & Hickman, 2003; Elbaum, Vaughn, Hughes, & Moody, 2000). Other researchers (McCombs et al., 2011) recommend a range of 80 hours to as much as 360 hours in total. These wide-ranging differences can be attributed to differences in quality and differentiation of instruction and in age or grade level of the students involved in the programs. Also, factors significant in maintaining high attendance rates were found to include providing engaging enrichment activities, providing transportation, and offering full-day programs.

OST Cost Considerations

An obvious response to helping less proficient students is to offer OST programs; however, cost can pose a significant barrier (McCombs et al., 2011). During times of educational budget constraints, OST programs often are among the first to be cut. According to the RAND Corporation (2011), the estimated cost of a high-quality six-hour-per-day, five-week summer school program ranges from $1,109 to $2,801 per child. Of note, this cost is minimal as compared to the average cost of retaining a student, and thus, providing an extra year of schooling ($12,612 in 2018) (Alonzo, 2020).

To maintain an OST program on a limited budget, school district and building-level administrators can consider a variety of creative options. When possible, they will do well to form creative partnerships with community-based organizations (McCombs et al., 2011), which offer the possibility of maintaining an OST program's quality and intensity while also reducing costs. To illustrate, perhaps librarians from the local public library can offer on-site or online summer reading activities and incentives that coordinate well with the summer school program; to make before-, after-, or summer school feasible for working parents, perhaps a nearby parks and recreation or childcare organization can coordinate to offer a full-day program. Perhaps the coordination with recreation activities would motivate students to enroll in and consistently participate in OST programs. Perhaps the community-based organization can transport students from the school to their facility instead of requiring the school to provide transportation.

After considering community-based partnership options, educators will want to examine other options for reducing costs while retaining OST program recommendations (i.e., alignment with the regular school day, engaging activities, high participation rates, individualized and targeted small group instruction). Hopefully, expenses can be cut while retaining the basic structure of the OST program.

We have identified six ideas for offering OST programs while reducing costs as follows:

1. **Shorten the program's length**. Rather than providing after-school reading intervention once per week for the school year, perhaps it can be offered for a semester. Rather than offering a 5-week summer program 5 days per week, perhaps the program can be provided for fewer days, 1–4 days per week. The amount of time students are engaged in a desired activity such as reading, writing, or math problem solving must be maximized. Intensity also can be increased by including online options (see idea 6).
2. **Increase class size**. Class size can be increased, but the research on small class size and importance of small groups must be considered in order to make gains. A better alternative is to use encore classes such as library read alouds or technology to offset targeted small group instruction as described in option 3. The priority is to maintain at least one homogeneous small group with a teacher-student ratio of no larger than 1:5 in Kindergarten and 1:6 overall.
3. **Reduce class size by using principles of Parallel Block Scheduling (PBS) and technology rotations**. Students can rotate from receiving small group literacy instruction with the classroom teacher, to receiving small group literacy review with a TA, to working in the computer lab. In some school districts, with training, TAs supervise students working on computers (see details in Chapter 7 of this book and also in Chapter 6 of Canady & Rettig, 2008).

4. **Reduce cost of staff**. Use trained teacher assistants, volunteers, or older students as helpers during Fluency or Writing intervention. Perhaps trained TAs can be strategically used for certain sight word or phonics interventions. Reserve highly trained educators to oversee the program and to introduce concepts and to help students transition from an emergent to a beginning reader and from a beginning reader to a transitional reader and beyond. During these transitions, a combination of reading abilities must come together to progress to the next level.

5. **Reduce the cost of materials**. Rather than purchasing individual classroom sets of student books and other materials, the LT can coordinate with the librarian to organize multiple copies of quality book titles containing recommended content and make them available for check out through a centralized Literacy Center. Instead of sending home expensive never-to-return trade books, a school or school district can organize a daily take-home system. When a book is returned, it is traded for a new book. Quality mini-books, such as Keep Books from Ohio State University, take-home books, available through Leveled Literacy Intervention, and student booklets printed from RazKids.com are inexpensive options; however, keep in mind that the cost of human resources to copy materials can outweigh the cost of purchasing books and materials.

6. **Expand online, including at-home and digital learning options**. Online options represent one way to reduce costs while also maintaining time engaged in reading, writing, and related activities. Online and visual learning options, especially when combined with teacher and/or peer interactions, have the potential to cut costs while also increasing student motivation. At-home and distant learning also is a possibility when school-based options are not feasible. This option will be discussed more fully in Option 4 of the next section.

Promising OST Time Options

Based on summer school research and with consideration to the importance of managing its expense, we have developed four types of summer school options. Option 1 represents a more intensive daily summer school option. Option 2 represents a weekly summer school option. Before- and after-school options are discussed in Option 3, and online learning and school-home contact options are discussed in Option 4.

Summer Option 1: Intensive Daily Summer School

We propose both half- and full-day intensive daily summer school options. As an intensive half-day summer school option, we propose a three-hour school day for 25 days, as shown in Figure 8.2 below.

Figure 8.2 Proposed 3-Hour Summer School Schedule with Two 30-minute ELGs

Teacher	30 Mins	30 Mins	60 Mins	30 Mins	30 Mins
A	1	2	Suggested Activities: • Read Alouds with Follow-Up Discussion or Activities** • Drama Activities** • Writing or Math Workshop** • Buddy, Partner, or Independent Reading • Movement • Snack/Break Time	1	2
B	3	4		3	4
C	5	6		5	6
D	7	8		7	8
E*	2, 4	1, 3		2, 4	1, 3
F*	6, 8	5, 7		6, 8	5, 7

*Instructors E and F supervise independent, small group, and computer based activities. F can be a Teacher Assistant (TA).

**For multiple reading, writing, and math ideas as well as application to social studies and science, see Appendix 2 of Canady and Rettig (2008), pp. 352-358.

Note 1: Each of the 1-8 groups consists of 3-6 students.

Within the 3 hours, students receive 2–30 minute periods of intensive ELG instruction, two 30-minute periods of computer-based activities, and 60 minutes of activities such as read alouds with follow-up activities, drama activities, writing or math workshop, buddy/partner, or independent reading, play/recess, and snack/break time.

ELGs in Intensive Daily Summer School

In the half- and full-day intensive daily summer school options, students receive ELG reading instruction twice daily. ELGs are based on goals identified through assessment. These summer school options are led by the LT leader, if possible, and staffed by trained LT members who are highly qualified to teach reading. LTs provide two daily 30-minute assessment-based lessons. This schedule is designed to accommodate a total of 30 students, assuming these students meet in ELGs with a teacher/student ratio of 1:5. ELG sizes in Grades PK–K can be smaller than in Grades 1-2, with ELGs in PK–K having 3–5 students and ELGs in Grades 1–2 having 4–6 students.

Literacy or Math Extension

During literacy or math extension, a small, modified or whole group of students works with teachers to engage in multiple reading, writing, and math activities as applicable to social studies and science content. On some days, literacy extension could involve viewing an informational video to build background knowledge in social studies or science. Before viewing the video, the teacher helps students connect with the topic and preview vocabulary. After the video, the teacher engages in a variety of follow-up oral and written activities to process and apply the content. On other days, literacy extension or math extension could employ Computer-Assisted Learning (CAL) as described in Option 4.

Whole-Group Options

During whole-group time, LT members can coordinate with project partners to offer PK–K storytelling and puppet show sessions in the library involving professional as well as student authors. At least one staff member could be trained in Writers Workshop and provide instruction to students on a rotating basis.

As another option, a trained mathematics team member could provide instruction in one or two daily 30-minute small group math sessions. The focus of the math instruction is to teach computation skills with application to problem solving. Also, technology could be used for building background knowledge in social studies and science, and for providing CAL. CAL would offer students individualized learning and practice opportunities in reading or mathematics. Principles of PBS would be employed to reduce small group sizes as explained in Chapter 7.

To motivate students to read, also through the Literacy Extension, students participate in a reading incentive program. Perhaps on Fridays, the teacher introduces and reads the beginnings of a few books out loud with expression until children are "hooked." Leveled books, including the read alouds, are available for check out. A sample Reading Rockets parent letter, reading log for parents to sign each week, and a graph of student progress can be accessed from our website. We recommend that students be allowed to read a book up to three times and still receive reading credit. When students return their signed reading logs, they earn weekly rewards related to literacy or family engagement. When they reach 100 books on their Reading Rockets graph, they receive an end-of-OST program reward such as blasting off rocket balloons.

Conversion from Half- to Full-Day Summer School

To accommodate full-time working parents, some school districts offer daycare on site or transportation to local park and recreation facilities or afternoon daycare programs after the morning summer school program. If this option is not available, the school can offer a full-day summer school option. The 3-hour morning block described in Figure 8.2 can be extended with an afternoon block as shown in Figure 8.3.

Figure 8.3 Proposed Full-Day Summer School Afternoon Schedule

Personnel	30 min	60 min	60 min	60 min
Teacher A	Lunch	Read Alouds/ Writing Workshop Class 1	Read Alouds/ Writing Workshop Class 2	Educational Videos with Follow-Up Activities/ Pack Up
Teacher B		Physical Ed. Class 2	Physical.Ed. Class 1	Educational Videos with Follow-Up Activities/ Pack Up

*For multiple reading, writing, and math ideas as well as application to social studies and science, see Appendix 2 of Canady and Rettig (2008), pp. 352-358.

A 30-minute lunch is followed by an expressive read aloud with a follow-up activity and supervised physical education activities focused on team-building, before returning to class for an educational video with a follow-up activity. Community and parent involvements are built into the program. Family outreach and student incentives encourage attendance and progress. Programs and classrooms are carefully monitored and adjustments are made on an ongoing basis.

LTs are specifically trained to provide the group they will be assigned to teach. They can quickly monitor to be sure students are reading appropriate leveled books or texts; they model excitement about and animation when reading; they are excellent with classroom management; they can coordinate and maintain a motivational reading incentive program. They plan and announce OST programs early, so parents can include the summer or before/after school program in their plans.

Summer Option 2: Weekly Summer School with Daily At-Home Reading

Option 2, a less expensive summer school option than Option 1, involves a 6-week summer school program where students meet with their teacher in person once per week. The amount of time can range from a more intensive 1-hour block of small group time to a half or full day of literacy instruction. The small group interventions are supervised by a highly-skilled educator. The highly-skilled educator and other LT members provide instruction.

Between weekly sessions, students participate in a monitored reading incentive program designed to encourage daily reading at home. As described previously, leveled books are available for check out. When students return to school with their books and signed book log, they can earn a prize. Local businesses often see the benefits of after-school and summer reading and are willing to donate prizes. At one school, a nearby ice cream store donated coupons for a free scoop of ice cream. Teachers, parents, and students frequented the store after school.

Option 3: Before-, After-School Options

As offered within Options 1 and 2, ELGs and Interventions can be offered before and after school. Also, before and after the regular school day, students can view online read alouds, book trailers, read books, and record themselves. They can write reading responses and respond to writing prompts designed to stimulate thinking about literacy or to retell daily school and home learning experiences. They can share them in class or include them in a class book.

These initiatives often can be improved if the after-school curriculum is connected with the regular school day. To illustrate, perhaps students who are learning about poetry during the regular school day participate in a poetry club before or after the school day. Use of technology also can increase student engagement and interest in learning. Rather than directing all K-5 students to the cafeteria as they arrive or depart from school, K-1 students could view an online read aloud in the gym; students in Grades 2 and 3 could view science videos in the cafeteria, and students in grades 4 and 5 could view more advanced science videos in the library. Perhaps this initiative would apply only to car riders who consistently wait to be picked up after bus riders. The same option could be offered to bus riders when they arrive early in the morning.

Option 4: Online Learning and School-Home Contact Options

To enhance other OST options or when in-person teacher-student contact is not viable, online learning with school-home contacts can be an option. Possibilities include, but are not limited to, providing virtual read alouds and online informational videos, and participating in CAL and online teacher and peer discussion groups, potentially including opportunities for online observation and feedback.

When considering use of at-home technology, issues of inequality surrounding its access must be overcome. Oreopoulos (2020) points out that about 9.4 million school-age children in the United States do not have at-home access to the Internet. To maximize effectiveness, we must ensure student access to the Internet by forming community-school partnerships with mobile and technology providers, and seeing that mobilization of technology resources has occurred. Expanded community-school partnerships to mobilize technology resources can help. Also, some evidence-based at-home learning strategies are inexpensive.

Virtual Read Alouds

Read alouds, when students listen as others read to them, are widely understood to be important for the development of vocabulary and higher level comprehension. When students view online read alouds, new possibilities arise. According to the Daily Progress (Knott, 2019), educators, parents, and students at an elementary school in Charlottesville, Virginia have enjoyed success with Read With Us (www.facebook.com/JacksonViaElementary), one of several programs developed to foster a love of reading and connect with families on their own time, at home. According to the school's principal,

"When you are home, we are still there with you" (p. A2). Teachers and staff volunteer to be videotaped reading a book or book chapter. The school takes suggestions on which books to read. The video is posted on the school's Facebook page each night at 7:30 p.m. As a parent reflected, "It's very exciting in our home when [the videos] come out; to my older daughter Sofia, these teachers are like rock stars" (A2). A younger daughter is still in preschool, but "she's getting excited about reading even though she can't read yet" (A2). At the onset of this program, each read aloud already is averaging 200 views, a high number, especially considering the school's population of 360 students. The stimulus for Read With Us in Virginia was a Washington Post article about a Texas elementary principal who would appear live on Facebook each week in her pajamas to read a book to students. The Virginia teachers wanted to expand this principal's effort to a schoolwide program.

Online Informational Videos

Background knowledge is required for comprehension of any topic (Neuman et al., 2014). Basically, the more we know about a topic, the easier it is to read, understand, and remember a given text. Building background knowledge is important, especially in an era of increased state standards and content demands. One recommendation for building background knowledge is embracing multimedia. Direct experiences (e.g., field trips, multimedia) are "the most compelling ways to build knowledge" (Neuman et al., 2014, p. 148). Multimedia does not replace real-life experiences, but they provide a wealth of information, contributing to a shared knowledge base useful for further classroom interaction. Students can build background knowledge by viewing quality informational science or social studies videos. A sample list of social studies and science videos is shown below.

Technology Sites for Building Background Knowledge

Social Studies

- National Geographic Kids: kids.nationalgeographic.com. Activities for children on various Social Studies and Science topics, includes videos and quizzes.
- National Geographic Society: www.nationalgeographic.com. Resources and activities for children; an educators' section with lesson plans and activities for all pages and grades.
- The History Channel: www.history.com. Many resources for students to conduct research.
- U.S. Library of Congress: www.loc.gov. Resources for students and teachers.
- U.S. Department of Education: www.ed.gov. Resources for teachers, including activities, simulations, and primary documents for students to use in their research.

Science

- Mystery Science: mysteryscience.com. Resources to support a K-5 Science curriculum.
- National Science Foundation: www.nsf.gov. Classroom resources for teachers in a broad list of curriculum subjects.
- U.S. Department of Energy: www.doe.gov. Resources for science teachers.
- National Aeronautics and Space Administration: www.nasa.gov. Games and activities for kids and resources for students and teachers.
- National Wildlife Federation: www.nwf.com. Resources, articles and information about global issues.

General Websites for Kids

Nonfiction books and videos also can be found on these more general websites.

- PBSKids: www.pbskids.org/video
- Scholastic's Watch and Learn Library: www.watchandlearn.scholastic.com
- World Book Online: www.worldbookonline.com/kids
- BrainPopJr: www.jr.brainpop.com/
- Tumblebooks: www.tumblemobile.com

Computer-Assisted Learning (CAL)

CAL programs are promising in helping students build literacy and math skills. Key elements of successful CAL programs are that they allow students to progress at their own pace, provide feedback, and offer help when prompted. As compared to teacher posts of Google Classroom assignments, Oreopoulos (2020) describes CAL programs as more motivating for students, because they are more interactive.

Teacher and parent interaction is important to student learning, which includes monitoring and rewarding progress. Although not a replacement for classroom learning, online and at-home options have the potential to provide supplemental learning.

With ASSISTments, a free online platform, teachers can assign individualized math homework and assess student progress remotely. Students also receive immediate feedback. With Khan Academy, students have free access to a library of courses across subjects and levels. Personalized feedback and help when prompted are offered within this program. With ITSS program, students learn text structure.

For beginning reading, Earobics, Lexia Reading, and Success Maker can be used in school technology or an at-home setting. Earobics is an interactive software that provides PK–3 students with "individual, systematic instruction in early literacy skills as students interact with animated characters" (WWC, 2009a, p. 1). Lexia Reading and Success Maker computerized programs provide supplemental instruction and independent practice in foundational reading skills (WWC, 2015; WWC, 2009b). Success Maker also has a math version. These software programs are available for purchase in general distribution markets.

Online Teacher and Peer Discussion Groups

As another possibility for encouraging daily reading and writing, particularly for transitional readers and beyond, peers respond to structured teacher prompts on a weekly book topic and engage in online blogs or structured online reading group dialogues. This type of after-school or summer program would be best suited for students who are beyond the beginning reader stage and who have basic technology and keyboarding skills.

Kidblog from kidblog.com, one such online discussion option, is designed to provide K-12 teachers with an individual blog for each student in a classroom. Within a secure classroom blogging community, students publish posts and participate in academic discussions. Teachers maintain control over student blogs and user accounts. Garbaccio (2015), a fifth grade teacher in Albemarle County, Virginia and a faithful user, has found students are much more motivated to read and write when blogging with peers than when filling out a reading log and responding to the teacher. In her words, "Kidblog is my way of generating excitement about reading at home."

How does it Work? The kidblog.org website details how it works. Basically, children log onto the site with a secure password in a section devoted to and viewed only by their class. Then, they discuss writing prompts the teacher has posted for the week such as "What part of your book has been confusing and why?" or "Pretend you are the protagonist in your book, what would you make happen next?" After showing students how to conduct research on a secure scholastic website, the teacher adds, "Find a review of your book and blog about whether you agree or disagree with it." After posting a response to the teacher's question, students then respond to a peer's entry. As the mediator for the blog, the teacher reviews each student's entry before approving its posting onto the site. So, the teacher's responsibility is to develop and post writing prompts, to review comments, and to give feedback to the students.

For those without Internet access at home, the teacher prints out the entry choices for the week and places copies in a designated space. Students without online access can write their responses in their writing journals and then type their responses on Kidblog during Technology Time at school. Also, the cost of materials can be reduced by using online books from Reading A-Z or Raz-Kids (www.raz-kids.com).

School-Home Communication

At-home or distant learning is more successful, especially for younger students, when regularly scheduled contacts are provided. Contacts could be in the form of text messages, e-mails, phone calls, or appropriate video platforms, depending on each family's accessibility and personal preferences. Teacher guidance and supervision can be provided at regular intervals during the school year, and especially during extended time away from school. Perhaps a teacher reviews reading logs and student work. Then, a teacher or a trained teacher assistant or college student contacts and dialogues with students and parents to establish reading and other goals, and to monitor and to reward progress. The critical factor is that every student is monitored and encouraged to read, complete assignments, and to develop strong study habits. As a reminder, time spent reading can double with the simple use of weekly reading goals, daily text reminders, and reading incentives related to literacy learning and family engagement.

Students can read appropriate independent level books on their own or with parent support, and then complete online reading logs or written journal responses. School-home communication by audio and video has exciting possibilities for student learning. With appropriate authorization, students can be video- or audio-taped as they engage with the teacher in literacy instruction such as making words, forming sentences, or reading a book. The video or audio can be sent to parents to show what their child already knows and needs to learn and how they can appropriately prompt their child at home. Children also receive a second chance to hear teacher prompts. Audiotaping actually is preferred when students need to focus on pointing under words while rereading text rather than simply viewing themselves on the screen. Parents also can be encouraged to share specific audio and video clips of their child's reading sessions, and they can receive individualized feedback on how to help their child progress as a reader.

Summary

In this chapter, we have documented potential positive effects of OST programs (i.e., before/after school, summer school). Based on research, we have described multiple options for accelerating literacy, ranging from intensive half- or full-day daily summer school, weekly summer school with an at-home reading incentive program, online school-home connections, and other before- and after-school options. Regardless of the option chosen, for maximum results, it is critical that OST programs be integrated with the regular school day program. We encourage school leaders to weigh the benefits versus costs of these various options. To help with decision making, a summary of program options, including cost and benefit considerations, is listed in Figure 8.4.

While not substituting for the regular school program, these OST options, along with the reflection questions, can help school personnel decide how to maximize out-of-school time at your own school or district.

Figure 8.4 OST Program Options

Options	Cost/Benefit Analysis
Option 1: Daily Summer School with Intensive Small Group Interventions	+ Highest level of intensity. + Requires highly-skilled educators each day. - Most expensive, largely due to staffing and transportation costs.
Option 2: Weekly Summer School with Intensive Small Group Interventions and Daily Reading at Home	+/- More structure/intensity than Option 3; less structure/intensity than Option 1. + Provides weekly face-to-face accountability. +/- Students need monitoring and provided instruction from a highly qualified educator at least once per week. - Requires weekly transportation.
Option 3: Before and After School Options	+/- Requires educators to tutor and/or monitor on a regular basis as with Options 1 and 2. Tutoring can provide need-based instruction. + Provides regular face-to-face accountability as with Options 1 and 2. + Before/after school videos can be high-interest for many students and can build background knowledge for social studies/science content. - Can require transportation costs at least once per week. - For after school options, some students have less perseverance to learn after being in school all day; for before school options, an intense before school experience can take from the regular school learning experience.
Option 4: Daily Online Reading with Teacher/ Online Peer Discussion and Regular/Weekly Online Accountability Checks and/or Contacts	+ Lowest level of structure or intensity. +/- Less reliance on educators; more reliance on students/parents/peers to follow-through with interventions. +/- Reliance on technology. + Technology can be motivating for many students and can individualize the learning experience. - Although adjustments are made for those without a computer, this option still highly relies on access to and ability to use technology. +/- Assuming technology is available without additional purchasing of technology equipment, this option is the lowest cost. Technology support would be required.

Reflection

Reflect on this chapter concerning OST programs.

1. Review your schoolwide data.
   a. In general, how did your school perform in reading? In math? In other academic areas?
   b. By grade level, how many students are not scoring proficient on reading and mathematics assessments? On state standards?
   c. Beyond listing overall reading and math levels, what informal literacy or math checks can you use to identify small group needs for OST programs?
2. Can community partners contribute to the success of any OST programs? Have they been contacted? Specifically, how will they help?
3. What grades will be served through summer school, before- and after-school, or other OST programs? How can students best be served? If funds are limited, students between Grades K and 1 should be served first, followed by students between Grades 1 and 2.

4. How can the OST schedule emphasize structured and engaging academic learning time? How can OST programs be integrated into academics of the regular school day and year? How can technology enhance the OST experience?

5. How can school-home connections and student supports be built into the OST program? How can consistent student attendance be encouraged?

6. How can OST program effectiveness be measured (i.e., demographic factors, reading or mathematics abilities, technology use, non-academic outcomes, reading incentives, community-partner and parent support)? Be sure to factor in attendance, time spent in intervention, and cost when evaluating OST program effectiveness.

Chapter 9

Literacy Program Evaluation and Closing Thoughts

In this book, we address *how* district and school administrators, Literacy Team (LT) leaders, LT members, school staff members, parents, and community partners can work together to implement these key initiatives for accelerating literacy achievement:

1. Commit to literacy acceleration and prioritize literacy in the master schedule.
2. Appoint a qualified LT leader, strategically train a team and use them to provide embedded professional development.
3. Select appropriate summative and formative assessments.
4. Offer a comprehensive literacy block, use selected assessments to drive literacy instruction and to group and regroup students into ELGs and I/Es.
5. Provide increased instructional time and extended time for common planning.
6. Create a master school schedule that reflects school priorities.
7. Consider parallel block scheduling options.
8. Consider out-of-school-time (0ST) options.
9. Evaluate the literacy program.

We aim high by expecting literacy progress at accelerated rates. We concur with Michelangelo (n.d.) who once wrote, "The great danger for most of us lies not in setting our aim too high and falling short; but in setting our aim too low, and achieving our mark." Even if virtually all students do not achieve at an accelerated level of progress initially, with refinement each year, we are on the path of continuous improvement, and dedication to continuous improvement is exciting and contagious! With consistency each year, our experience is that accelerated literacy performance by the end of Grade 3 is a likely result.

Program Evaluation

District and school administrators work together with the LT leader to develop and refine an effective literacy program evaluation process. This process starts with development of an evaluation plan (Beckett, 2009. The evaluation plan should include both formative and summative evaluation. Formative evaluation is weighted more heavily for new programs, whereas summative evaluation receives more weight for more established programs. The evaluation plan also should describe outcomes that will be used in the evaluation, data to be collected to measure the outcomes, and who is responsible for gathering the data by established due dates, and how the evaluation will be shared and used to improve the program. After developing the evaluation plan, responsible stakeholders collect program and student performance data, and analyze data, and use findings for future program improvement. All LT members should be included in the evaluation process, but stakeholders outside of the LT should be utilized as well. Once program and performance data have been collected and analyzed, they conduct a summative evaluation of the program.

As part of a summative evaluation and consistent with key initiatives detailed in this book, we have developed this Literacy Program Evaluation Survey as shown in Form 9.1 below.

Form 9.1 Literacy Program Evaluation Survey

<u>Directions</u>: For each statement about our school literacy program, check 1 = Strongly disagree; 2 = Disagree; 3 = Agree; or 4 = Strongly Agree.	1	2	3	4
Commitment to Literacy Acceleration (Intro and Chapter 1)				
We have accelerated literacy expectations for less proficient and proficient readers.	❑	❑	❑	❑
Literacy receives priority in the early grades.	❑	❑	❑	❑
Our budget reflects a commitment to early literacy acceleration.	❑	❑	❑	❑
Commitment to PLC/Literacy Teams (Chapter 2)				
We have Literacy Teams (LTs) that provide daily ELGs and Interventions for students in the early grades.	❑	❑	❑	❑
LTs provide embedded professional development throughout the school year.	❑	❑	❑	❑
Student Assessment and Progress Monitoring (Chapter 3)				
Summative assessments are used to establish initial student groups and to evaluate literacy program effectiveness.	❑	❑	❑	❑
Formative assessments are used frequently to identify student needs, to flexibly group students, and to plan instruction.	❑	❑	❑	❑
Literacy Instruction Factors (Chapter 4)				
The literacy block is 160–180 minutes in the primary grades. Students in Grades K-1 receive at least 60 minutes of targeted Early Literacy Groups (ELGs) or Interventions daily.	❑	❑	❑	❑

Form 9.1 Literacy Program Evaluation Survey (*Continued*)

The literacy block is comprehensive (modeled/shared reading, ELGs, independent time/Interventions, literacy essentials).	❏	❏	❏	❏
Teachers provide appropriate scaffolding from higher to lower levels of support.	❏	❏	❏	❏
LT members provide structured lessons focused on assessment-based literacy goals.	❏	❏	❏	❏
Students proficient in reading and math receive enrichment. LT members provide in-depth multidisciplinary enrichment units with a primary focus on social studies and science content.	❏	❏	❏	❏
We have a shared Literacy Center. Teachers have access and can quickly check out books and materials they need.	❏	❏	❏	❏
Scheduled Time Factors (Chapters 5–7)				
All K-1 students are scheduled for ELG daily instruction.	❏	❏	❏	❏
Less proficient readers are scheduled for double or triple ELG or intervention periods.	❏	❏	❏	❏
Students who are proficient in reading and mathematics receive enrichment during an enrichment period.	❏	❏	❏	❏
For all LT members, daily planning time of at least 40 minutes is built into our master schedule.	❏	❏	❏	❏
On a rotational basis, LT members also have extended planning time built into our master schedule.	❏	❏	❏	❏
We use Parallel Block Scheduling (PBS) to reduce groups and also to integrate technology with ELG and I/E goals.	❏	❏	❏	❏
Commitment to Outside-of-School Time (OST)				
Our OST program is aligned academically with the school day, and pacing is appropriate.	❏	❏	❏	❏
We are maximizing student participation and attendance.	❏	❏	❏	❏
We adapt instruction to individual and small group needs, and we provide engaging learning experiences.	❏	❏	❏	❏
Program Evaluation				
Our evaluation plan is effective and equitable.	❏	❏	❏	❏
We collect student and program evaluation data, and we use these data for continuous program improvement.	❏	❏	❏	❏
Our less proficient readers achieve at accelerated rates.	❏	❏	❏	❏
Our proficient readers progress to advanced levels in enrichment areas.	❏	❏	❏	❏

This survey is intended to be used with program and student data to generate discussion. Success is celebrated, and ideas for future program improvement are generated.

Closing Thoughts

When you find yourself overwhelmed by the time, energy, coordination, and funding required to make the changes we advocate, which are backed by research–our closing plea is this: consider the costs of *not* accelerating literacy achievement during the early years of school. Consider the millions of dollars now being spent on interventions and retention. In addition to the cost to individuals who do not become proficient readers during the early grades, consider the multiple costs to society as described in our Introduction and in Chapter 1.

We close with thoughts from Ron Edmonds (1979), an early leader of the effective schools movement, who advocated – we know enough to successfully teach all children whose schooling is of interest to us. Stated more succinctly, Edmonds expressed the underlying issue as primarily one of *will*. Do we have the *will* to fully invest in PK–3 literacy? Are we willing to advocate for the needed changes? If so, the payoff for investing in early literacy can reap huge dividends for students, schools and society at large.

References

Adler, C. R. (2001). Put *reading first:* The research building blocks for *teaching children to read* (pp. 49–54). National Institute for Literacy.

Afferbach, P., & Cho, B. (2009). Identifying and describing constructively responsive comprehension strategies in new and traditional forms of reading. In S. E. Israel & G. G. Duffy (Eds.), *Handbook of research on reading comprehension* (pp. 69–90). New York: Routledge.

Alexander, K. L., Entwisle, D. R., & Olson, L. S. (2007). Lasting consequences of the summer learning gap. *American Sociological Review, 72*(2), 167–180. https://doi.org/10.1177/000312240707200202.

Alkin, M. C. (1992). Scheduling and school organization. *Encyclopedia of educational research* (6th ed.). New York, NY: Macmillan Publishing Company.

Allen, M. (1999). *Sing-Song Sid,* Dr. Maggie's Phonics Reader. Creative Teaching Press. www.creativeteaching.com

Allington, R. L. (2002). What I've learned about effective reading instruction from a decade of studying exemplary elementary classroom teachers. *Phi Delta Kappan, 83*(10), 740–747. https://doi.org/10.1177/003172170208301007.

Allington, R. L. (2009). *What really matters in response to intervention: Research-based designs.* Boston: Allyn & Bacon.

Allington, R. L. (2011). What at-risk readers need. *Educational Leadership, 68*(6), 40–45. Retrieved from www.ascd.org/publications/educational_leadership/mar11/vol68/num06/What_At-Risk_Readers_Need.aspx.

Allington, R. L. (2012). *What really matters for struggling readers: Designing research-based programs* (3rd ed.). Boston, MA: Pearson.

Allington, R. L. (2014). How reading volume affects both reading fluency and reading achievement. *International Electronic Journal of Reading Education, 7*(1), 13–26.

Allington, R. L., & McGill-Franzen, A. (Eds.). (2012). *Summer reading: Closing the rich/poor reading achievement gap.* New York: Teachers College Press.

Allington, R. L., & Walmsley, S. A. (Eds.). (1995). *No quick fix: Rethinking literacy programs in America's elementary schools.* New York: Teachers College Press and the International Reading Association.

Almy, S., & Theokas, C. (2010). Not prepared for class: High poverty schools continue to have fewer in-field teachers. *The Education Trust.* Retrieved from https://pdfs.semanticscholar.org/5ba1/e1dcb33bbed00c331deca86b91e505830daf.pdf?_ga=2.258211210.107325090.1566746659-531537429.1566746659.

Alonzo, F. (2020). Spending per pupil increased for 6th consecutive year. U.S. Census Bureau. RELEASE NUMBER CB20-TPS.21.

Annie, E. Casey Foundation. (2010). *EARLY WARNING! Why reading by the end of third-grade matters*. Retrieved from www.aecf.org/m/resourcedoc/AECF-Early_Warning_Full_Report-2010.pdf.

Barth, P. (2004). The real value of teachers: If good teachers matter, why don't we act like it? *Thinking K-16, 6*(), 1–42. Retrieved from http://files.eric.ed.gov/fulltext/ED494819.pdf.

Beaver, J., & Carter, M. (2019). *Developmental reading assessment* (3rd ed.). Pearson.

Bear, D. R., Invernizzi, M., Templeton, S., & Johnston, F. (2020). *Words their way: Word study for phonics, vocabulary, and spelling instruction* (7th ed.). Upper Saddle River, NJ: Pearson.

Beck, I. L., & McKeown, M. G. (2007). Increasing young low-income children's oral vocabulary repertoires through rich and focused instruction. *The Elementary School Journal, 107*(3), 251–271.

Beck, I. L., Kucan, L., &McKeown, M. G. (2013). Bringing words to life (2nd ed.): *Robust vocabulary instruction*. New York: The Guilford Press.

Beckett, M., Borman, G., Capizzano, J., Parsley, D., Ross, S., Schirm, A., & Taylor, J. (2009). *Structuring out-of-school time to improve academic achievement: A practice guide* (NCEE #2009-012). Washington, DC: National Center for Education Evaluation and Regional Assistance, Institute of Education Sciences, U.S. Department of Education. Retrieved from http://ies.ed.gov/ncee/wwc/publications/practiceguides.

Black, A. R., Doolittle, F., Zhu, P., Unterman, R., & Grossman, J. B. (2008). *The evaluation of enhanced academic instruction in after-school programs: Findings after the first year of implementation* (NCEE 2008- 4021). Washington, DC: U.S. Department of Education, Institute of Education Sciences, National Center for Education Evaluation and Regional Assistance.

Black, P., & Wiliam, D. (1998). Assessment and classroom learning. *Assessment in Education: Principles, Policy, & Practice, 5*(1), 7–74. https://doi.org/10.1080/0969595980050102.

Blackwell-Bullock, R., Invernizzi, M., Drake, E. A., & Howell, J. L. (2009). *Concept of word in text: An integral literacy skill*. Retrieved from https://pals.virginia.edu/pdfs/login/Reading_in_VA_COW_2009.pdf.

Blevins, W. (2019). *Meeting the challenges of early literacy phonics instruction*. Literacy Leadership Brief. International Literacy Association. https://www.literacyworldwide.org/docs/default-source/where-we-stand/ila-meeting-challenges-early-literacy-phonics-instruction.pdf

Bodrova, E., Leong, D. J., & Semenov, D. (1998). *100 most frequent words in books for beginning readers*. Aurora, CO: McREL International.

Bogner, K., Raphael, L., & Pressley, M. (2002). How grade 1 teachers motivate literate activity by their students. *Scientific Studies of Reading, 6*(2), 135–165. https://doi.org/10.1207/S1532799XSSR0602_02.

Bonstingl, J. J. (1992). The quality revolution in education. *Educational Leadership, 50*(3), 4–9.

Breslow, J. M. (2012). *By the numbers: Dropping out of high school*. Retrieved from www.pbs.org/wgbh/frontline/article/by-the-numbers-dropping-out-of-high-school.

Canady, C. E., & Canady, R. L. (2012). Catching readers up before they fail. *Educational Leadership: Strong Readers All, 69*(9). ASCD. Retrieved from www.ascd.org/publications/educational-leadership/jun12/vol69/ num09/Catching-Readers-Up-Before-They-Fail.aspx.

Canady, R. L. (1988). *A cure for fragmented schedules in elementary schools.* Alexandria, VA: Association for Supervision and Curriculum Development.

Canady, R. L. (1990). Parallel block scheduling: A better way to organize a school. *Principal, 69*(3), 34–36. ERIC Number EJ402340.

Canady, R. L., Canady, C. E., & Meek, A. (2017). *Beyond the grade: Refining practices that boost student achievement.* Bloomington, IN: Solution Tree Press.

Canady, R. L., & Rettig, M. D. (2008). *Elementary school scheduling: Enhancing instruction for student achievement.* New York: Routledge.

Carlberg, C., & Kavale, K. (1980). The efficacy of special versus regular class placement for exceptional children: A meta-analysis. *The Journal of Special Education, 14*(3), 295–309. http://dx.doi.org/10.1177/002246698001 400304.

Carver, P. R., & Iruka, I. U. (2006). *Afterschool programs and activities: 2005 (NCES 2006-076).* Washington, DC: U.S. Department of Education, National Center for Education Statistics.

Chard, D. J., Vaughn, S., & Tyler, B. (2002). A synthesis of research on effective interventions for building fluency with elementary students with learning disabilities. *Journal of Learning Disabilities, 35,* 386–406.

Compton, D. L., Fuchs, D., Fuchs, L. S., & Bryant, J. D. (2006). Selecting at-risk readers in first grade for early intervention: A two-year longitudinal study of decision rules and procedures. *Journal of Educational Psychology, 98,* 394–409. http://dx.doi.org/10.1037/0022-0663.98.2.394.

Connor, C. M., Morrison, F. J., & Katch, L. E. (2004). Beyond the reading wars: Exploring the effect of child-instruction interactions on growth in early reading. *Scientific Studies of Reading, 8*(4), 305–336. http://dx.doi. org/10.1207/s1532799xssr0804_1.

Conradi, K., Jang, B. G., & McKenna, M. C. (2014). Motivation terminology in reading research: A conceptual review. *Educational Psychology Review, 26,* 127–164.

Cooper, G., & Sweller, J. (1987). Effects of schema acquisition and rule automation on mathematical problem-solving transfer. *Journal of Educational Psychology, 79*(4), 347–362. http://dx.doi.org/10.1037/0022-0663.79.4.347

Cooper, H., Charlton, K., Valentine, J. C., Muhlenbruck, L., & Borman, G. D. (2000). Making the most of summer school: A meta-analytic and narrative review. *Monographs of the Society for Research in Child Development, 65*(1), i–127.

Cooper, H., Nye, B., Charlton, K., Lindsay, J., & Greathouse, S. (1996). The effects of summer vacation on achievement test scores: A narrative and meta-analytic review. *Review of Educational Research, 66*(3), 227–268. https://doi.org/10.3102/00346543066003227.

Cunningham, P. M., & Allington, R. L. (2011). *Classrooms that work: They can all read and write.* London: Pearson.

The Daily Progress. (April 21, 2019). Teachers bring books to students with nightly videos. Retrieved from www.dailyprogress.com/news/local/jackson-via-teachers-bring-books-to-students-with-nightly-videos/article_ddb275fc-63d1-11e9-871e-2fbfab6ab8a2.html.

Darling-Hammond, L., Wei, R. C., Andree, A., Richardson, N., & Orphanos, S. (2009). Professional learning in the learning profession: A status report on teacher development in the United States and Abroad. *National staff development council*. School Redesign Network at Stanford University. https://learningforward.org/docs/default-source/pdf/nsdcstudy2009.pdf

Denton, C. A., Fletcher, J. M., Taylor, W. P., Barth, A. E., & Vaughn, S. (2014). An experimental evaluation of Guided Reading and explicit interventions for primary-grade students at-risk for reading difficulties. *Journal of Research on Educational Effectiveness*, 7(3), 268–293.

DeWitt, P. (2019). How collective teacher efficacy develops. *Educational Leadership*, 76(9), 31–35.

Dexter, D. D., & Hughes, C. (n.d.). *Progress monitoring within a response-to-intervention model*. Retreived from www.rtinetwork.org/learn/research/progress-monitoring-within-a-rti-model.

DiSalle, K., & Rasinski, T. (2017). Impact of short-term intense fluency instruction on students' reading achievement: A classroom-based, teacher-initiated research study. *Journal of Teacher Action Research*, 3(2). https://www.timrasinski.com/presentations/impact_of_short_term_intense_fluency_instruction.pdf

Dolch, E. W. (1936). A basic sight vocabulary. *The Elementary School Journal*, 36, 456–460.

D'Orio, W. (2017). Will teacher microcredentials upend the $8 billion PD industry? *Education Update*, 59(6), 1–5.

Downing, J. A., & Anderson, D. (2006). In or out: Surprises in reading comprehension instruction. *Intervention in School and Clinic*, 41(3), 175–179. https://doi.org/10.1177/10534512060410030801.

DuFour, R. (2004). What is a professional learning community? *Educational Leadership*, 61(8), 6–11.

DuFour, R. (2015). *In praise of American educators: And how they can become even better*. Bloomington, IN: Solution Tree Press.

DuFour, R., DuFour, R., Eaker, R., Many, T., & Mattos, M. (2016). *Learning by doing: A handbook for professional learning communities at work* (3rd ed.). Bloomington, IN: Solution Tree Press.

DuFour, R., & Marzano, R. J. (2011). *Leaders of learning: How district, school, and classroom leaders improve student achievement*. Bloomington, IN: Solution Tree Press.

Duke, N. K. (2004). The case for informational text. *Educational Leadership*, 61(6), 40–44.

Duke, N. K., & Varlas, L. (2019). Turn small reading groups into big wins. *ASCD Education Update*, 61(7). Retrieved from www.ascd.org/publications/newsletters/education-update/jul19/vol61/num07/Turn-Small-Reading-Groups-into-Big-Wins.aspx.

Dunn, D. M. (2019). *Piedmont picture vocabulary test* (5th ed.). Bloomington, MN: NCS Pearson.

Dweck, C. S. (n.d.). The power of believing that you can improve. Video File. Accessed at www.ted.com/talks/carol_dweck_the_power_of_believing_ that_you_can_improve on August 2, 2020.

Edmonds, R. (1979). Effective schools for the urban poor. *Educational Leadership*, 37(1), 15–24.

Elbaum, B., Vaughn, S., Hughes, M. T., & Moody, S. W. (2000). How effective are one-to-one tutoring programs in reading for elementary students at-risk for reading failure? A meta-analysis of the intervention research. *Journal of Educational Psychology*, *92*, 605–619. doi: 10.1037/0022-0663.92.4.605.

Esbaum, (2010). *Everything Spring*. National Geographic Kids.

Foorman, B., Beyler, N., Borradaile, K., Coyne, M., Denton, C. A., Dimino, J., Furgeson, J., Hayes, L., Henke, J., Justice, L., Keating, B., Lewis, W., Sattar, S., Streke, A., Wagner, R., & Wissel, S. (2016). *Foundational skills to support reading for understanding in kindergarten through 3rd grade* (NCEE 2016-4008). Washington, DC: National Center for Education Evaluation and Regional Assistance (NCEE), Institute of Education Sciences, U.S. Department of Education. Retrieved from the NCEE website: http://whatworks.ed.gov.

Foorman, B. R., Schatschneider, C., Eakin, M., Fletcher, J. M., Moats, L. C., & Francis, D. J. (2006). The impact of instructional practices in Grades 1 and 2 on reading and spelling achievement in high poverty schools. *Contemporary Educational Psychology*, *31*(1), 1–29. https://doi.org/10.1016/j.cedpsych.2004.11.003

Ford, M. P., & Opitz, M. F. (2011). Looking back to move forward with guided reading. *Reading Horizons*, *50*(4), 225–240.

Fountas, I. C., & Pinnell, G. S. (2016). *Guided reading: Responsive teaching across the grades* (2nd ed.). Portsmouth, NH: Heinemann.

Fountas, I. C., & Pinnell, G. S. (2017a). *Benchmark assessment system* (3rd ed.). Portsmouth, NH: Heinemann.

Fountas, I. C., & Pinnell, G. S. (2017b). *Progress monitoring by instructional text reading level*. Retrieved from https://www.fountasandpinnell.com/Authenticated/ResourceDocuments/ProgressMonitor-10mos%20-%20 by%20level_OCT2017.pdf

Fountas, I. C., & Pinnell, G. S. (2020). *Fountas & Pinnell leveled books website*. Portsmouth, NH: Heinemann. www.fandpleveledbooks.com.

Fry, E. (1980). The new instant word list. *The Reading Teacher*, *34*(3), 284–289.

Fuchs, D., & Fuchs, L. S. (2006). Introduction to response to intervention: What, why, and how valid is it? *Reading Research Quarterly*, *4*, 93–99. doi:10.1598/RRQ.41.1.4.

Fuchs, D., Fuchs, L. S., Compton, D. L., Bouton, B., Caffrey, E., & Hill, L. (2007). Dynamic assessment as responsiveness to intervention: A scripted protocol to identify young at-risk readers. *Teaching Exceptional Children*, *39*(5), 58–63. https://doi.org/10.1177/004005990703900508.

Fuchs, D., Fuchs, L. S., Vaughn, S., Denton, C.A., Shanahan, T., Stecker, P. M., & Taylor, B. M. (2008). *Response to intervention: A framework for reading educators*. Newark, DE: International Reading Association.

Fuchs, L. S., Fuchs, D., Hosp, M. K., & Jenkins, J. (2001). Oral reading fluency as an indicator of reading competence: A theoretical, empirical, and historical analysis. *Scientific Studies of Reading, 5*(3), 239–256. https://doi.org/10.1207/S1532799XSSR0503_3.

Fulton, K., Yoon, I., & Lee, C. (2005). *Induction into learning communities.* Washington, DC: National Commission on Teaching and America's Future.

Fry, E. B. (1980). The new instant word list. *The Reading Teacher, 34,* 284–289.

Gamse, B. et al. (2008). Reading First Impact Study Final Report. NCEE 20094038. Accessed May 14, 2020 from https://ies.ed.gov/pubsearch/pubsinfo.asp?pubid=NCEE20094038

Garbaccio, B. (October 2, 2015). *Kid blog.* Albemarle County, VA.

Ganske, K. (2014). *Word journeys: Assessment-Guided phonics, spelling, and vocabulary instruction* (2nd ed.). Guilford Press.

Gewertz, C. (2020a) States exerting new control over reading. *Education Week, 39*(24), 1–15.

Gewertz, C. (2020b). States to schools: Teach reading the right way. *Education Week,* Web Only.

Gill, J. T. (2019). *Concept of Word Scale.* Unpublished manuscript.

Gillon, G. (2004). *Phonological awareness: From research to practice.* New York: Guilford Press.

Graham, S., Bollinger, A., Booth Olson, C., D'Aoust, C., MacArthur, C., McCutchen, D., & Olinghouse, N. (2012). *Teaching elementary school students to be effective writers: A practice guide* (NCEE 2012- 4058). Washington, DC: National Center for Education Evaluation and Regional Assistance, Institute of Education Sciences, U.S. Department of Education. Retrieved from http://ies.ed.gov/ncee/wwc/publications_reviews.aspx#pubsearch.

Graham, P. (2007). Improving teacher effectiveness through structured collaboration: A case study of a professional learning community, *RMLE Online, 31*(1), 1–17, DOI: 10.1080/19404476.2007.11462044.

Hanford, E. (2019). *At a loss for words: How a flawed idea is teaching millions of kids to be poor readers.* APM Reports. https://www.apmreports.org/story/2019/08/22/whats-wrong-how-schools-teach-reading

Hanushek, E. A. (1992). The trade-off between child quantity and quality. *Journal of Political Economy, 100*(1), 84–117.

Hanushek, E. A. (2011). The economic value of higher teacher quality. *Economics of Education Review, 30*(3), 466–479.

Hanushek, E. A. (2016). *The economic impact of good schools.* Retrieved from www.uschamberfoundation.org/blog/post/economic-impact-good-schools.

Hanushek, E. A., Rivkin, S. G., & Jamison, D. T. (1992). *Improving educational outcomes while controlling costs.* Carnegie-Rochester Conference Series on Public Policy 3i, 205–238. Retrieved from http://hanushek.stanford.edu/sites/default/files/publications/Hanushek%2BRivkin%2BJamison%201992%20CarRocConSerPubPol%2037.pdf.

Harold, B. (2016). Comparing paper and computer Testing: 7 key research studies. *Education Week.* Retreived from http://www.edweek.org/ew/articles/2016/02/23/comparing-paper-and-computer-testing-7-key.html

Hartnett-Edwards, K. (2011). Helping the adults learn. *Educational Leadership, 69*(2), 60–63.

Hasbrouck, J. E., & Tindal, G. (2006). Oral reading fluency norms: A valuable assessment tool for reading teachers. *The Reading Teacher, 59*, 636–644.

Hasbrouck, J. E., & Tindal, G. (2017). *An update to compiled ORF norms* (Technical Report No. 1702). Eugene: Behavioral Research and Teaching, University of Oregon.

Hattie, J. (2017). 250+ influences on student achievement. Visible Learning. Available at www.visiblelearningplus.com.

Hayes, L., & Flanigan, K. (2014). *Developing word recogniFtion.* New York: The Guilford Press.

Hernandez, D. J. (2011). *Double jeopardy: How third-grade reading skills and poverty influence high school graduation.* Baltimore, MD: Annie E. Casey Foundation. Retrieved from www.aecf.org/resources/double-jeopardy.

Hiebert, E. H., & Kamil, M. L. (2005). *Teaching and learning vocabulary: Bringing research to practice.* Mahwah, NJ: Lawrence Erlbaum Associates.

Holmes, C. T., & Matthews, K. M. (1984). The effects of non-promotion on elementary and junior high school pupils: A meta-analysis. *Review of Educational Research, 54*(2), 225–236. doi:10.3102/00346543054002225.

Hughes, C., & Dexter, D. (2020). Response to Intervention: A research review. Response to Intervention Action Network. http://www.rtinetwork.org/learn/research/researchreview

Hull, J. (2012). *Starting out right: Pre-k and kindergarten: Full report.* Retrieved from www.leg.state.nv.us/App/InterimCommittee/REL/Document/5412.

Lapp, D. (2020). Children experiencing reading difficulties: What we know and what we can do. *Literacy leadership brief.* International Leadership Association (ILA).

International Dyslexia Association (IDA). (2020). Effective reading instruction. https://dyslexiaida.org/effective-reading-instruction/

Intercultural Development Research Association. (2018). Failing in-grade retention: How an ineffective practice with lasting consequences, high price tags and civil rights implications can be wiped out by schools doing what schools do best. Retrieved from www.idra.org/wp-content/uploads/2018/05/ eBook-Failing-In-Grade- Retention-IDRA-2018.pdf.

Invernizzi, M., Meier, J., & Juel, C. (2007). *PALS 1-3: Phonological awareness literacy screening 1-3* (6th ed.). Charlottesville: University of Virginia.

Invernizzi, M., Sullivan, A., Swank, L., & Meier, J. (2004). *PALS-PreK: Phonological awareness literacy screening for preschoolers* (6th ed.). Charlottesville: University of Virginia.

Invernizzi, M., Swank, L., & Juel, C. (2007). *PALS-K: Phonological awareness literacy screening-kindergarten* (6th ed.). Charlottesville: University of Virginia.

Jenkins, J. R., & Johnson, E. (2008). Universal screening for reading problems: Why and how should we do this. *RTI Action Network.* Retrieved from www.rtinetwork.org/essential/assessment/screening/readingproblems.

Johns, J. (2017). *Basic reading inventory: Pre-primer through grade twelve and early literacy assessments* (12th ed.). Dubuque, IA: Kendall Hunt Publishing.

Johnson, D., & Rudolph, A. (2001). *Critical Issue: Beyond social promotion and retention—Five strategies to help students succeed*. Naperville, IL: Learning Point Associates, www.learningpt.org.

Jolly, J. L., & Makel, M. C. (2010). No child left behind: The inadvertent costs for high-achieving and gifted students. *Childhood Education, 87*(1), 35–40. doi: 10.1080/00094056.2010.10521436.

Juel, C. (1988). Learning to read and write: A longitudinal study of 54 children from first through fourth grades. *Journal of Educational Psychology, 80*(4), 437–447.

Kasaza, K. (1996). *The wolf's chicken stew*. New York: G.P. Putnam's Sons.

Kavale, K. A. (2005). Effective intervention for students with specific learning disability: The nature of special education. *Learning Disabilities: A Multidisciplinary Journal, 13*(4), 127–138.

Kavale, K. A., Forness, S. R., & Siperstein, G. N. (1999). *Efficacy of special education and related services*. Washington, DC: American Association on Mental Retardation.

Kay, N., & Pennucci, A. (2014). *Early Childhood Education for low-income students: A review of the evidence and benefit-cost analysis*. Olympia, WA: Washington State Institute for Public Policy.

Kirby, Nell. (1996). *How the chick tricked the fox*. Modern Curriculum Press.

Kilpatrick, D. (2015). *Essentials of assessing, preventing, and overcoming reading difficulties*. (Essentials of Psychological Assessment series). Hoboken, NJ: Wiley and Sons.

Knott, K. (2019). Jackson-Via teachers bring books to students with nightly videos. *The Daily Progress*. Retrieved from www.dailyprogress.com/news/local/jackson-via-teachers-bring-books-to-students-with-nightly-videos/article_ddb275fc-63d1-11e9-871e-2fbfab6ab8a2.html.

Kohn, A. (2000). *Standardized testing and its victims*. Retrieved from www.alfiekohn.org/article/standardized-testing-victims.

Kunn, M. R., & Stahl, S. A. (2003). Fluency: A review of developmental and remedial practices. *Journal of Educational Psychology, 95*, 3–21.

Kvande, M. N., Bjørklund, O., Lydersen, S., Belsky, J., & Wichstrøm, L. (2018). Effects of special education on academic achievement and task motivation: a propensity-score and fixed-effects approach. *European Journal of Special Needs Education, 34*(4), 409–423. https://doi.org/10.1080/08856257.2018.1533095.

Laberge, D., & Samuels, S. J. (1974). Toward a theory of automatic information processing in reading. *Cognitive Psychology, 6*, 293–323.

Lance, K. C., & Loertscher, D. V. (2001). *Powering achievement: School library media programs make a difference: The evidence*. Farmington Hills, MI: Linworth Publishing.

Lance, K. C., Rodney, M. J., & Hamilton-Pennell, C. (2005). *Powerful libraries make powerful learners: The Illinois study*. Canton, IL: Illinois School Library Media Association.

Lauer, P. A., Akiba, M., & Wilkerson, S. B. (2006). Out-of-school-time programs: A meta-analysis of effects for at-risk students. *Review of Educational Research, 76*(2), 275–313. https://doi.org/10.3102/00346543076002275.

Leslie, L., & Caldwell, J. S. (2006). *Qualitative reading inventory* (4th ed.). London: Pearson.

Leslie, L., & Caldwell, J. S. (2017). *Qualitative reading inventory* (6th ed.). London: Pearson.

Lipson, M. Y., & Wixson, K. K. (2013). *Assessment of reading and writing difficulties: An interactive approach.* London: Pearson.

Lynch, M. (2017). Pass or fail: The real cost of student retention. *The Advocate.* Retrieved from www.theedadvocate.org/pass-fail-real-cost-student-retention.

Lyman, F. (1987). Think-Pair-Share: An Expanding Teaching Technique. MAACIE, Cooperative News 1, 1.

Mathematica Policy Research. (2017). WWC Intervention Report: A summary from findings of a systematic review of the evidence. Leveled Literacy Intervention. Institute of Education Sciences. Washington, DC: U.S. Department of Education. Retrieved from https://ies.ed.gov/ncee/wwc/Docs/InterventionReports/wwc_leveledliteracy_091917.pdf

Marzano, R. J. (2003). *What works in schools: Translating research into action.* Alexandria, VA: Association for Supervision and Curriculum Development.

McCombs, J. S., & Marsh, J. A. (2009). *Lessons for boosting the effectiveness of reading coaches.* RAND Corporation.

McCombs, J. S., Augustine, C. H., Schwartz, H. L., Bodilly, S. J., McInnis, B., Lichter, D. S., & Cross, A. B. (2011). *Making summer count: How summer programs can boost children's learning.* Santa Monica, CA: RAND Corporation.

McDaniel, S. C., McLeod, R., Carter, C. L., & Robinson, C. (2017). Supplemental summer literacy instruction: Implications for preventing summer reading loss. *Reading Psychology*, 1–14. https://doi.org/10.1080/02702711.2017.1333070.

McGill-Franzen, A., & Allington, R. L. (1993). Flunk 'em or get them classified: The contamination of primary grade accountability data. *Educational Researcher*, 22(1), 19–22. https://doi.org/10.3102/0013189X022001019.

McGill-Franzen, A., Allington, R. L., Yokoi, L., & Brooks, G. (1999). Putting books in the classroom seems necessary but not sufficient. *The Journal of Educational Research*, 93(2), 67–74. doi: 10.1080/00220679909597631.

McNamara, J. K., Scissons, M., & Gutknecht, N. (2011). A longitudinal study of kindergarten children at risk for reading disabilities: the poor really are getting poorer. *Journal of Learning Disabilities*, 44(5), 421–30. doi: 10.1177/0022219411410040.

Mesmer, H., Mesmer, E., & Jones, J. (2014). *Reading intervention in the primary grades: A common-sense guide to RTI.* New York: The Guilford Press.

Michelangelo. (n.d.). *Top 25 quotes by Michelangelo.* Accessed on May 13, 2020 on https://www.azquotes.com/author/10049-Michelangelo.

Miksic, E. (n.d.). *Nonfiction in the early grades: A key to reading success.* Retrieved from www.globalreadingnetwork.net/news-and-events/blog/nonfiction-early-grades-key-reading-success-0.

National Assessment of Educational Progress (NAEP). (2019). The National Center for Education Statistics, U.S. Department of Education.

National Center for Education Statistics (NCES). (1997). Time spent teaching core academic subjects in elementary schools: Comparisons across community, school, teacher, and student characteristics. Retrieved from https://nces.ed.gov/pubs/97293.pdf.

National Center for Education Statistics (NCES). (2020). The condition of education. Retrieved from https://nces.ed.gov/programs/coe/indicator_cgg.asp.

National Public Radio. (July 13, 2019). States are ratcheting up reading expectations for 3rd-graders.

The Nation's Report Card (n.d.). NAEP Reading Report Card National Average Scores. https://www.nationsreportcard.gov/reading_2017/nation/scores?grade=4.

National Institute of Child Health and Human Development (NICHD). (2000). Report of the National Reading Panel. Teaching children to read: An evidence-based assessment of the scientific research literature on reading and its implications for reading instruction. Washington, D.C.: U.S. Government Printing Office.

Neuman, S. B., Kaefer, T., & Pinkham, A. (2014). Building background knowledge. *The Reading Teacher*, *68*(2), 145–148. https://doi.org/10.1002/trtr.1314.

Nilsson, N. L. (2008). A critical analysis of eight informal reading inventories. *The Reading Teacher*, *61*(7), 526–536. https://doi.org/10.1598/RT.61.7.2.

North Central Regional Education Laboratory. (2000). A study of the differences between higher and lower performing schools in Indiana. Retrieved from https://learningunlimitedllc.com/wp-content/uploads/2018/02/Characteristics-of-Schools-that-Beat-the-Odds-in-Teaching-Children-to-Read.pdf.

O'Neill, J., & Conzemius, A. (2006). *The power of SMART goals: Using goals to improve student learning*. Bloomington, IN: Solution Tree Press.

Obiakor, F. E., Harris, M., Mutua, K., Rotatori, A., & Algozzine, B. (2012). Making inclusion work in general education classrooms. *Education and Treatment of Children*, *35*(3), 477–490. doi: 10.1353/etc.2012.0020.

Oczkus, L. (2018). *Reciprocal teaching at work: Powerful strategies and lessons for improving reading comprehension* (3rd ed.). Alexandria, VA: Association for Supervision and Curriculum Development.

Ohio Department of Education. (2015). *Individuals with Disabilities Education Act & maintenance of effort*. Retrieved from http://education.ohio.gov/Topics/Special-Education/Special-Education-Data-and-Funding/Special-Education-Part-B-Allocations/UPDATED-Individuals-with-Disabilities-Education-Ac.

Opitz, M. F., & Rasinski, T. V. (2008). *Good-bye round robin, updated edition: 25 effective oral reading strategies*. Boston: Heinemann.

Oreopoulos, P. (2020). The best research on online learning. *Education Week*, *39*(30), p. 20.

Orton, S. T. & Gillingham, A. (2020). *Orton Gillingham Training Manual*. Southfield, MI: Institute for Multi-Sensory Education (IMSE). Retrieved from https://www.orton-gillingham.com/.

Pappano, L. (2008). Small kids, big words: Research-based strategies for building vocabulary from preK to grade 3. *Harvard Education Letter*, *24*(3). Retrieved from www.hepg.org/hel-home/issues/24_3/helarticle/small-kids,-big-words.

Paunesku, D. (2019). Stop measuring student deficits. Measure systemic ones. *Education Week, 38*(37), 22.

Peavler, J. (2014). Marooney Foundation. http://www.marooneyfoundation.org/library/documents/PL-Docs/Training-Manual-w-Appendix-3-20-14-rs.pdf

Peske, H. G., & Haycock, K. (2006). *Teaching inequality: How poor and minority students are shortchanged on teacher quality.* Washington DC: Education Trust. Retrieved from http://files.eric.ed.gov/fulltext/ED494820.pdf.

Phillips, G. W. (2016). National benchmarks for state achievement standards. *American Institutes for Research.* Retrieved from www.air.org/sites/default/files/downloads/report/National-Benchmarks-State-Achievement-Standards-February-2016_rev.pdf.

Pianta, R. C., Belsky, J., Houts, R., & Morrison, F. (2007). Opportunities to learn in America's elementary classrooms. *Science, 315*(5820), 1795–1796. doi: 10.1126/science.1139719.

Pinnell, G. S. (1989). Reading recovery: Helping at-risk children learn to read. *The Elementary School Journal, 90*(2), 160–183. https://doi.org/10.1086/461610.

Pressley, M. (1998). *Reading instruction that works: The case for balanced teaching.* Guilford Press.

Presley, J. B., White, B. R., & Gong, Y. (2005). *Examining the distribution and impact of teacher quality in Illinois.* Retrieved from https://files.eric.ed.gov/fulltext/ED493170.pdf.

Pressley, M., & Woloshyn, V. (1995). *Cognitive strategy instruction that really improves children's academic performance.* Cambridge, MA: Brookline Press.

Pressley, M., Wharton-McDonald, R., Allington, R., Block, C. C., Morrow, L., Tracey, D., et al. (2001). A study of effective first-grade-1 literacy instruction. *Scientific Studies of Reading, 5*, 35–58. https://doi.org/10.1207/S1532799XSSR0501_2.

Project CRISS (2010). What Works Clearinghouse. https://ies.ed.gov/ncee/wwc/Docs/InterventionReports/wwc_projectcriss_061510.pdf

Rasinski, T. (2013). From Phonics to fluency: Effective teaching of decoding and fluency in the elementary school.

Rasinski, T. V., Reutzel, C. R., Chard, D., & Linan-Thompson, S. (2011). Reading fluency. In M. L. Kamil, P. D. Pearson, B. Moje & P. Afflerbach (Eds.), *Handbook of reading research* (Vol. 4, pp. 286–319). New York: Routledge.

Rettig, M., & Canady, R. (2012). *Scheduling RTI and special services in elementary schools: No more "When can I have your kids?"* Retrieved from www.schoolschedulingassociates.com/handouts/Rettig%20and%20Canady%20ASCD%202012.pdf.

Richardson, J., & Lewis, E. (2018). *The next step forward in reading intervention: The RISE framework.* New York: Scholastic.

Richardson, J., (2016). *Next Step Forward in Guided Reading (NSGR) Assessment.* Scholastic.

Riedel, B. W. (2007). The relationship between DIBELS, reading comprehension, and vocabulary in urban first-grade students. *Reading Research Quarterly, 42*, 546–567. doi: 10.1598/RRQ.42.4.5.

Rivkin, S. G., Hanushek, E. A., & Kain, J. F. (2005). Teachers, schools, and academic achievement. *Econometrica, 73*(2), 417–458. https://doi.org/10.1111/j.1468-0262.2005.00584.x.

Ronan, A. (2017). Why reading comprehension in the content areas is so important. *Edudemic.* Retrieved from www.edudemic.com/reading-comprehension-content-areas-important.

Ronfeldt, M., Farmer, S. O., McQueen, K., & Grissom, J. A. (2015). Teacher collaboration in instructional teams and student achievement. *American Educational Research Journal, 52*(3), 475–514. https://doi.org/10.3102/0002831215585562.

Rosen, P. (2020). MTSS: *What you need to know.* Reviewed by Musgrove, M. Director, Office of Special Education Programs (OSEP). U.S. Department of Education. Retrieved April 19, 2020 from https://www.understood.org/en/learning-thinking-differences/treatments-approaches/educational-strategies/mtss-what-you-need-to-know

Rowe, K. (2003). The importance of teacher quality as a key determinant of students' experiences and outcomes of schooling. *Australian Council for Educational Research.* Retrieved from http://research.acer.edu.au/research_conference_2003/3.

Rumberger, R. W. (2013). Poverty and high school dropouts. *American Psychological Association.* Retrieved from www.apa.org/pi/ses/resources/indicator/2013/05/poverty-dropouts.

Ryder, R. J., Sekulski, J., & Silberg, A. (2003). *Results of direct instruction reading program evaluation first through second grade, 2000-2002.* Madison, WI: Wisconsin Department of Public Instruction. https://ies.ed.gov/ncee/wwc/Docs/InterventionReports/wwc_readmast_081010.pdf.

Safer, N., & Fleischman, S. (2005). Research matters/how students progress monitoring improves instruction. *Educational Leadership, 62*(5), 81–83. Retrieved from www.ascd.org/publications/educational-leadership/feb05/vol62/num05/How-Student-Progress-Monitoring-Improves-Instruction.aspx.

Sahlberg, P. (2011). *Finnish lessons: What can the world learn from educational change in Finland?* New York: Teachers College Press.

Sanders, W. L., & Rivers, J. C. (1996). *Cumulative and residual effects of teachers on future student academic achievement.* Knoxville, TN: University of Tennessee Value-Added Research and Assessment Center.

Scanlon, D. M., Anderson, K. L., & Sweeney, J. M. (2017). *Early intervention for reading difficulties: The interactive strategies approach* (2nd ed.). New York: Guilford Publications.

Scanlon, D. M., Gelzheiser, L. M., Vellutino, F. R., Schatschneider, C., & Sweeney, J. M. (2010). Reducing the incidence of early reading difficulties: Professional development for classroom teachers versus direct interventions for children. In P. H. Johnston (Ed.), *RTI in literacy: Responsive and comprehensive* (pp. 257–295). Newark, DE: International Reading Association.

Scharlach, T. D. (2008). These kids just aren't motivated to read: The influence of pre-service teachers' beliefs on their expectations, instruction, and evaluation of struggling readers. *Literacy Research and Instruction, 47*(3), 158–173. doi: 10.1080/19388070802062351.

Schatschneider, C. (2006). *Reading difficulties: Classification and issues of prediction.* Paper presented at the Pacific Coast Regional Conference. San Diego, CA.

Scherer, M. (Ed.). (2011). Coaching: The new leadership skill. *Educational Leadership, 69*(2).

Schmoker, M. (2011). *FOCUS: Elevating the essentials to radically improve student learning.* Alexandria, VA: Association for Supervision and Curriculum Development.

Serravallo, J. (2015). *The reading strategies book: Your everything guide to developing skilled readers.* Portsmouth, NH: Heinemann.

Shanahan, T. (2010). *Improving reading comprehension in Kindergarten through Third Grade.* Washington, DC: U.S. Department of Education, Institute of Education Sciences, National Center for Education Evaluation and Regional Assistance, Regional Educational Laboratory Southwest.

Shanahan, T. (2019a). How would you schedule the reading instruction? Online Blog. https://shanahanonliteracy.com/blog/how-would-you-schedule-the-reading-instruction.

Shanahan, T. (2019b). Which texts for teaching literacy: decodable, predictable, or controlled vocabulary? https://shanahanonliteracy.com/blog/which-texts-for-teaching-reading-decodable-predictable-or-controlled-vocabulary.

Shapiro, E. S. (2008). *Tiered instruction and intervention in a response-to-intervention model. RTI Action Network.* Retrieved from www.rtinetwork.org/essential/tieredinstruction/tiered-instruction-and-intervention-rti-model.

Shields, M. K., & Behrman, R. E. (2000). Children and computer technology: Analysis and recommendations. *The Future of Children, 10*(2), 4–30. doi: 10.2307/1602687.

Shephard, L. A., & Smith, M. L. (1990), Synthesis of research on grade retention. *Educational Leadership, 47,* 84–88.

Sisson, D., & Sisson, B. (2016). *Re-envisioning the literacy block: A guide to maximizing instruction in grades K-8.* Routledge.

Slavin, R. E. (1986). *Ability grouping and student achievement in elementary school: A best evidence synthesis. Report 1.* Baltimore, MD: Center for Research on Elementary and Middle Schools. (ERIC Document Reproduction Service N. ED348174)

Slavin, R. E. (1987). Ability grouping and student achievement in elementary school: A best evidence synthesis. *Review of Educational Research, 57,* 328.

Slepian, J., & Seidler, A. (2001). *The hungry thing.* New York: Scholastic.

Smith, C., & Gillespie, M. (2007). Research on professional development and teacher change: Implications for adult basic education. In J. Comings, B. Garner, & C. Smith (Eds.), *Review of adult learning and literacy: Connecting research, policy, and practice* (Vol. 7, pp. 205–244). Mahwah, NJ: Lawrence Erlbaum Associates.

Snyder, T. D., de Brey, C., & Dillow, S. A. (2019). *Digest of education statistics 2018* (NCES 2020-009). Washington, DC: National Center for Education Statistics, Institute of Education Sciences, U.S. Department of Education.

Snow, C.E., Burns, M.S., & Griffin, P. (1998). *Preventing reading difficulties in young children*. National Research Council. Washington, DC: The National Academy Press. https://doi.org/10.17226/6023.

South Carolina Department of Education. (n.d.). *Read to Succeed frequently asked questions*. Retrieved from https://ed.sc.gov/instruction/early-learning-and-literacy/read-to-succeed1/read-to-succeed-frequently-asked-questions.

Sparks, S. D. (2015). RTI practice falls short of promise, research finds. *Education Week, 35*(12) 1–12. Retrieved from www.edweek.org/ew/articles/2015/11/11/study-rti-practice-falls-short-of-promise.html.

Sparks, S. D. (2018). Are classroom reading groups the best way to teach reading? Maybe not. *Education Week*. Retrieved from www.edweek.org/ew/articles/2018/08/29/are-classroom-reading-groups-the-best-way.html?intc=main-mpsmvs.

Stahl, K. A. D., & Bravo, M. (2010). Contemporary classroom vocabulary assessment for content areas. *The Reading Teacher, 63*, 566–578.

Stahl, K. A. D., Flanigan, K., & McKenna, M. C. (2020). *Assessment for reading instruction* (4th ed.). Guilford Press.

Stanovich, K. E. (1986). Matthew effects in reading: Some consequences of individual differences in the acquisition of literacy. *Reading Research Quarterly, 21*(4), 360–407. doi: 10.1598/RRQ.21.4.1.

Starr, A. (2019). States are ratcheting up reading expectations for 3rd-graders. *National Public Radio*. Retrieved from www.npr.org/2019/07/13/741156019/states-are-ratcheting-up-reading-expectations-for-3rd-graders.

Stiggins, R. J. (2002). Assessment crisis: The absence of assessment for learning. *Phi Delta Kappan, 83*(10), 758–765. https://doi.org/10.1177/003172170208301010.

Strebe, J. D. (2010). *Engaging mathematics students: Using cooperative learning*. Eye on Education.

Stuhlman, M. W., & Pianta, R. C. (2009). Profiles of educational quality in first grade. *The Elementary School Journal, 109*(4), 323–342. https://doi.org/10.1086/593936.

Taylor, B. M. (2004). Tier 1: Effective classroom reading instruction in the elementary grades. In D. Fuchs, L. S. Fuchs, & S. Vaughn (Eds.), *Response to intervention: A framework for reading educators* (pp. 5–26). Newark, DE: International Reading Association.

Taylor, B. M., Fuchs, L. S., Fuchs, D., Vaughn, S., Denton, C. A., Stecker, P. M. et al. (2008). In D. Fuchs, L. S. Fuchs, & S. Vaughn. (Eds.), *Response to Intervention: A framework for reading educators*. Newark, DE: International Reading Association.

Taylor, B., Pearson, D., & Clark, K. (1999). *Beating the odds in teaching all children to read*. Ann Arbor, MI: Center for the Improvement of Early Reading Achievement.

Taylor, B. M., Pearson, P. D., Clark, K., & Walpole, S. (2000). Effective schools and accomplished teachers: Lessons about primary-grade reading instruction in low-income schools. The Elementary School Journal, 101(2), 121–165..

Taylor, B. M., Pressley, M., & Pearson, D. (2000). ERIC Document: ED450353.

Taylor, J., Roehrig, A. D., Hensler, B. S., Connor, C. M., & Schatschneider, C. (2010). Teacher quality moderates the genetic effects on early reading. *Science, 328*(5977), 512–514. doi: 10.1126/science.1186149.

Templeton, S., & Gehsmann, K. (2014). *Teaching reading and writing: The developmental approach.* London: Pearson.

Thompson, S., Provasnik, S., Kastberg, D., Ferraro, D., Lemanski, N., Roey, S., & Jenkins, F. (2012). *Highlights from PIRLS 2011: Reading achievement of U.S. fourth-grade students in an international context (NCES 2013–010 Revised).* National Center for Education Statistics. Retrieved from https://nces.ed.gov/surveys/pirls/pirls2016/tables/pirls2016_figure01.asp

Tivnan, T., & Hempill, L. (2005). Comparing four literacy reform models in high-poverty schools: Patterns of first-grade achievement. *Elementary School Journal, 105*(5), 419–441. https://doi.org/10.1086/431885.

Tucker, M. (2019). Let teachers work and learn in teams–like professionals. *Educational Leadership, 76,* 48–54.

Tyner, B. B. (2009). *Small-group reading instruction: A differentiated teaching model for beginning and struggling readers.* Newark, DE: International Reading Association.

Ustine, H. L., Schwartz, S. J., Bodilly, B. M., Dahlia, S., & Lichter, A. B. (2011). *How summer programs can boost children's learning.* Santa Monica, CA: RAND Corporation.

Vaughn S., Linan-Thompson S., & Hickman, P. (2003). Response to instruction as a means of identifying students with reading/learning disabilities .*Exceptional Children, 69,* 391–409.

Vaughn, S., Wanzek, J., Woodruff, A. L., & Linan-Thompson, S. (2007). A three-tier model for preventing reading difficulties and early identification of students with reading disabilities. In D. Haager, J. Klingner, & S. Vaughn (Eds.), *Evidence-Based reading practices for response to intervention* (pp. 11–28). Baltimore: Brookes.

Vellutino, F. R., & Scanlon, D. E. (2002). The interactive strategies approach to reading intervention. *Contemporary Educational Psychology, 27*(4), 573–635.

Vellutino, F. R., Fletcher, J. M., Snowling, M. J., & Scanlon, D. M. (2004). Specific reading disability (dyslexia). What have we learned in the past four decades? *Journal of Child Psychology and Psychiatry, 45*(1), 2–40. doi: 10.1046/j.0021-9630.2003.00305.x.

Walberg, H. J., & Tsai, S. (1983). Matthew effects in education. *American Educational Research Journal, 20*(3), 359–373. doi: 10.3102/00028312020003359.

Walpole, S., & McKenna, M. C. (2006). The role of informal reading inventories in assessing word recognition. *The Reading Teacher, 59*(6), 592–594. doi: 10.1598/RT.59.6.10.

Walpole, S., & McKenna, M. C. (2009). *How to plan differentiated reading instruction: Resources for grades K-3.* New York: The Guilford Press.

Walpole, S., & McKenna, M. C. (2013). *The literacy coach's handbook: A guide to research-based practice* (2nd ed.). New York: The Guilford Press.

Walpole, S., & McKenna, M. C. (2016). *Organizing the early literacy classroom.* New York: The Guilford Press.

Walpole, S., & McKenna, M. C. (2017). *How to plan differentiated reading instruction: Resources for grades K-3* (2nd ed.). New York: Guilford Press.

Wattenberg, R., Hansel, L., Hendricks, S., & Chang, J. (2004). Waiting rarely works: 'Late bloomers' usually just wilt. *American Educator*, 10–11.

Wei, R. C., Darling-Hammond, L., Andree, A., Richardson, N., & Orphanos, S. (2009). *Professional learning in the learning profession: A status report on teacher development in the United States and abroad*. Retrieved from https://learningforward.org/docs/default-source/pdf/nsdcstudy2009.pdf.

Weyer, M. (2019). *Third-grade reading legislation*. Retrieved from www.ncsl.org/research/education/third-grade-reading-legislation.aspx.

What Works Clearinghouse. (n.d.). *Leveled literacy intervention*. U.S. Department of Education. Retrieved from https://ies.ed.gov/ncee/wwc/InterventionReport/679.

What Works Clearinghouse. (2009a). Earobics. U.S. Department of Education. Retrieved from https://ies.ed.gov/ncee/wwc/Docs/InterventionReports/wwc_earobics_011309.pdf

What Works Clearinghouse. (2009b). Lexia Reading. U.S. Department of Education. Retrieved from https://files.eric.ed.gov/fulltext/ED505846.pdf

What Works Clearinghouse. (2013). Reading Recovery. U.S. Department of Education. Retrieved from https://ies.ed.gov/ncee/wwc/Docs/InterventionReports/wwc_readrecovery_071613.pdf.

What Works Clearinghouse. (2015). Successmaker. U.S. Department of Education. Retrieved from https://ies.ed.gov/ncee/wwc/Docs/InterventionReports/wwc_successmaker_111715.pdf

Williams, K. T. (2019). *Expressive vocabulary test* (3rd ed.). Bloomington, MN: NCS Pearson.

Wood, A. (1999). *Silly Sally* (1st ed.). Minneapolis, MN: Red Wagon Books.

Wren, S. (2000). *The cognitive foundations of learning to read: A framework*. Austin, TX: Southwest Educational Development Laboratory.

Yoon, K. S., Duncan, T., Lee, S. W.-Y., Scarloss, B., & Shapley, K. (2007). Reviewing the evidence on how teacher professional development affects student achievement (Issues & Answers Report, REL 2007–No. 033). Washington, DC: U.S. Department of Education, Institute of Education Sciences, National Center for Education Evaluation and Regional Assistance, Regional Educational Laboratory Southwest. Retrieved from http://ies.ed.gov/ncee/edlabs.

Yopp, H., & Yopp, R. (2000). Supporting phonemic awareness development in the classroom. *The Reading Teacher*, 54(2), 130–143.

Yopp, H., & Yopp, R. (2009). Phonological awareness is child's play! *Young Children on the Web*. http://www.anchorageaeyc.org/wp-content/uploads/2019/02/Phonological-Awareness-Is-Childs-Play-Handouts.pdf

Made in the USA
Monee, IL
24 August 2022

12335420R00105